The World of Russian Borsch
Explorations of Memory, People, History, Cookbooks & Recipes

NIKOLAI BURLAKOFF

With a Foreword by Angus Kress Gillespie

AElitaPress.org
Ossining, New York

Copyright © 2013 by Nikolai Burlakoff. All rights reserved.
Printed in the United States

Library of Congress Control Number: 2013916025
CreateSpace Independent Publishing Platform, North Charleston, SC

Burlakoff, Nikolai
The World of Russian Borsch
Explorations of Memory, People, History, Cookbooks & Recipes
ISBN-10: 148402740X
ISBN-13: 978-1484027400

Edited by: Gail S. Burlakoff

Cover photo N. Olefer, Jr.

Illustration: Heracleum sphondylium; Family:Apiaceae Original book source: Prof. Dr. Otto Wilhelm Thomé "Flora von Deutschland, Österreich und der Schweiz" 1885, Gera, Germany. Permission granted to use under GFDL by Kurt Stueber

For additional copies visit:
https://sites.google.com/site/aelitapressorg/Home

DEDICATION

To Gail Shaw Burlakoff (wife), Olga Vladimirovna Kazanetskaya née Rybakova (*babushka*), Anna Alexandrovna Osetrova (*krestnaya*), and Sergey Matveevich Osetrov (*dyadya Serezha*).

These were the true heroes of my life. They all were forced to abandon a home, a country, a culture and to go forth into the world in hopes of a future. Twice, in the course of their lives, everything was ripped away from them. By life, in one case, and by forces of war and revolution in the others; twice they rebuilt from nothing never forgetting to care for others, to love the best in what they left behind, and to transmit that to new generations.

This work is an acknowledgement of that journey and their efforts.

Variety of Borsch Plant

CONTENTS

	AKNOWLEGEMENTS	i
	FOREWORD by ANGUS KRESS GILLESPIE, Ph.D.	v
	PREFACE	ix
1	HOW THIS BOOK BEGAN	1

Anna Alexandrovna's Borsch

2 EVOLUTION & HISTORY OF BORSCH   9
Cow Parsnip (*Borschevik*) Borsch
White Borsch *(Barszcz biały)* or *żurek*
Ciorbă de perişoare (Romanian Soured Meatball Soup)
Nick's Green Sorrel Borsch
Anna's *Šaltibarščiai* (Lithuanian Cold Beet Soup)
"Lazy" Slow Cooker Borsch-Russian
Crock Pot Russian Beef Borscht-American

3 BORSCH: REGION, ETHNICITY, CLASS, OCCUPATION   21
Nick's Vegetarian *luo song tang* (Russian Soup) or Chinese Borsch
Nick's Living Food Raw Borsch
Zaporozhian Borsch [Brezhnev's Favorite]
Prune Borsch
Carême's Borsch for Tsars
Louis P. de Gouy's Bortsch Polonaise
Jellied Bortsch I
Russian borshch *(Potage bortsch à la Russe)*
British Royal Navy Bean Borsch
Nina Nicolaieff's Maritime Borsch *(Flotski Borsch)*
Lake Smelt Borsch-Pskov Style
Galina's Ukrainian Borsch

4 RELIGION & BORSCH   31
Christmas Eve Borsch *(Wigilia Barszcz)*
Sea Cabbage (Kelp) Borsch
Beet Borsch with Barley (Lenten Memorial Borsch)
Cold Borsch with Farmer's Cheese

Borsch with Radish
Smolensk Borsch
Borsch with Turnip
Turkish Borsch
Cossack Happiness Lenten Borsch
Lil's Doukhobor Borsch
Kommst Borscht (Cabbage Soup)
Zhure Kommstborscht (Sauerkraut Soup)

5   RUSSIAN COOKBOOKS - *Medieval Times to the Empire's Fall*   43
Celery Borsch
Baked Beet Borsch with Wine
Borsch with Fried Herring (Lenten Dish)
"Little Russian" Borsch as it is Prepared in Petersburg

6   RUSSIAN COOKBOOKS - *Soviet to Post-Soviet Periods*   51
Ukrainian Borsch (*The Book*)
Borsch with Pickled Beets (*The Book*)
Lenten Borsch with Fish
Ukrainian Borsch (*Cookery*)
Byelorussian Borshch with String Beans and Apples
Kiev (*Kyiv*) Borsch with Chicken
Onion Borsch
"Autumn-Winter" Turkey Borsch with Fettuccini

7   DIASPORA COOKBOOKS OF THE "BORSCH MIGRATION" - *Commercial Press Books*   63
Borsht
Cabbage Borsch
Borsch with Fresh Cabbage

8   DIASPORA COOKBOOKS OF THE "BORSCH MIGRATION" - *Addressing Differing Cultural Needs*   71
Lenten Borsch II
Passover Russell Borscht (Fermented Beets)
Moscow Borsch
The Red Soup
Princess Alexandra's Quick Borsch
Russian Borsch

9	DIASPORA COOKBOOKS OF THE "BORSCH MIGRATION" - *Charity or Community Cookbooks*	83

Borsch (No Meat)
Posnee [Lenten] Borsch (Vegetarian)
Borsch for a Large Church Dinner
Old Country Borsch
Sara's Borsch
Matushka Gizetti's Borscht
Vegetarian Borsch
Borshch
Meatless Borshch

10	BORSCH GOES INTERNATIONAL	93

Borshch ukrainsky (Ukrainian-style Beet Soup)
Potage Bortsch (Borscht Soup)
Blender Borsch II
Russian Cabbage Borscht
Barszcz-Poland
Chlodnik (soupe froide aux betteraves)-France Kholodnik
Borsch
Borscht with Sour Cream
Borsch

11	BORSCH IN THE AGE OF THE INTERNET	103

Alan Ginsberg's Cold Summer Borsch
Siberian Borsch
Cossack Borsch
Green Borscht Mama Regina's Way-Bessarabian Stew with Lamb Ribs

12	COOKING WITH MATZA	119

	APPENDIX: BORSCH RECIPES & COOKING TIPS	127
	BIBLIOGRAPHY	209

ACKNOWLEDGEMENTS

Silent gratitude isn't much use to anyone
Gladys Berthe Stern

The romantic notion of a lonely author sitting in some garret creating a masterpiece that somehow finds its way to an unsuspecting but eternally grateful readership is firmly planted in popular mythology. Some authors cultivate that image. Hemingway did so when he so lovingly described his early working regimen in Paris. Kerouac is perhaps the poster child for that sort of disinformation. His *On the Road* has the reputation of having been written in three weeks on a single scroll of tracing paper. In fact, it went through several drafts over a number of years, the very first of which is believed to have been written in French. More realistic is the story of Leo Tolstoy's *War and Peace*, a novel considered by many to be the quintessence of the form, and which in its various manifestations was copied, by hand, some dozen times by his wife, Sofia.

The blunt fact is that a written work is the product of many forces and people. Without people in the surrounding world alternately supporting and challenging a writer, no work would ever be produced. Every writer has two fundamental needs: one is literacy and the other is readers. I would even go so far as to say that readers are more important than literacy. A writer can, after all, adapt and become a storyteller, so literacy is not strictly a requisite; but without a reader (or listener) a writer-storyteller is lost. So my first expression of thanks is to my most loyal reader who throughout all our life together has continually egged me on to write, and write, and write. And loyally, she keeps reading, and reading, and reading. And she keeps correcting when needed and trying to bring out the best in my writing. Thanks wif.

In terms of this specific work, I want to thank Marcy Quinney, Catia Klick, Aaron Doyle, Janet Reale, Janet Freed, Alexandra Winthrop, Barbara Kirshenblatt-Gimlett, my long-time friend Angus Gillespie, and my late friend Shelley Blitstein, who two weeks before his death was helping me with his critiques. The early readers, the ones who come before the work has set its voice, are pure gold and no work is improved without their comments and judicious silences. I also need to thank Eduardo Barrios for his help with the graphics, as well as, Matza Andreyev, Doris in Thailand, Lil

Potapoff, her daughter Michelle Barabonoff, and Lady Di for their recipes and reminiscences.

The book would not even have been contemplated had Grandmother not left her apartment in Belgrade after World War II to join Mother and me in Germany. Grandmother was the one who made sure I knew how to read and write. She was a toughie. I still have a postcard from her, sent to me at the age of four, in which she laments that I am "still" illiterate and therefore unable to read her card and ask Mother why she is not writing more often. She was the principal person who raised me from the age of six until I was fifteen, so it is no wonder that I have inherited a measure of her toughness.

I can only hope that I inherited also a measure of her heart. She lost one child and a husband to pestilence and war, talked-down a rapist soldier and chased him out of her apartment by sheer force of will. She also gave her all for her daughter and her daughter's children. Olga Vladimirovna, our mother's mother, abandoned the coziness of her Belgrade home and the affection of her students and friends to come to the cold comfort of a refugee camp, in a conquered nation, to raise her grandson, a task her daughter gave. And again, decades later, in yet another country she began that job once more, with a new set of grandsons, as Mother grew a new family.

At a crucial point in our lives the Osetrovs, Godmother Anna and "Uncle" Serge, materially helped our family of two women and a child. Most importantly, they spent countless hours reading, telling stories, sharing food, and creating a vision of a place and time only accessible by language and imagination, a world at once both past and future. With their life they modeled the values of hard work, uncompromising integrity, love of land, as well as adjusting with dignity to life's twists and turns, and generously sharing what they had. For decades they single-handedly cared for the paraplegic Vladimir Georgevich Strogov, simply because he was a *zemlyak*—a fellow Cossack. The borsch I tasted with this family is what started me on this particular odyssey.

Our family joke, which I use from time to time, is to remind my brothers, Al and Adrian, that I knew Mom at least a decade before Dad did. These brothers are a gift of Mother's second marriage, which also gave me a father who cared and who did all he could to make me into a decent human. Without him, his boundless openness and giving, who knows whether these lines would ever have been written.

Mother gave me life and breath, a love and knack for cooking, and a sister, Nina, whose own skills converted her husband to the world of borsch. And I am thankful for a niece who has inherited her mother's and grandmother's talent for the arts (and who loyally read some initial chapters of this book).

Without our father, Peter, neither Nina nor I would have our present incarnation. I am thankful for the two times in my life he reached out to me, and still remember the borsch the three of us shared on our last visit together.

And then there is my friend Angus, who happily agreed to write the foreword, provided that I acknowledge his borsch "fieldwork" and share his recipe for "Filipino borsch." Thanks, Angus, for the "fieldwork," the television interview, and the recipe, but most of all for the friendship. Here is the recipe: *"My Jewish friend uses the glass jar of ready-made Borsch and then mixes in sour cream. In the bottom of the soup bowl, place a small baked potato, opened with knife and spread out with fork. Pour the borsch and sour cream mixture over the baked potato. The Philippine version--pour the mixture over cooked white rice."*

Finally, I need to thank the millions of cooks who helped make this dish a world phenomenon, ascribing it to Russia. And I need to thank those who wrote about the dish and through that mirrored their lives, and who through that work became friends and teachers. All of their efforts have made possible a better understanding of history, cultural evolution, foodways, and basic humanity. I can only hope that I have served as an adequate catalyst of their experiences.

МИР РОССИЙСКОГО БОРЩА

FOREWORD

In the spring of 2012, after I agreed to contribute a foreword to my friend Nick Burlakoff's labor of decades, *The World of Russian Borsch*, my wife and I had occasion to go to the Russian restaurant in New York's Flatiron District, *Nasha Rasha*—an interesting place with atmosphere and attitude.

The atmosphere is particularly noticeable at the bar, where a wide variety of military jackets are draped on the backs of bar stools. The jackets are, without exception, too small for most of the middle-aged male patrons, leading one to suspect that they may be destined to be modeled by others during the hours when the bar is approaching closing time. The dozen military hats, on the other hand, are of sizes that could accommodate the most inflated ego or luxurious hairdo. The male waitstaff was dressed in Russian Special Forces (*Specnaz*) shirts. The militaristic décor was reinforced by coasters advertising in cherry-red print and image, "Hammer and Sickle Vodka." To soften the edges, the female waitstaffers were dressed in school girl and scout uniforms.

The attitude is supplied by customers. While enjoying a drink, I was addressed in Russian by a fellow imbiber. To my apologetic, "I'm sorry but I don't speak Russian," I got the rejoinder, "So vat are you doing here?" I was perplexed: is this Russian or New York attitude? Before we finished our drinks, however, we were fast friends, musing about the best Russian restaurants in the City. My companion insisted that that honor belongs to *Rasputin* in Brooklyn.

The martini craze of recent years has transformed itself into a craze for vodka infusions. *Nasha Rasha* has a vodka menu of over 100 different flavors, including such dubious sounding choices as bacon, bacon and chocolate, salmon, root beer, and chicken. Gone were the traditional flavorings of buffalo grass (*zubrovka*) and red pepper (*pertsovka*); only the perennial favorite *limonovka* (lemon vodka) remains from the old pantheon. A completely unexpected, and surprisingly popular, drink proved to be the borsht-infused vodka. It comes with an edible spoon and a dollop of sour cream. Though I was not adventurous enough to try this combination, I did procure a vodka menu for Nick's collection of borsch items, and gave it to him after he agreed to give me fieldworker credit in his book.

The meal proved interesting and my wife and I enjoyed our visit although, once more, I failed to meet the challenge and did not try the House borsch. It was advertised on the menu as vegan. I also skipped "Ukrainian sushi," described as *salo* (pork belly) served Japanese style, whatever that means. And my Scot's blood would not allow me to spend $150 for four pancakes with fish-eggs (Caspian caviar). But we enjoyed our less exotic choices and appreciated the imagination that created this isle of culinary and cultural adaptation.

The worth of an author is not limited to skillful use of language or to a vivid imagination. In addition, a good author needs both courage and integrity: integrity, to wrestle with vague notions until they form a coherent vision, which then needs to be honestly conveyed, and the courage to go past the constraints of a particular genre when its limits abridge the vision. These two qualities separate notable authors from others. Perhaps Matthew Arnold, the critic responsible for bringing awareness of Lev Tolstoy to the English reading public, expressed it best in his famed essay on *Anna Karenina*, in which Arnold lauds Tolstoy for going beyond the bounds of "art" and bringing "life." Bringing life is much more challenging than staying within the bounds of an art form.

Nick book attempts to bring life to readers in an unusual way. In a modest volume of some 100 plus pages (not counting the appendix) the author reflects on many decades of his own life, as well as the life of others. But this is neither a memoir nor a period piece. It bears little resemblance to classics of Russian literature of family history, ethnography, and nostalgia, such as Sergey Aksakov's *Family Chronicle* or Pavel Melnikov's (Andrey Pechersky) *In the Forests* and *On the Hills*, and it bears no likeness whatsoever to Vladimir Nabokov's *Speak Memory*. If there is any literary connection between this book and Russian literature, the most likely candidate would be Alexander Solzhenitsyn's *One Day in the Life of Ivan Denisovich*.

The story of Ivan Denisovich is the story of an average convict, in an average concentration camp, on an average day. It is a story of a decent and hard-working person surviving in a difficult situation. Within that context Solzhenitsyn draws a quiet and sympathetic portrait of his "Everyman." *One Day in the Life of Ivan Denisovich* is not the story of Job with his histrionic appeals to God.

Solzhenitsyn created his protagonist, Ivan Denisovich. The protagonists of Nick's book, many varieties of borsch, have been and continue to be created daily by people all over the world. So, it becomes suddenly obvious that the book is not really about soup, although there are enough recipes in it to keep a family eating borsch for some time. The book is about people who have two traits in common: they have some knowledge of borsch, and their lives and activities have intrigued the author enough for him to explore those lives and join them to the web of personal experience.

The book explores the history and geographic distribution of the dish. It is also a view of Russian, European, and American history and includes a bit of social and gender history. It is a review of some classic works in the Russian, Ukrainian, Jewish, and Soviet culinary traditions and it is a book on cultural and personal transformation.

Nick has evolved from his strong dislike of borsch as a child to becoming its champion. (He cared enough to research the authenticity of a Chinese recipe, cook it, and then sell it at a Chinese festival to determine whether the Chinese consider it authentic.) And the soup itself transforms from a concoction of fermented hogweed, cabbage, and meat to a highly regional celebratory dish current among Eastern-European peasantry, to the tables of notables, nobility, and even royalty. And even, as my wife and I discovered, as a vodka infusion in the financial capital of the world.

Whenever there is something new in the humanities a bit of research often shows that a folklorist is at the cutting edge of that phenomenon. The noted folklorist Barbara Kirshenblatt-Gimlett was among the pioneering academics to laud the social and cultural significance of so-called "charity cookbooks" in her seminal article, "Kitchen Judaism." Nick's book, however, goes beyond showing the role of "charity" or "community" cookbooks in an ethnic community. His ambition is to show food as a social phenomenon that simultaneously reflects and affects cultures and everyday realties beyond a single group. One can read the work as a case history on the globalization and glocalization phenomena, as those phenomena affect one dish.

Although serious research and analytic synthesis are both integral to this book, Nick does not consider himself an academic writer. The question that inevitably arises is "Who is the reader for this book?" The answer: Someone special, who is comfortable with reflection and ideas, who loves food and, especially, someone who can always perceive the best in people and life and who, through hard work and ethical behavior, transcends the evil in the world. In short, the reader for this book is, like those who contributed to it, the reading Ivan Denisovich.

More than this I cannot say. I am glad that I had the opportunity to spend some time in *The World of Russian Borsch*.

Angus Kress Gillespie
Professor of American Studies
Rutgers—The State University of New Jersey
February, 2013

PREFACE

The cookbook author rarely confines himself to the kitchen; whether consciously or not, his work may also prove to be a study of manners, or aesthetics, or social climbing, or politics, or it may be a comic work of a very high order. ... any good cookbook is likely to be mainly a work of moral philosophy. ... any thoughtfully written cookbook, concerned as it must be with the satisfaction of one of our deepest needs, will have gone into this matter deeply.
Maria Bustillos, "Soul Food: Cookbooks as Literature"

Historically, books on cookery do not teach cooking techniques—technique is ignored, or assumed. Rarer still are books that consciously look at cookery as a cultural phenomenon. Most unusual are books that look at a single dish and attempt to examine its history and evolution, its cultural role, salient elements, and connections to spiritual life. The question arises: Why do that? The answer is not complex: by doing that one can learn a lot about the variety of factors that underlie a seemingly simple cultural object—a particular soup.

In the Russian language the words "Russia"(*Rossiya*) and "Russia" (*Rus'*)have two distinct meanings, and two different words are used to indicate that difference. One word refers to a multiethnic state, the Russian Federation (*Rossiyskaya Federatsiya),* commonly called "*Rossiya*" ("Russia"), and the other refers to a nation founded on an ethnic group called the *Rus'*. For simplicity's sake we will just say that any transliteration from Russian that begins "Ross" references the multiethnic state (either pre- or post-Soviet), while the prefix "Rus" denotes a specific ethnicity. Obviously, in English the ambiguity remains. Many countries that today are independent political entities were at various points in the past 400 years part of the Russian Empire, the Soviet Union, or affiliated with them. This includes Finland, Latvia, Estonia, Lithuania, Poland, Moldova, and Ukraine—countries of the "Borsch Belt."

The distinction between a narrow ethnicity based national entity and a multiethnic cultural "umbrella" is important both to the title of this book and to its contents because the term "Russian" is used here in its multi ethnic sense. It reflects the contributions made to the creation and dissemination of borsch, a dish deemed by many to be quintessentially Russian, by many different cultural and language groups that are, or have been, part of that state.

Borsch is inexorably linked to Russian culture. The seemingly solid connection of borsch with Russia is a bit askew, however, because Russians themselves consider *schi* (a hearty cabbage soup) to be the prototypical Russian soup. The proverbs *schi da kasha pishcha nasha* (schi and porridge are our food) and *schi da kasha mat' nasha* (schi and porridge are our mother) are concise expressions of that notion. Ukrainians, on the other hand, lay claim to borsch as their creation and as their national dish. Most Russians cede the point.

Facts and attitudes, however, have no effect on lessening the identification of borsch with Russia and Russians. Perhaps featuring borsch as one of the dishes on the menu for the grand dinner at the 1867 International Exposition in Paris played a role in identifying the dish as Russian in the eyes of others. Perhaps the notorious recipe for borsch created by the first celebrity chef, Marie-Antoine Carême, started its international journey. Maybe Auguste Escoffier's love for the dish (primarily because he loved its ruby-red color) is responsible for its standing. Maybe serving it at the coronation banquet of Tsar Nicholas II helped solidify that image. Who can say, with any assurance, that they actually know?

For my purposes, however, it is sufficient to note that my relationship to borsch has, over the years, been complex and that it motivated a twenty-year quest to delve into the mysteries of the dish. When I tell folks that I spent twenty years carrying a book about borsch in my consciousness I usually get an incredulous laugh. "A book—about borsch? Twenty years?" And those are good questions. Only a poet, whom I met recently, nodded his approval and said, "Yes, I write slowly too."

It is hard to describe this book in terms of standard genres. By focusing on one dish, it is an attempt to tell the story of people whose lives were touched by that dish. Joyce Toomre has said in her translation of the classic 19th century Russian cookbook, *A Gift to Young Housewives*: "All cookbooks start as manuals of instruction, but some develop an extra richness as they age." This book began as a reminiscence of a time, place, and people. Historically, and in terms of this work, the dish initially described in that recounting evolved to become an organizing symbol to help transmit the "extra richness" found in cookbooks of which Toomre writes.

Part of this story is my own; part is that of people I have known; much is the story of those whom I've met only through books. This is also a story about cookbooks; a genre often dismissed as modest, yet one that is rumored to go back to the 1st century CE, making it one of the oldest known kinds of books. This book introduces and reviews some remarkable cookbooks and as Toomre writes:

> *In such books, it is the asides or the glimpses of another culture that come to captivate us as much as their antiquated directions for frying an egg or roasting a pig. Embedded in the language of every recipe are assumptions about the reader and his or her milieu, skills, and resources. A collection of recipes is even more informative, both for what it includes and for what it omits. Recipes are rooted in time and space; essentially static, they function as snapshots of culture. Like translations, they usually serve the needs of a particular group of people in a particular locale.*

My quest began with a desire to share a bit of the lives of people close to me, people whose rich and challenging lives were filled with generosity but ended in isolation. I did not want their lives to go unremarked. I could not do much to alter their karmic path when they were alive, but I can tell their story, as I experienced it, and through that hope to repay a debt with gratitude.

But my quest also became a journey of discovery and wonderment. Imagine my surprise when, on a trip to Vietnam in 2008, I found a Russian restaurant in Ho Chi Minh City (Saigon) that (even in this humid, hot, tropical country) offered a hearty meat and cabbage version of borsch. The taste of the soup was not much different from what can be had in a restaurant in Moscow or New York.

Here I share recipes from different sources and their stories, and attempt to set a context for both. My goal is to show, on the strength of a single dish, how people can interact within time, space, and cultural conventions, and how they form realities of great depth and complexity in the pursuit of an essentially simple end: cooking a particular soup. All too often, we fail to grasp the significance of such small, ephemeral things.

Sometimes, however, it is the ephemeral that proves to be connected to the deepest yearnings of people and therefore remains stable through space and time. This story, therefore, is a story of extraordinary ordinary people and the legacy of a dish that has attempted to maintain its essential taste elements over hundreds of years in different settings and cultures. Obviously, a dish itself cannot do that.Iit is the people who cook and eat the dish that put forth the effort and carry those elements through generations and who by those exertions create a spiritual phenomenon, or value.

This brings up the point about books on cookery as a literary genre. They are a representation of reality at its very warmest and most welcoming. In that way they serve as affirmations of the positive in the world and, because they involve the reader's imagination, they are a kind of magic tale: "If you follow the path (recipe) you will live happily ever after (enjoy the dish)." It is interesting to note that some of the most important early 19th century Russian cookbook authors were also collectors of folktales.

A number of recipes are embedded in the text itself. Others, marked in the text by boldface type, are included in the appendix. They could not all be included without making the book unwieldy. I've chosen to share over three-score representatives. In my opinion, reading the Appendix, almost as if it were a chapter, will give a feel for the range of recipe types, the authors, the intended audience, and the time of the recipe's creation. My editor found one recipe so disturbing that she asked me if I would consider eliminating it—I didn't. But be warned a recipe can upset even a professional editor.

Before beginning to examine borsch as a culinary and cultural phenomenon, I need to address a purely technical issue—how to transliterate the word used by Russians, Byelorussians, and Ukrainians to designate *борщ* (borsch). In American English the transliteration varies depending on the author and the author's cultural references. So, for example, Kyra Petrovskaya, Princess Alexandra, Nina Nicolaieff, Irma S. Rombauer and I have used "sch," while Joyce Toomre, Lynn Visson, Darra Goldstein, the *Russian Cookbook for American Homes,* and the Time-Life book used "shch," Mary Henderson and Louis P. De Gouy used the French "tsch." Not surprisingly, Norma Jost Voth, in her Mennonite cookbook used the German "scht" and Florence Kreisler Greenbaum in *The International Jewish Cookbook* used "sht."

In short, authors for whom Russian is native prefer the "sch" ending; scholars or those who follow one of the ten officially recognized transliteration systems sometimes use "shch," while others use the transliterations used in a specific non-English languages. This (not lack of a proofreader) accounts for the differences in spelling throughout this book.

In the book I refer to the soup as "borsch" but in recipes or titles I will adopt the author's usage, except in cases when I have done the translation from Russian myself. For example, since I translated the Marie-Antoine Carême French recipe from Russian I use my convention instead of the French.

Over the decades it took to research and bring this book to its final form, it transformed itself from a book conceived as a narrative based on folkloric fieldwork to one that is based on more varied exploration. The original intent is still there, as evidenced in the first and twelfth chapters, but the chapters in between are filled with presentations of history, cultural studies, rituals, and writings associated with analysis. There is purpose to this approach—I really would like the reader not only to learn some interesting facts about borsch and the cultures in which it finds itself, but also be motivated to understand that virtually all events in life, as represented in Chapter 1, have similarly complex histories and associations. Buddhists call the sum of all possible influences on a particular phenomenon *karma*, and I believe that this word conveys well the complexity of a dish I am interested in presenting.

1. HOW THIS BOOK BEGAN

> ... *Pelagia Antonovna carried in a steaming pot. With a single glance at it, one could surmise that within, in the thick of the fiery borsch, there is to be found something of which there is nothing tastier in the world—a marrow bone.*
> Mikhail Bulgakov, *Master and Margarita*

    For many years I never liked cooked beets. And since most modern versions of borsch involve beets, I did not particularly care for it. As a child, whenever Mother or Grandmother would cook it, I would try my best to minimize the amount of the beet root that found its way to my plate. And I devised a number of stratagems to deal with the beets once they were there. Usually I would try to avoid the issue and eat everything except the beets, heaping the julienned pieces into a purplish-red pile, perhaps hoping that they understood their unpopularity and would disappear on their own, somehow. That never happened, nor was I ever able to persuade any of our dogs—who often happily rescued my taste buds from assault by an unloved food—to soldier in my stead.

    Since the beets refused to disappear of their own accord, I would break the pieces on my plate into the smallest possible bits. Finally, accepting the inevitable, and after nearly driving my parents mad with my dawdling, I would swallow the bits without chewing, endeavoring mightily not to taste that which passed through my mouth. This practice led, in later years, to an enviable ability to swallow, without water, virtually any pill made by modern medicine.

    After finishing the last bits of beets, there came a coda from Mother or Grandmother that would go something like this: "You see, that wasn't so bad; I don't understand why you always make things so difficult." From experience, I knew that any utterance from me at this point would lead to no good end, and I would keep silent until the first moment I could escape from this field of battle and perpetual defeat. I liked the slightly sweet/sour taste of the broth, potatoes, and meat and, except for the beets, I might have liked borsch.

My attitude toward beets began to change in college. The bland red discs, called Harvard beets, that appeared as a side dish in the dining hall were not offensive, though they offered little to recommend themselves. They also added color, if not flavor, to any salad made at a salad bar. But the real change in attitude came about with the help of my godmother when I was in graduate school.

For a number of years while I attended Indiana University I would visit my godmother and her family in Shamokin, Pennsylvania. Many years earlier they had helped my mother when she was growing up in Yugoslavia. Later, they helped her while all of them were tossed from refugee camp to refugee camp in Austria and Germany, then they helped her and me in Germany, and after they immigrated to the United States they helped us come to the United States also. Finally, once we got here, they helped us by finding a place next door to them for my grandmother and me to live. During my visits from Indiana I was repaying a moral family debt by helping them, in turn, when their strength flagged while I was filled with energy and vigor.

Normally, I would spend a week in the summer, during school break, in Shamokin. My stay had two functions: the acknowledged one, of catching up with maintenance that had been neglected due to their age and lack of funds, and the even more important one, never acknowledged, of providing a week of outside companionship, political arguments, and the transfer of energy and optimism that I exuded. The physical work was welcome after a semester of classroom and library study, and knowing that I was repaying kindness with kindness was deeply satisfying.

The days there had an invariable structure and rhythm. I would be the first one to wake on my bed, the short couch in the tiny foyer by the kitchen. With each passing year the couch seemed to grow a bit moldier, and I would often start the day with a bout of allergic coughing. Then I would wash up, brush my teeth, boil water for a cup of instant coffee, which I drank black with no sugar. I would take the cup and my first cigarette of the day outside and walk around the property. On the first day I would observe the changes from the previous year and make mental notes of things that seemed to need attention.

By the time I finished my third cup of coffee and cigarette, godmother Anna Alexandrovna would come downstairs to the kitchen. If I was still outside she would come out the kitchen door and call me to breakfast. We would greet each other, and I would inquire about how the night was for her and Vladimir.

Vladimir, as I was allowed to call him (but always with a formal "you" form of address), guided me in the acquisition of English my first months in-country, read to all of us, taught me how to sharpen a knife, how to mix concrete, and watched me as I built my Soap Box Derby car—careful not to "help" but always ready with a suggestion of how to reach my intended goal.

Vladimir, a few years older than my mothers was part of a group of young people in Yugoslavia who had found welcome in the home of Anna Alexandrovna and her husband Sergey Matveevich. All of them went through World War II together, retreated from Yugoslavia with the German Army, survived in the same refugee camps, and after Anna and her husband came to America, Vladimir came to live near them. Bad luck followed him and he had a work accident that left him a paraplegic. Anna and Sergey took care of him from that time on. After Sergey died, Anna continued to care for Vladimir by herself.

Usually the night would not have gone well, and Anna would still have the marks of sleep on her face. Nevertheless, her deep chestnut-colored wig and lipstick were impeccable, and she would go about breakfast preparations with the gusto of a 20-year old. Breakfast usually consisted of slices of Stella D'Oro Italian bread, butter, cheese, cold cuts, and more coffee. After breakfast I would drink a second cup with her (my fifth cup of the morning!). As I aged and started to gain some excess pounds she would chide me about "letting myself go," but meanwhile each meal was a battle in which Anna was determined to feed me much more than I could ever hope to eat. Coming from a country that for centuries had periodic famines, and where the word "diet" for much of the 20th century meant enhanced feeding, overfeeding guests is still a mark of hospitality and caring

On the first day of the visit, after breakfast, I would take care of some of the minor projects and wait until Vladimir came downstairs, so that we could discuss the plan of action and I could tackle the most critical projects in an agreed-to sequence. One could tell when Vladimir was about to appear because the steel chain in the homemade elevator would begin to make noises as he lowered himself from upstairs. Usually he would make his appearance around 10 AM. He would have a cup of instant Kava (coffee with the acid removed) and his first cigarette. I would approach him and after exchanging morning greetings we would lay out the projects that needed to be completed that year. Usually the work was minor but necessary, such as repair of the back stairs, replacement of light bulb housing, repair of the laundry drying pole, trimming of branches, etc. The most important, but also the most onerous task, however, was the initial unplugging and then annual maintenance of the house's sewer line.

Soon after uncle Sergey's death the line had completely plugged up and I had to make a special trip from Indiana to take care of the ensuing emergency. My main tool for the job was a 50-foot hand snake, completely inadequate for covering the hundreds of feet of sewer line that crossed the property. First, access holes needed to be dug and chipped into the ceramic pipe (without inadvertently cracking it); and then the laborious and dirty task of snaking followed. That first time it took three full days to unplug the pipe; after that, annual maintenance took about a day.

As I was engaged in these various projects, once a week, around 11AM or so, Mr. Beaver would arrive with his olive green panel truck grocery store. When I heard the truck arriving I would wash my hands and go and visit with Jim Beaver. When Grandmother and I lived in Shamokin he and his wife Pat showed us many kindnesses and during my summer visits I never failed to visit with him and exchange family information. In my last few visits to Shamokin I missed Mr. Beaver; he finally retired, and he and his wife moved to Florida to help ease her arthritis, which was exacerbated by the cold Pennsylvania winters.

Anna would purchase whatever she needed for the week as well as the ingredients she lacked for the borsch I named **Anna Aleksandrovna's Borsch**.[1] In the first years of my visits most vegetables came from her sizable garden but then, as life took its toll, vegetables would also be bought. Having been forewarned about my arrival, Mr. Beaver would bring fresh rib roast for the soup's stock (usually he sold frozen meat) because Anna insisted that this was the only meat that made good borsch. After handing over the purchased food, and most important, cigarettes for Vladimir, Mr. Beaver would enter the balance due into his ledger and continue on his way.

In the meantime Vladimir would prepare the homemade hibachi (*mangalka*) stove right by the kitchen door. The use of this little stove outdoors helped keep the temperature down inside the un-air conditioned house and also saved money on the propane that fueled the regular stove. Scrap lumber was free.

In its Shamokin incarnation, the *mangalka* became a "Mongolian" stove made out of a small galvanized steel pail that had outlived its usefulness and had been transformed: a small access opening had been cut out with tin snips on one side, toward the bottom; it was lined with a good one-inch thickness of leftover cement and topped by a grate made of scrap pieces of steel rods. Vladimir used leftover scrap lumber to make large wood splinters with which he would start a fire in this stove.

Anna would put water and the meat in a large white enamel cooking pot with a thin red rim. The pot had an 8- or 10-quart capacity and was one of those that could be bought for a few dollars at Woolworth's or on a special cookware promotion at Acme supermarkets. Despite its low cost (and perhaps because the days of itinerant tinkers who soldered small holes in pots were long gone), the pot was treated with great care lest a bit of enamel be chipped off. Inevitably, over the years, some small chips did appear, but the pot nevertheless remained a treasured member of the cooking ensemble. The concern was not to burn a hole through the unprotected thin steel wall where the chip was.

It was my job to carry the heavy pot to the *mangalka*, place it carefully on the steel rods, and then go about my appointed tasks. It was Vladimir's job to tend to the stove and the cooking pot and prepare the vegetables for the soup. These jobs he did while sitting in his blue-backed wheelchair, smoking cigarettes. There was a ritual: first, Vladimir would get the old, worn-down whetstone, spit on it,

---

[1] Recipe names in bold indicate a recipe in the Appendix.

and begin to sharpen the little paring knife he would use. After sharpening the knife he would test it by running his thumb along the blade's edge and then shaving a few hairs off his arm. Once satisfied that the knife was sharp he would begin to prepare the various roots, leaves, stalks, and bulbs for the pot. Anna, meanwhile, was working on the dough for the *pirozhki*—a savory pastry filled with meat (in this version)—and perhaps my favorite Russian dish.

In Russian culinary tradition borsch is most commonly eaten with bread, vegetable-stuffed *pirozhki*, or *pampushki*—a yeast roll popular in Ukraine. It is unusual to serve meat *pirozhki* with borsch, but Anna knew how much I loved them, and she always prepared a large batch for me to take home. Packed in empty cardboard boxes from medical cotton, interleaved with paper towels, these delectable morsels of fried dough and meat would begin to disappear on the drive back to Bloomington. It was a heroic effort to be able to bring home half of the initial number entrusted to me by Anna. As we worked, there was a hum of activity, a dance of sorts, with Vladimir peeling, cutting, and chopping on a small board placed on his lap— constantly wheeling in and out between the kitchen and the outside—while Anna was pouring and mixing and complaining about her angina; and I would be trimming, cutting, digging, moving, sawing, or hammering.

Then, at a certain point, Anna would decide that the stock was done and I would be called to help bring the pot into the kitchen. There are two basic approaches to making broth: one is the slow simmering of bones, meat, and aromatics (onion, garlic, celery), and the other is a fast boil of meat and bones, sometimes without any other additives. Anna's approach was of the latter type; it gave a rich meat-tasting broth with the additional benefit of providing boiled meat with enough flavor in it to be tasty in the soup and in other applications. Traditionally, after eating the soup, the meat from stock-making is served accompanied by grated horseradish and mustard.

Anna would remove the meat and bones from the broth, and braised vegetables would be placed in the pot. I would take the pot back outdoors. And Vladimir would continue his task of tending the fire. He also had the additional task of putting the chunks of boiled meat through the meat grinder, grinding them by hand so that a filling for the *pirozhki* could be made.

By mid-afternoon the soup would be done, the *pirozhki* would be prepared and deep fried, and all of us would be hungry and pretty tired. The last step before we began to eat would be for me to go to the garden to pick a few hot peppers, snip some dill, chives, and garlic greenery. These were the condiments that were finely chopped and available to add to the borsch.

Usually we ate outside on the homemade concrete deck under the pergola, which was made of salvaged lumber and galvanized steel pipes. The grape-covered pergola was painted a light blue, and the grape leaves and immature grapes gave a bit of Mediterranean feeling to this corner of coal-country Pennsylvania.

Dinner would be leisurely, with more talk than eating, although the latter was by no means neglected. It is during these hours that I learned much of my family history, of my parents' youth, stories of my grandparents, and in general, of life in the Russian émigré community in Yugoslavia in the years between the wars. It is during these dinners that I learned how to place direct familial experience in a larger context and see the fate of our family as part of a community. It is also during these dinners that I overcame my antipathy toward beets and learned to appreciate the incredibly rich symphony of flavors that came out of the garden's dirt, the truck grocery store, a stove made out of a pail, and the efforts of folk who manifested in their daily being centuries of human experience and deep caring for others.

Only years later did it occur to me that in enacting our borsch ritual we were unconsciously following the tradition of serving borsch on special, celebratory occasions. We were celebrating our reunion and reaffirming bonds of culture, love, and family. Who could have imagined in 1895 or 1905, the years Sergey Matveevich and Anna Aleksandrovna were born, that thanks to borsch a project conceived to share those moments would, more than a century later, make their story part of the literary record.

2. EVOLUTION AND HISTORY OF BORSCH

BORSCH-*masc. Soured beet. Type of schi, pottage made out of fermented beet juice with beef and pork or with pork fatback. The plant Acanthus or Heracleum (sphondylium et sibiricus).*
Vladimir Dal'. *Explanatory Dictionary of the Living Great Russian Language*, 1880

While borsch is eaten throughout Russia, Ukrainians claim that borsch is their national dish. This claim is easily accepted; no other nation has the sheer multiplicity of varieties of the soup or has brought it to a similar height of perfection. It seems that there is no region, or town, that does not have its own version. And in the recent past Ukraine has been suffused with borsch festivals vying for world records in borsch cookery: for numbers of different versions served at one venue; for the largest quantity of borsch cooked (the current record is 4,000 liters, or about 1,000 gallons); or for the creation of the largest ceramic borsch cooking pot (somewhere in the 1,000-liter range).

The importance of borsch in Ukraine can be seen in a reminiscence in Kyra Petovskaya's *Kyra's Secrets of Russian Cooking*:

I helped my hostess prepare huge meals for her big family and farmhands. The main staple of their diet was borsch, which my hostess cooked almost daily in a pot of at least ten gallon capacity.

At meal time, 12 to 15 of us would sit around this large pot, each with his own wooden spoon, waiting for the head of the family to start. Crossing himself piously several times, the head of the family would dip his spoon into the huge pot. His wife would be the next, and so on down the line to the youngest child. It took me, a city-bred girl, a long time to get used to this manner of eating. ... I had to learn how to hold a piece of bread under my chin, as I saw the peasants do, to catch any drippings from the round, wide spoon, which was too big even for the biggest mouth.

The question of the soup's origin, however, is a bit more complex. There is an extant legend, for example, among Don Cossacks that borsch was invented by them during the siege of Azov in the 17th century. According to that tale the initial borsch was a mix of foodstuffs available to the defenders during the siege, and the name of the dish was an anagram of the Don Cossack term for fish soup "*scherba*." Furthermore, the legend claims that Zaporozhian (Ukrainian) Cossacks learned how to cook borsch during the siege and took that knowledge afterwards to their homeland. The legend may be hard to accept as factual truth, given that the use of the term "borsch" for a soup goes back at least to the 16th century, and that the recipe that accompanies this tale contains tomatoes, a vegetable that did not enter wide use in Russia until the 19th century, at a time when Ukraine was part of Russia.

Of course, there is also a counter-legend. According to it, in 1683 the Ottomans were laying siege to Vienna. The Polish king sent troops to help the city and in that army there were Zaporozhian Cossacks who failed to provision themselves. They lived off the land and at one of their stops began sautéing beets in bacon fat. This culinary discovery, the precursor of the tradition of sautéing beets, the technique that gives the soup its characteristic color and flavor, became a war prize which was transmitted orally by the Cossacks to their brethren. The preeminent Russian food writer—William Vasilyevich Pokhlyobkin, stated unequivocally that borsch finds its origin in the Ukraine.

The Dictionary of the Russian Language of the 11th to the 17th Centuries defines the word *borschevik*, also called "borsch," as "A species of edible plant." The definition goes on to cite two early usages, both from the 16th century: "At that time and until the autumn the borsch is cut and dried and into braids braided, it will always be useful in the future and into the year. Carrots, turnip, beets are salted for storage, borsch and all kinds of garden vegetables."

The borsch plant is closely related to the common hogweed (*Heracleum sphondylium*) and has a large reddish root. As the name implies, hogweed was fed to pigs, and all parts of the vegetable (leaves, young stems, and roots) were eaten also by humans. In Russia, *Heracleum sibiricum* was the variety most commonly consumed, with other varieties such as cow parsnip (*Heracleum maximum*) serving various flavoring roles. According to Pokhlebnikov, *Heracleum sibiricum*, which has an identifiable mushroom taste, was in particular use among populations whose dietary culture did not include mushrooms. Today, borsch recipes with *borschevik* are difficult to find. In this book I present one **Cow Parsnip Borsch** recipe.

The earliest Russian references to the borsch plant and soup are found in the medieval compendium *Domostroy* (*Domestic Order*, 1547) attributed to archpriest Sylvester:

By the fence, around the whole garden, where the nettle grows, sow borsch. From springtime on cook it frequently. You won't be able to buy the same kind in the market and here you'll always have some. And for the Lord's sake share it with those in need. If it grows abundantly sell it, exchanging it for another ingredient.

In writing about the Polish borsch (plant and soup), Maria Dembinska wrote in her *Food and Drink in Medieval Poland*:

… it was not even made from beets in its original form, but from the European cow parsnip—also called barszcz in Polish—that grows on damp ground. Its roots were collected in May for stewing with meat, the shoots and young leaves were cooked as greens, and the unopened flower penduncles were eaten as a vegetable or added to soups and pottages. Szymon Syrennius discussed this plant in his herbal and further stated that soups made with it were highly valued in Poland, Lithuania, and Russia. During the Middle Ages it was prepared in soup by itself or was cooked in chicken stock with such additions as egg yolks, cream, or millet meal. The dry leaves exude a sweet substance that was used to create sweet-sour flavors, especially when used with vinegar. The adaptation of cow parsnips to Polish cookery appears to have come from Lithuania.

According to Dembinska, *żurek*, rye-kvas based soup (without beets), also known as **White Borsch**, appeared in Polish chronicles in 966 C.E.

The beet came from Byzantium to Rus' (a precursor state, which both Russians and Ukrainians claim as theirs) somewhere between the 10th and 11th centuries. Initially, beets were solely used for their greens; it took some time until the beetroot was bred to be edible. We know that turnips were the staple root vegetable in Russia throughout the medieval period, but it is safe to state that by the 16th

and 17th century beets were commonly used, and that borsch with beets as an ingredient was consumed. It appears that the greens were initially of prime importance and later the soured (fermented) beetroot. Given that the beet came from Byzantium via Ukraine, it seems logical that the beet variety of borsch did, indeed, originate in the Ukraine, but the geographical origin of the cow parsnip version is not clear.

The term "soup" did not enter the Russian vocabulary until the time of Peter the Great (17th and 18th centuries) and initially referred only to soups of foreign (Western) origin. Only in the 19th century did the term begin to refer to Russian as well as non-Russian dishes, but even then soup was a term of disdain and referred only to clear soups.

The native Russian terms used were *shchi*, *kalya* or *rassolnik*, *ukha*, *solyanka* or *selyanka*, *borsch*, and *pokhlebka*. Each of these types of soups has a specific characteristic that identifies it. *Schi*, for example, must contain cabbage as its main ingredient; *pokhlebka* is always based on a vegetable broth; *ukha* is a fish soup; *rassolnik* or *kalya* has pickle brine as the distinguishing ingredient; and *solyanka* or *selyanka* is a variety of spicy soup. Borsch, therefore, is not simply a particular kind of soup, but a category of soups, and one ought to find what specifically makes it this type of soup. Borsch soups, along with *schi*, *rassolnik*, and some others, belong to what is called in Russian *zapravochye* soups. While no English word adequately translates this term, the meaning of it is "filled," and the reference is to the fact that *zapravochye* soups are those in which braised and/or sautéed vegetables are added to a broth—the broth is "filled." The base stock or broth can be made from meat or vegetables (in the latter case, often with dried *boletus* mushrooms), or a fermented liquid called "kvas."

Zapravochnye soups were the oldest soups in the Russian, Byelorussian, and Ukrainian culinary practice and are the result of the peculiarities of the way the Russian/Byelorussian/Ukrainian stove/oven (*russkaya pech*) is built. The classic Russian stove consisted of a huge piece of masonry that took up somewhere between one-third to half of the interior of a peasant's hut. Initially made of clay, and later of brick, it was a marvel of folk engineering. In essence it was a fire box surrounded by masonry, and honeycombed by an intricate system of internal ducts and baffles to allow smoke and gasses to give up their heat before being vented. The stove is extremely efficient in its use of fuel and provides a long-term and steady heat.

The stove was used for baking, frying, cooking, and heating. Because of its size and manner of construction it was also used as a sleeping surface in winter. Obviously, such a stove was a disadvantage in the summer; there is a long-standing tradition of stand-alone summer kitchens in Russia and similar countries.

Anything that requires long-term cooking on such a stove is cooked at slowly decreasing heat levels, somewhat like modern slow cookers. Anyone who has used a slow cooker to cook vegetables knows that it takes much longer to cook them than to cook meat, and in order to have all be done in the same span of time, the vegetables need to be pre-cooked to a degree. This is what braising and sautéing vegetables before adding them to a broth accomplishes; it breaks down the fibers so that, when simmered, ingredients reach doneness together. Soups that require "pre-processing" through braising of vegetables to accommodate the requirements of the Russian *pech*, as a *zapravochnyi* borsch does, clearly indicate their ancient lineage, which predates the appearance of beets in the cookery in Russia in the 1500s.

The central ingredients for the oldest Russian and Ukrainian borsch soups are not beets, but some sort of greens, the sweetness of which is combined with a souring agent, usually *kvas*. *Kvas* is a fermented liquid, principally made from rye; in borsch, however, beet-based *kvas* is most traditional. It is also interesting that in Romania *borş* (fermented wheat bran) is used in the making of sour soups such as **Ciorbă de perişoare (Romanian Soured Meatball Soup)**. The term *borş* is derived from the Russian or Ukrainian borsch. One important invariable in borsch, therefore, appears to be the presence of an acidic (sour) taste in combination with a sweet ingredient. Sweet, dried *borschevik* leaves and sour kvas would be the classical combination.

One can trace this evolution linguistically. In 1863 and 1880, the famous *Dictionary of the Living Russian Language,* by Vladimir Dal', defined borsch in its secondary meaning as "a type of schi: soup from sour beet juice with beef, pork or pork fat," or as a particular type of soup within the larger schi category. But in *The Practical Dictionary of the Russian* Language (1934-1940), by Dmitri Ushakov, borsch is defined as "soup with beets and other vegetables." This latter definition seems to show that by the middle of the 20th century borsch had established itself as a soup distinct from schi.

The early connection and centrality of kvas to borsch is clearly indicated as early as the 10th century CE by the existence of the Polish White Borsch (**Barszcz biały**), also known as **Żur** (a name said to come from the German *sauer*, or sour). Normally a very rich Polish Easter soup, *Żur* (with rye-based kvas) or *Barszcz biały* (wheat flour kvas) contains sausages, and the water in which the sausages are cooked is used for broth. The sour flavor of fermented grain liquid in the soup is considered to be important. That significance was clearly indicated in a particular recipe I found on the Internet. The author had listed all the ingredients for a first-class white borsch and had written very clear directions for making the soup. The first response from a reader, however, was, "Your recipe is no good; you need fermented flour liquid in white borsch."

The importance of greens and a sour taste in borsch is indicated by the existence of a whole category of non-beet borschs: green and onion borsch. The classic green borsch is made with sorrel, although spinach, chard, or nettles (*Urtica*) can be added to the sorrel or used alone after the spring and early summer season for sorrel has passed. **Nick's Green Sorrel Borsch** is my interpretation of this classic summer dish. In Jewish cookery, green borsch is called *schav*.

Sorrel is an intensely acidic green with a smaller, thinner leaf than spinach. Borsch made with sorrel is radically different from the modern varieties of beet borsch. While a good Ukrainian beet borsch is rich and full of complex flavors, visually somehow reminiscent of an overstuffed Victorian sofa, green sorrel borsch is light, clean tasting, and closer to the ideal of a Danish modern chair.

It appears, therefore, that beet greens replaced the leaves of the *borschevik* plant while the root provided the kvas needed for souring. The initially ancillary role of beets in borsch is suggested also by the fact that in some versions of Lenten borsch not only are meat, butter, and other dairy products not used (all are proscribed in Orthodox and Eastern Rite Catholic Lenten dishes) but even vegetables such as beets, carrots, tomatoes, and red peppers are avoided. These vegetables have bright colors and were therefore seen as *skoromnye* (immodest). Usually these Lenten soups, also called *borschok* or "little borsch," have either rye kvas or dried porcini (*Boletus edulis*) or "white" mushrooms, in Russian, for the base stock.

Although beet roots are not used in this soup, beet greens are an essential traditional ingredient.

Another characteristic of *borschok* is that the vegetables are placed in this soup raw and are not first sautéed, as they are in meat-based borsch. This would indicate that *borschok* is meant to be cooked quickly, probably over an open fire, and not in a Russian stove. Since there is no meat involved there is no need to pre-cook the vegetables.

The importance of sautéing vegetables for meat-based borsch was brought home to me some years ago, when I made a beet borsch using a newer recipe that did not call for sautéing the vegetables. A family friend, who was born and lived for a good portion of her life near the city of Oryol, in Central Russia, made the following comment: "This is a very nice soup, but this is not borsch, this is *borschok*." It seems, based on that comment, that another invariant of a traditional borsch is not the presence of beetroot, but rather the sautéing of the vegetables, which adds a certain richness and depth of flavor to the dish.

It is interesting that when, by the 18th century, the fundamental elements of contemporary borsch became established, the new ingredients mimicked the flavor and texture elements of the medieval dishes. This process of attempting to maintain flavor and texture continued into the 19th century when even more changes in ingredients came about. Borsch traditionally is an extremely local dish, key ingredients sometimes can be limited to a single lake (to a type of smelt), but as the dish evolved and its area of distribution widened a "patchwork" of borsch traditions emerged, some varieties maintaining ancient ways while others incorporated the innovations and created new traditions. The same process continues to this day, when food products and cooking techniques have changed even more, and the dish has now experienced a much wider geographic distribution than ever before.

As an example, the sweet-sour flavor imparted to medieval borsch pottages by dry leaves of the borsch plant being mixed with vinegar or by fermentation, was maintained in the 18th century when fermented red beets replaced hogweed as the fundamental ingredient in the soup. Sometimes fermented beet juice (kvas) was made from the beets and added to the soup; at other times, the prepared soup itself would be allowed to sour. The latter method was cumbersome, requiring anywhere from three to seven days for completion of the dish. Today, the sweet-sour taste is normally achieved by use of beets for sweetness, tomatoes for acidity, and sugar and lemon or vinegar to help stabilize the red color of the soup and get the intended balance of flavors.

One last point on this theme: a popular summer soup in Eastern Europe is the Polish *Chłodnik*, also known as **Šaltibarščia** in Lithuanian, and *svekolnik* (beet soup) in Russian. This cold version of Polish beet borsch is usually not referred to as borsch in Russian and Ukrainian, although the term *kholodny borsch* (cold borsch) is gaining in popularity.

The point of this forensic exploration is to show that the current definition of borsch as a type of beet soup represents an evolution from the original hogweed/cow parsnip soup, and that for a very long time the definitional invariables of borsch depended, in part, on cooking technique (sautéing of vegetables) and in part on the presence of greens and an acidic taste usually created by some form of kvas or brine. A secondary point that emerges is that if kvas and greens are the salient traits of a borsch, then the dish could have originated in some part of East Central Europe other than Ukraine, such as Lithuania or Poland. It is plausible to think that the original hogweed borsch, which could have arisen anywhere in East Central Europe, was displaced by beet borsch as that vegetable and soup migrated from the south.

By itself, this point is not earth-shattering, but it is important to underline that all ethnicities in the area made their contributions to the origin and development of this dish that has become a worldwide phenomenon. It is also important to show that borsch with beets did not appear out of nowhere; rather, it is a dish that is part of an ongoing evolution. It appears that originally borsch was much closer to the greens soups found in the Southern United States than to the ruby-red consommé found in some elite restaurants in Moscow today.

After the development from a hogweed- to a beet-centered soup, the next new vegetable that became a staple in borsch-making was the potato. The introduction of the potato to Russia is credited to Peter the Great, but that attribution may be more legendary than factual. As in most European countries, the potato was initially more of a curiosity than a diet staple; in some documented instances potatoes were cultivated for their flowers which, included in the corsages of fashionable ladies, were deemed to be the height of fashion. As a food item, initially the potato was limited to the highest social circles. Resistance to wide-spread cultivation was intense, but eventually it spread all over Eastern Europe, and today Russians consider their country to be the second home of the potato, after the Andes; I even remember singing songs in Russian camp, in my youth, about the wonderful qualities of the potato.

The potato replaced the staple root vegetable of Russian and Ukrainian medieval times: the turnip (*Brassica rapa*). To this day, Russian traditionalists shed tears into their meads and kvas over the displacement of that food by the more prolific and calorically richer, but nutritionally less beneficial, tuber. But the fact remains that the potato has become, since the 19th century, a key player in the borsch ensemble. Except for some extremely regional versions, only specialists and purists still add turnips to a borsch today, and that usually in combination with potatoes.

The other important new vegetable (technically, a fruit) that transformed borsch preparation is the tomato. The tomato entered the Russian Empire toward the end of the 18th century. It migrated to the shores of the Black Sea (primarily Crimea and Georgia), the Caspian Sea (Astrakhan area), and the Baltic (St. Petersburg). In the north tomatoes were initially raised as decorative plants and curiosities, and as herbal medicinal plants. In Georgia, Crimea, and the Astrakhan area, however, they were used as food. But it was not until the beginning of the 20th century that most of European Russia and parts of Siberia saw the cultivation of this plant. Today, the tomato is second only to the potato in the hearts of Russians, Ukrainians, and other denizens of Central and Eastern Europe.

In most contemporary borsch recipes from Russia and the Ukraine the tomato is an essential ingredient. Depending on the recipe, it is added to the soup raw, canned, and/or as tomato paste. In some recipes, such as in Russian Mennonite borsch, the tomato is on a par with cabbage and potato. Mennonites do not use beetroot in their borsch, and beet greens used in summer borsch are the only beets found in their varieties of the soup.

The tomato also replaced kvas as the major source of acidity in borsch. (In addition, making kvas takes anywhere from two to five days, depending on ingredients, weather, and temperature.) One seldom sees recipes that call for both ingredients. Vinegar or powdered citric acid was used to help keep the beet color in braising, and tomato added the needed sourness to the soup as a whole. In some Ukrainian recipes lemon juice is also added towards the end to help balance and brighten the flavors.

The adoption of new ingredients reflected the changes in cooking techniques that resulted from growing urbanization, industrialization, and other social transformations. In the 19th century the urban dweller went from the traditional Russian stove to a coal-fired cast iron stove. In the communal apartments of the Soviet era one often had to rely on a one-burner (kerosene) Primus stove, so there was little room for multi-utensil cookery, or time and fuel to slow-cook a dish. In the oldest recipes, borsch cooking was often a two-day affair, and the recipe of 19th century French chef Carême calls for a cooking time of more than five hours.

In short, modern life has forced significant changes in Russian cookery in general and borsch in particular. Much of the pressure has been towards simplification of recipes and the shortening of cooking times. Today one can even purchase freeze-dried borsch and a panoply of dried borsch soup varieties. But these "helpers" do not mean that people are willing to forego the soup made "from scratch."

There are also counter-trends to the tendency towards simplification. A few years ago, I began experimenting, using our slow cooker to imitate borsch cooked in a Russian stove. I discovered that the qualitative difference between a borsch cooked on a stove top and in a slow cooker is substantial. The texture of the latter soup is velvety and the flavors are extremely mild and rich. At the time I also noticed that more and more traditional borsch recipes, including some that call for a slow cooker, were being posted on the Internet by American, English, or Canadian contributors—a possible attempt to imitate the *tomlenie* (languor) of the ancient Russian stove. Two recipes, **"Lazy" Slow Cooker Borsch,** by a Russian contributor, and **Crock Pot Russian Beef Borscht** by an American, are two tasty versions. Technology, it seems, can serve not only to speed the pace of life but also help to re-create old flavors and textures within a modern cultural context.

The post-Soviet era of private entrepreneurship has also resulted in the appearance of an active guild of master Russian-stove builders in Moscow and other localities. One can even order a

Russian stove in kit form; and there are companies that will build one specifically designed for a given architectural space. In short, while simplification and evolution of borsch recipes continues there are also attempts to hearken back to ancient times. The growth and popularity in virtually every Russian metropolitan area and in many provincial towns of restaurants that serve native dishes based on old recipes and techniques is a sign of a hunger for an experience of heritage and authenticity.

While the evolution of borsch has occurred since its first mention in Russian sources in 1547 and Polish in 966, its role as a special, celebratory, and ritual dish has stayed remarkably consistent over the centuries. Even when used as an everyday food, as indicated in Kyra Petrovskaya's reminiscence, it is surrounded by ritual, elevating it from the role of a simple utilitarian cultural artifact to one imbued with significant spiritual values.

3. BORSCH: REGION, ETHNICITY, CLASS, OCCUPATION

"I can't begin to tell [Toronto friends] that when I was six, those whirling girls with the hair ribbons in Dauphin were princesses to me. I can't fill their tongues with the tart sensation of borshsh.
Tanis MacDonald's *"Social Studies,"* 1992

In June of 2011, Campbell Soup Company announced that it planned to withdraw from the Russian market. It appears that 80 percent of Russians believe that prepared soups are fine for camping trips but are a sign of bad breeding when served to a guest, or family, at home. It is curious, however, that while abandoning the Russian market and apparently not pursuing plans to open in Ukraine, Campbell is marketing a canned borsch to the Chinese community as **luo song tang**, or Russian soup.

There is a most curious story to *luo song tang* (罗宋汤), which is known not only as Russian Soup but also as Chinese Borsch. The dish, which is now quite popular in Hong Kong restaurants, originally came from Harbin, a city in Northeast China founded by Russians in 1898. The Chinese borsch that originated there, also called Red Soup, lacks beets as an ingredient but has generous portions of cabbage and tomatoes and is very similar to Mennonite borsch from the Volga region. (It is interesting to note that in 1929 a few hundred Mennonites emigrated from Harbin to the U.S.)

When I first learned of this recipe I was quite skeptical, and decided to test its authenticity. In May of 2012, I volunteered to sell my homemade Chinese borsch at a Chinese Buddhist monastery in

Carmel, New York, during the Buddha's birthday celebration. I sold quite a few bowls, modified to be vegetarian and without garlic to reflect the monastery's dietary rules. My Chinese customers recognized it as a familiar soup, although almost all of them informed me that they make it slightly differently (not surprising, considering that I left out two normally key ingredients). That is how **Nick's Vegetarian *luo song tang* (Russian Soup)** was created.

My only complaint came from a non-Chinese customer who said, "This is not how my mother's borsch tastes." When I responded, "But, ma'am this is Chinese Monastery Borsch," she shook her head and walked away with her bowl. I understand that a version of Chinese borsch with cobra meat as an ingredient can be purchased at a stall opposite Restaurant Number 369 in Jakarta, Indonesia. Some claim it to be tasty. And, of course, one can always order (online) cans of Campbell's Borsch with Chinese lettering.

Borsch, like Buddhism, is perfectly suited to a global culture. In each, within a global phenomenon local variants are so numerous and diverse that it is hard sometimes for a non-specialist to grasp that any single example of it is something that is part of a unified tradition. Borsch is an almost perfect example of the recently coined term "glocalization"—a phenomenon that is global in distribution but reflective of local needs and ways in its variants and adaptation. One way that borsch differs from the standard concept of "glocalization" is that, unlike modern counterparts that begin as global initiatives and then are adapted to local conditions, borsch was a highly localized product that became globalized, and in the process adapted to conditions other than the original ones. It is a truism among borsch enthusiasts that there are as many recipes as there are cooks, and yet there are fusing elements that help create soups of national, regional, ethnic, and religious cultures.

William Pokhlebkin claimed that there are twenty variants of the soup. Traditionally, people from the Central European Borsch Belt—a geographical swath in Europe that starts with Poland, goes north to the Baltic Sea, east to Siberia and south to the Black Sea—count four: hot and cold, green and red. I like this simpler set of categories, but would add to them vegetarian and animal protein-based broths and slow-cooked versus fast-cooked versions. I also would slightly recast the color distinction into red and non-red variants so as to allow the Polish White Borsch to be included.

Most often borsch is classified by nationality or ethnic group, even when it becomes traditional in a country or group other than the ascribed one. I can't remember the last time I ate a Ukrainian borsch prepared by an actual Ukrainian, as opposed to a Russian or an American.

A few summers ago I received, from a member of our class on Buddhism, a request to help a noted monk by cooking for a few days. The monk was trying a raw food diet, hoping that it would ease a chronic medical condition, and therefore was not eating at the monastery's dining hall. The nun who was helping him with his food had to be away for some days. I liked this monk, was quite willing to give a hand, and was intrigued to learn something about a food universe I had no inkling about. So I offered my services and was asked to talk to a volunteer who was coordinating these matters.

I talked to her. Despite my accurate description of a respectable cooking competence, my lack of knowledge of the raw food "cooking" made her uncomfortable, and my query, "If you know how to cook, then how hard can raw food cooking be?" during our conversation did not set her mind at ease. But I guess no one else came forward and so, with some trepidation evident in her voice, she accepted my offer.

The monk and I have known each other for some years, always had a positive relationship, and I was even involved for a short while with a project that was dear to his heart. When I arrived at the monastery on the appointed afternoon with my toilet kit, change of clothes, small computer, and camera, my friend the monk was happy to see me. And that is how I entered the world of Living Foods, developed by Dr. Ann Wigmore.

The first evening was simple; as a member of a Buddhist sangha my friend did not eat after the noon hour, and just had had a cup of miso soup with dulse seaweed flakes and a light chiffonade of scallion, to give a bit of freshness to the beverage. Later that evening I began to study the cookbook from the Creative Health Institute in Michigan to see what I could prepare in the days to follow.

As I studied the book I became intrigued by some of the staples involved in Ann Wigmore's regimen. Somewhere in all of this information, scattered between Vitamix blenders, Himalayan Sea Salt (an intriguing concept in itself), the Excalibur food dehydrators, Agave nectar, Hurom or Omega wheat grass juicers (Champion juicers for other foods), for an initial capital outlay well north of $1,000, there was something awfully familiar, with a distinct scent of history. A key ingredient of the daily diet, present in many dishes, was something called "Rejuvelac"—to me—a mild form of kvas; another was "Veggiekraut," or fermented cabbage, often with beets. The daily regimen included consumption of wheat grass juice. Something that also fascinated me was the prevalence of garlic in many recipes, and even in the enemas that are to be administered regularly.

The Internet helped resolve my questions and premonitions. It turns out that Dr. Ann Wigmore was a Lithuanian immigrant who deeply respected, imitated, and adapted to modern American living some of the ancient Lithuanian foods and health practices modeled by her grandmother. "Rejuvelac" is a mild form of kvas, and I even learned from her writings that to get the silky smooth texture of naturally fermented sauerkraut that I love, one has to pound the cabbage in the crock as it is filled to capacity. I could just picture a Lithuanian housewife pounding cabbage in a crock with a "Louisville slugger."

And even wheat grass juice suddenly fell into a traditional context, as I remembered that Kalmyks—pastoral nomads living in Russia since the 17th century—would often use as medicine, meat broths cooked from animals slaughtered at various times of the year to ensure that the curative powers of herbs would be part of the broths. How many micronutrients modern wheat grass has, raised as it is in a soil composed of perlite and sphagnum moss, is an open question. I was inspired: I would create a borsch recipe using the "Living Foods" principles and see if it helped my friend or, at least, gladdened his heart. That is the story of **Nick's Living Foods Raw Borsch**.

The next morning, after breakfast, I suggested borsch for the meal of the day. I expected an enthusiastic response, since my friend was originally from Brooklyn and of Jewish heritage, but I got a more circumspect one. It turned out that my friend, who was being very careful of sugar intake, expected the sweet all-beet consommé that he had experienced in his youth, while I was thinking more along the lines of Russian or Ukrainian vegetable soup, with beets only giving their flavor and color.

I assured him that in this version of borsch beets would serve mostly a flavoring role and he agreed to try. The experiment went well enough so that when the coordinator called for a report on my cooking I got a positive evaluation, which assuaged her concerns and resulted in subsequent warm and friendly conversations.

During the monk's and my discussion it became clear that we had two different expectations when we heard the word "borsch." I realized, in an instant of comprehension, that for people who grew up with a particular soup version that borsch becomes iconic. I fully understood at that moment the non-material dimension of food as an evocator of emotions.

While borsch originated with and was mostly eaten by the peasantry, it migrated to the tables of the highest reaches of society. In Russia, Catherine the Great, Tsar Alexander II, the ballerina Anna Pavlova, and the General Secretary of the Communist Party, Leonid Brezhnev, liked borsch immensely. Brezhnev's wife, who is said to have continued to cook even when they lived in the Kremlin, was quoted by Larisa Vasilievas in *Kremlin Wives* as having said:

Leonid Ivanovitch loved my borsch. You know there are different kinds of Ukrainian borsch: cold, hot, Lenten, and with meat stock. For the first course, for the most part, we would have borsch—Ukrainian borsch; hot or cold. Nowadays I only cook borsch in vegetable oil—sunflower oil, we need lighter, Lenten food. But in those years I cooked borsch with beets, potatoes, cabbage, tomatoes, garlic, fatback; and, in addition, a nice piece of meat. I cooked "day-long borsch" for two, three days—it's tastier when it can steep.

Brezhnev's reputedly favorite **Zaporozhian Borsch** and his wife's **Borsch with Prunes** recipe clearly speak of his humble Ukrainian beginnings.

By the time Brezhnev had an opportunity to enjoy borsch in the Kremlin, the dish had been part of international high society since the days of Marie-Antoine (Antonin) Carême, who in 1819 worked for a short while for Tsar Alexander I in St. Petersburg. This "king of chefs, and chef of kings" published during his lifetime a notorious borsch recipe, along with a number of other "Russian" dishes, and was instrumental in setting the understanding of Russian cuisine in Western Europe.

This recipe, easily found in *Larousse Gastronomique* of 1938 in French, was translated late in the 19th century into Russian and is currently making the Internet rounds under the title of **Borsch for Tsars**, to the amusement of many Russian cooks because of its astounding number and combination of ingredients. What modern readers fail to grasp is that Carême was less interested in the authenticity of the recipe than in creating an exotic dish that would appeal to French diners of the time.

We also see that already in 1855 two much more traditional recipes (Lithuanian Borsch Made with Green Celery and Little Russian Borsch) found their way to *Gastronomer's Almanac*, a cookbook published that year by N. M. Radetsky. The presence of borsch in this work shows the currency of the dish in the highest circles of Russian and international society. Radetsky was the maître d'hôtel for HH Grand Duke Maximilian of Leuchtenberg (husband of Grand Duchess Maria Nikolaevna, daughter of Nicholas I).

One can argue that Radetsky's work was more authentic because he was part of the Russian social scene, but looking at the borsch recipe developed by August Escoffier, who was not in that orbit, the excesses of Carême were toned down to a minimum wholly in keeping with Escoffier's "Faites simple" (Keep it Simple) mantra.

Escoffier's legacy was passed on to Louis P. De Gouy who as an internationally acclaimed chef with experience in the premier hotels in France, England, and Spain, was for 30 years at the Waldorf-Astoria in New York. The height of his influence ranged from the 1930s through the 1950s. He apprenticed with Escoffier, worked for a year as chef on J.P Morgan's yacht *Wild Duck*, wrote 20 cookbooks, and was the first chef for *Gourmet* magazine. As shown by **Bortsch Polonaise**, his borsch recipes make borsch non-exotic, and fully in line with the elite American cooking practices of the time. His **Jellied Bortsch** is a combination of simplicity and elegance.

Of all the versions of cookbooks created for high society with borsch recipes, my favorite is Mary Henderson's *Paris Embassy Cookbook*, published in 1980. Mary was born in Greece in 1919 as Mary Xenia Cawadias. She was the daughter of the doctor to the King of Greece. When Mary was five her family moved to London and Mary studied there, but her father prevented her from attending Oxford University. In 1939, when WWII broke out, she was staying with her mother in Greece and became a Red Cross nurse. Later she was arrested by the Gestapo and condemned to death for aiding the Allies (a sentence she managed to avoid). Between 1946 and 1949 she was a war correspondent for *Time* and *Life* magazines during the Greek Civil War, and in 1951 she married British diplomat and Ambassador Nicholas Henderson. Mary and Nicholas served at the embassies in Vienna, Santiago, Madrid, Warsaw, Bonn, Paris, and Washington.

Physically, Mary Henderson's book is most attractive—a hard-bound tome with sewn pages that lie absolutely flat when opened; coated heavy-weight paper; wonderful historic illustrations; "acres" of white space. It is published by Weidenfeld and Nicolson, an imprint begun in 1940 and noted for some daring ventures, including the publication of Nabokov's *Lolita* (an act that cost Nigel Nicolson his seat in the British Parliament) and Weidenfeld's autobiography, *Portrait of a Marriage,* a more honest view of marriage than was common at the time. In short, the book speaks of political connectedness and a progressive bent, combined with elegance, quality, diplomacy, and attention to detail. The book is written in close cooperation with the embassy chef, Monsieur Viaëne, whose son shares the book's dedication.

Paris Embassy Cookbook has two borsch recipes: one, Polish Borshch, and the other, **Russian Borshch**. I found it particularly interesting that in this work borsch is written about as a French dish and not as some glamorous import, as it was to Carême. It is no longer a food of some exotic "Calmouck" kingdom, as Russia was seen through much of the 19th century in Western Europe (perhaps as a result of Kalmyk cavalry entering Paris in 1814), but as an indigenous product. The book's subtitle, *200 distinctive Anglo-French recipes,* clearly indicates borsch's acceptance in the high social circles of Western Europe.

In short, a peasant dish from East-Central Europe, over time, found recognition not only among the upper classes in that region but also internationally, and even began to viewed as part of the cultural legacy of those other countries.

British diplomats were not the only social group that quietly accepted borsch as part of their own culture; other social groupings seem to have adopted it also. The British navy, long the mightiest naval force in the world, has a tradition of bean and "portable" soups (a type of dehydrated food functionally similar to contemporary bouillon cubes). It does not, however, have a tradition of bcet soups, but in **British Royal Navy Bean Borsch** I found a recipe that combines the British naval bean tradition with beet borsch. I don't know how popular it is, but it is similar to a recipe for a Russian Army borsch I have found, circa 1900, and the standard recipes of the Russian ***Flotskiy borsch*** most commonly called Navy Borsch. "Fleet Borsch" would be a literal translation of *Flotskiy borsch*, and **Maritime Borsch** is probably more accurate. Food tastes being extremely conservative, the migration and acceptance of a foreign dish by different classes of another nation was not common until very recently, making borsch a kind of pioneer.

My exposure to a plateful of genuine Russian Maritime Borsch occurred in the late 1990s when I was doing economic development work in Yonkers, New York, and also was a volunteer for the Seamen's Church Institute. One day I received a call asking me to provide interpreting assistance for a minister who was about to visit a Russian bulk freighter that was docked at the Domino Sugar factory in Yonkers, with a load of sugar from South America. The problem, it appeared, was that the crew had not been paid their wages in months, and the Seamen's Church Institute wanted to see whether we could help the crew with that problem.

The problem of owed wages in not uncommon in the maritime world and the Institute has a good track record of ensuring that ships' crews get paid. So the minister and I met and proceeded to the ship berthed at the sugar factory. We did not solve the major problem the crew had, largely because crew members were afraid to take legal action against the ship owners, but we made a significant positive difference in their lives by providing them with fresh food, cigarettes and vodka. Especially appreciated was a supply of fresh dill used for borsch and other dishes. In the bustle of the events I never thought of asking the cook for her borsch recipe but the one I include in this book, by Nina Nicolaieff, is similar to the one I tasted that first day on the freighter.

Two characteristics identify a Russian maritime borsch: one is the presence of frankfurters as the chief meat ingredient and the other is the cut of the cabbage. In any recipe for maritime borsch the cabbage is cut into diamonds, or squares, and never julienned. While the manner in which you cut the cabbage will affect the way borsch tastes I never gave the difference much thought until I began volunteering at the Chinese monastery. In that kitchen our crew of half-a-dozen volunteers, under the guidance of the cook, would produce during the course of the morning vegetarian food for a few hundred visitors on weekends to literally thousands on major holidays. There I learned how to chop a cabbage in about 12 cuts into bite-sized pieces—they turned out to be diamond shaped. The apparent answer to the question of "why diamond-shape cabbage pieces?" appears to be simple and pragmatic.

My time in Yonkers also resulted in learning a modern Ukrainian borsch recipe. **Galina Chernych's Ukrainian Borsch** is a contribution made by Galina Chernykh, a young woman who self-identifies as a Russian, but who was born and raised in the Crimea, Ukraine. Galina, a recent immigrant to the US at the time, was a library volunteer for our non-profit and conducted a course in Russian cooking. Galina's recipe maintains the traditional two-step cooking process, but by beginning with prepared stock she significantly reduces the time of preparation from two or three hours to no more than one.

While borsch, at present, is an occupational, national, and international dish we should remember that it is also a soup of great localization. Two local recipes that I find particularly intriguing-- for **Sea Cabbage (Kelp) Borsch**, and for **Lake Smelt Borsch**—show this clearly. It is obvious that sea cabbage borsch is most likely found near the seacoast and is much less likely in areas with no sea. What is less obvious and not widely known outside of Russia is that lake smelts, until very recently, were predominantly harvested in one area, the *Beloe ozero* (White Lake), so the range of borsch with smelt is confined to a small region of Russia.

By no means is this localization unique to the borsch versions mentioned. Virtually every Ukrainian city or region has its own version of borsch. Borsch varieties, such as a Mennonite borsch from Bolivia that contains green papaya as a cabbage substitute, are definitely localized variants. Other borsch types that specify particular ingredients, such as garlic from Starocherkasskaya or water from the Aksaysk springs, immediately peg the recipe to the Rostov Oblast, a region between Ukraine and Kalmykia. And, since this is the ancestral home of the Don Cossacks, any such recipe would in all probability be a Cossack borsch. Likewise, a Lenten borsch recipe that lacks any oils would most likely be from a monastery where, during Lent, even vegetable oils are not allowed on days of strict fast.

But it is not only ingredients that signal borsch localities. Cooking techniques do also—anything from how one cuts the cabbage, what heat source one uses, number of stages of cooking, etc. German Mennonites, for example, do not have a tradition of the

Russian stove; their recipes, as a result, do not call for a two-stage cooking process. The Doukhobors, on the other hand, who come out of the old Russian tradition, still maintain that technique (even in Canada, where few Russian stoves exist).

I can only hope that this brief excursion is sufficient to illustrate that the many varieties of the borsch and the difference in ingredients and techniques in its preparation are frequently not accidental or done at the whim of a particular cook but are a reflection of a complex sociocultural process that often can be traced quite clearly.

Many people in modern societies are not aware that traditionally, consumption of food was very much intertwined with religious practice. In today's life in America we see remnants of these practices in the ritual of communion, and in the post-services meals that are often part of a congregation's religious celebration. We all have experienced, or know of, special foods that are associated with specific religious holidays in a variety of faiths, but we tend to forget that everyday food has traditionally been viewed as sacred and accorded respect. This dimension of food is not often discussed, but it is important if one tries to understand the various means by which social groups define themselves. It is therefore important to look at the connection between borsch and religious expression.

4. RELIGION AND BORSCH
"I can't eat any more nettle borsch""
Klavdia, *"Breaa Day"*

Most Americans know that Muslims and Jews do not eat pork, and that Hindus avoid beef. Obviously, Catholic Americans know about Lenten periods, and many Buddhists are vegetarians.

Little is known in America about Eastern Orthodoxy or Eastern Rite Catholics by people who are not affiliated with these religious traditions. Eastern Rite Catholics are Roman Catholics who follow some cultural and religious practices normally found among the Eastern Orthodox. For example, Eastern Rite Catholics, also known as Byzantine Catholics, are allowed to have married clergy, something that is part of Eastern Orthodoxy. The Eastern Orthodox are a number of independent (autocephalous) Christian churches that originated in Byzantium and represent the second largest Christian denomination after Roman Catholicism. Today's Russia is the world's largest Orthodox nation, with some 80 million believers.

The ethnic groups that inhabit the cultural area called the "Borsch Belt" in Central Europe encompass the major international religious traditions. Generations of official atheism in the area throughout most of the 20th century have without a doubt affected these traditions and related customs, but it is remarkable how much has remained, and how strong the hunger to reconnect with old cultural habits has been. To cite just one graphic example, in June of 1991, months before the Soviet Union dissolved in December of that year, the voters of the city of Leningrad approved the return of the city's tsarist name of St. Petersburg.

While there is no doubt that government policy affected religious traditions it is far from clear whether policies, or facts of modern living, had the dominant influence. Did cultural traditions change because of official atheism, or because of three major wars that killed more than ten percent of the population, the physical dislocations of many ethnic groups, major urbanization and chronic shortages of living space, and a literacy rate that country-wide went from less than fifteen percent to nearly one hundred percent within one generation?

When thinking about the actual impact that policies have on people's spiritual life I am reminded of an anecdote told during the antireligious campaigns in the 1930s. According to the story a peasant emerging from an antireligious lecture given at his collective farm was heard to mutter, "Maybe there is no God, but as long as we have St. Nicholas we will be OK."

It is not well known that the early Bolsheviks were not uniform in their opposition to religion. There is little doubt that there was nearly universal opposition to the established religious institutions but many, like the writer Maxim Gorky, were involved in Spiritualism. The first People's Commissar for Education, Anatoly Lunacharsky, was a proponent of an idea of a new humanistic religion called *bogostroitelstvo* (God-building). He thought that Marxism by itself was too abstract and inflexible to win over the loyalty of the population and therefore he hoped that a religious base could be given to Marxism so as deepen its roots in the peoples' psychology.

Even the fully convinced materialist and atheist, Lenin, took his bride on their honeymoon trip to visit a Kalmyk Buddhist temple. Perhaps most surprising is that the wife of the head of the secret police in the 1930s, Nikolai Yezhov, who implemented the brutal antireligious campaigns of the 1930s, was a Theosophist. Quite intriguing was that in the 1970s the Brezhnev administration made quiet inquiries of the Russian Orthodox hierarchy on the appropriate depth at which a corpse needs to buried, and afterwards the government lowered Lenin's sarcophagus to conform to that standard.

The list of early Communists who were involved with religion could go on, and if we examine what actually occurred during the Soviet period then we see that the persecution of believers was not as intense as it was towards church and clergy. In large part antireligious activities were aimed at religious institutions because they were seen as possible political challengers and inculcators of values contradicting those of the Party hierarchy.

The staunchly Roman Catholic Poles, as well as Eastern Rite Ukrainians (Uniats) and Carpatho-Rusins have particularly noteworthy traditions and recipes for Christmas Eve and Easter, which they maintained during the years of official atheism. Even under Communism the traditional Christmas Eve dinner would be served after the first star appeared in the sky, and the normally twelve-course meal would begin among the Poles with a meatless **Christmas Eve Borsch *(Wigilia Barszcz)*** with a type of ravioli, shaped like pig's ears *(uszki)*. The Lemkos called the same ritual *Sviata Vecheria* (Holy Supper).

Fast, or Lenten, days are the hallmark of traditional Orthodox practice in Russia, Byelorussia, and the Ukraine. Like Western Christians, the Orthodox have a 40-day Lenten period before Easter; additionally, however, they have another 150 to 170 day of fasting practices associated with other holidays. The Christmas or Nativity Fast, for example, is another 40-day Lenten period, in which Christmas Eve is a particularly strict day of abstention that calls for refraining from food for the whole day until the appearance of the first star of the evening. The Apostolic (Pentecost to June 29th) and Dormition of Mary Fasts (two weeks prior to August 15th) are the other two major periods of fasting.

In the Orthodox tradition, fasting includes abstention not only from meat, but also from eggs and dairy. In strict interpretations, even vertebrate fish are avoided. The emphasis in Orthodox fasting is on refraining from consuming products of warm-blooded animals; in particularly strict interpretations, this prohibition extends to red vegetables, such as beets and carrots. In this belief system, fish, particularly shellfish, are not considered to be warm-blooded animals.

Lenten fare, however, does not mean dull eating, as Katherine Czapp points out in her wonderful article, "Eating by the Seasons in Russia." A sample menu she shares illustrates the point:

Menu 1

Mushroom and sturgeon marrow pirog	Plum soup with wine
Sturgeon head soup	Pike in yellow sauce
Potatoes with herring	Potato cutlets with mushroom sauce
Cranberry kissel	Stewed fruit compote

Fasting periods in Orthodoxy are lengthy and very complex, in part because of moveable holidays and in part, because of various exceptions and complexity of dietary rules. This necessitated special calendars and churchmen were expected to publish dietary advice. The tradition of indicating fast periods and suggesting appropriate dishes for them goes back at least to archpriest Sylvester's *Domostroy* of 1547. In this compendium of religious, moral, and everyday advice two chapters illustrate this point clearly. Chapter 18 is entitled "The Master's Directive to the Housekeeper on How to Prepare Lenten and Meat Dishes, and How to Feed the Family During Meat-Eating Days and Lent," and Chapter 64 is entitled "Notes for the Entire Year on What to Serve at the Table, from Easter Sunday's Meat-Eating Onward."

The demise of the Soviet Union in 1991 led to an explosion of interest in things prerevolutionary. Among other expressions of interest in the old ways were books on Orthodox cookery. *On the Days of Lent: Recipes from the Orthodox Kitchen* (1994) was compiled and published by the sisters of the Holy Presentation Women's Monastery in Ivanovo, Russia. The nunnery was founded in 1991 and the book was printed in December of 1994 in a surprisingly large print run, for a young nunnery, of 30,000 copies—a fundraiser.

Unlike conventional Western cookbooks that divide dishes according to kinds of foods, this book follows the Orthodox liturgical year and the schedule of Lenten weeks. Each week is further subdivided into menu categories: Appetizers, 1st Course (usually soups), 2nd Course (entrée), and Beverages. Within each category there are seven or eight specific dishes, roughly one for each day of the week. Interestingly, some weeks offer dessert, while others do not. Since, like most Russian books, this one lacks an index, finding a specific dish such as borsch requires going through the whole book, page by page.

In all, there are five borsch recipes. The first recipe, for **Sea Cabbage (Kelp) Borsch**, is listed for the second week of the Great Lent (pre-Easter). This is a particularly severe recipe; normally during Lent vegetable oils are allowed, but this version offers no oils. For Palm Sunday a Lenten feast dish of a vegetarian Ukrainian borsch is suggested. In this recipe oils are a concession to "feasting." A fascinating borsch variant is a "memorial" borsch. While the **Beet Borsch with Barley** is a Lenten memorial borsch which the book's authors recommend for the Ancestor Day Remembrances during Lent, other memorial borsch recipes can be based on meat stock. The recipe for memorial borsch is in line with the Ukrainian traditional belief that the soul of the departed leaves a home on the steam from borsch since that soup is cooked for the post-funeral meal. In fact, throughout most of Ukraine and in many parts of Russia a borsch is the traditional first course at a memorial dinner.

The **Borsch svekolnyi s perlovoi krupoi** is intended for Saturdays dedicated to the memory of ancestors commemorated during the Orthodox Great Lent. The recipe is interesting because of the inclusion of barley. In Orthodox funeral and memorial rites grain dishes play an important role. The addition of grain makes this particular soup appropriate for remembering ancestors.

Another Orthodox cookbook that appeared shortly after the fall of the Soviet Union is Lidia Ivanovna Nichiporovich's *Orthodox Culinary*, published in 1995. Again, the recipes are grouped according to the liturgical calendar cycle, but with a bit of a difference; ingredients and dishes in this work are associated with specific holidays but offer a choice of similar dishes made with different ingredients for each holiday. For the Assumption Lent, known in folk usage as "Honey Lent" (*Medovyi spas*), for example, five different borsch recipes are offered. All of the recipes are Lenten, but each is distinct from the others. Since this time of year is the height of summer, the recipes concentrate on cold varieties of borsch. **Cold Borsch with Farmer's Cheese** and **Borsch with Radish** are representative of that kind of borsch.

The difference between *Recipes from the Orthodox Kitchen* and *Orthodox Culinary*, then, is that one is a guide for specific dishes to be prepared and served at specific times and the other allows more choice for the cook.

A different kind of cookbook with a religious theme, published in 1996 in a large initial print run of 30,000 copies, was *Orthodox Kitchen*, by Vladimir Sergeevich Mikhailov, a book that focuses on traditional recipes gleaned from Orthodox monasteries.

Orthodox Kitchen is a fascinating book for anyone interested in Russian history or the sociology of foodways in a compact form. It effectively summarizes the immense role of monasteries in the food culture of the country. There were some 1,025 monasteries before 1917, with some tracing their origin to the first millennium of the current era. Their impact cannot be underestimated; monasteries were not only the main institutions in constant contact with the populace but they were also part of formal political life. In terms of food culture, they served as emergency food stores for times of famine, and as a place where one could always get a simple but nutritious meal.

Most importantly, they were the place where the traditions of using local foodstuffs for healthy and sustaining diets that could be available to most people were developed and shared. Lastly, the monasteries also had extensive experience in medicinal herbs and food as medicine.

Monasteries were also places of pilgrimage. The oldest among them developed "brand" dishes, many of which were lost in the Soviet period when monasteries were destroyed. Some monastery recipes, however, were preserved. *Orthodox Kitchen* offers a borsch recipe from the Avramiev Monastery, founded around 1210 and currently being restored in Smolensk.

Its **Smolensk Borscht** is a far cry from the vegetarian severity of a Lenten recipe. The other recipe, for **Borsch with Turnip,** is prepared specifically to celebrate the "First Vegetables" Holiday (July 14), which is also the feast day of the martyrs Saints Cosmas and Damian. The recipe illustrates the syncretism of formal religious holidays with folk celebrations which may go back to pagan practices.

Of course, in addition to borsch being included as a menu item in religious celebrations and as recipes found in books of the official Orthodox Church, it was also part of other religious traditions that shared the overall cultural space. The **Turkish Borsch** recipe discovered as part of research for this book appears to be the product of the settlement of a group "Old Ritualist" Cossacks, called "Nekrasovsty," in the Ottoman lands after their 1708 revolt was crushed. The Old Ritualists arose out of vehement opposition to the reforms instituted in the 17th century by Patriarch Nikon of the official Russian Orthodox Church. The schism lasted until 1971, when the Russian Church officially lifted the anathema imposed in 1656. But the division between the churches is still there, because the Old Ritualists, in turn, view the official church as heretical and avoid any interaction with it. At the time of the Russian Revolution and Civil War about ten percent of the population belonged to the Old Ritualist denomination.

After the schism, many believers fled to remote parts of northern Russia or to Siberia and established tiny settlements. There also were settlements in the Ukraine and Turkey. As the persecution of the Ritualists continued throughout the 19th century and until the 1905 Edict of Toleration, many practitioners moved to the periphery of the Empire including what today are the Baltic republics, regions of Austro-Hungary, and Finland. As a result of the Russian Revolution and consequent repressions, communities of Old Ritualists scattered all over the world. In the United States a few communities are in the Eastern U.S. (Millville, New Jersey; Erie, Pennsylvania; Detroit, Michigan) but most are located in Oregon and Alaska (approximately 10,000 individuals, in all).

Maintaining traditions is a hallmark of their lifestyle and it is challenging. They adhere to traditional customs, including peasant-style clothing. Women wear headscarves and long dresses, and adult males do not shave their beards. They observe 40 annual religious celebrations, making employment with local businesses nearly impossible. Thus, many Old Ritualists own businesses and farms. They are not allowed to eat from the same dishes as nonbelievers, so if they eat outside their homes they will eat only at fast-food restaurants, which use disposable containers. Nonetheless, there are signs of social compromise. Today, they drive automobiles and watch television. They are also very present on the Internet.

It was the Internet that led me to the happy discovery of the vibrant Vereya community that survived the vicissitudes of history in the very heart of Russia, some 50 miles southwest of Moscow. It existed there for a long time and, according to local legend, its wooden prayer house was burned down during the War of 1812. In 1814 the community built a brick chapel and has continued to practice from that time to this. It survived the religious repression of the 1930s, World War II, the antireligious campaigns of the 1950s, and today appears to be a thriving center of the Old Ritualists community in the Moscow area, welcoming fellow religionists from the City. I was thrilled to read a nice Lenten borsch recipe posted by the parishioner Elizabeth, titled **Cossack Happiness**.

Among the many other nonconformist Christians in Russia are the *Molokans* (Milk Drinkers), *Skoptsy* (Castrates), *Subbotniki* (Sabbath Worshipers), *Pryguny* (Jumpers), *Dukhobory* (Spirit Wrestlers), and a number of others. All of these small denominations are essentially Protestant, in the sense that they rejected the dominant Orthodox Church and its teachings, and evolved interpretations of Christianity that in spirit and practices are more closely aligned with such Western European faiths as Quakers and Mennonites.

The Molokans are of particular interest to Americans since members of the Molokan community emigrated to the U.S. and settled on the West Coast. After a while a group from that area moved to Guadalupe Valley in Baja California, Mexico. A number of Molokans in Mexico have married locally, and Mexican women married to Molokan men had to learn to cook "el borsch" from their mothers-in-law. The Molokans follow the food laws of Moses that prohibit non-scale seafood, pork, and other "unclean" foods. **Molokan Borscht** in this book is an unusual variant because many Molokans do not use beets in their borsch.

The story of the Doukhobors is particularly compelling, in part because of their radical egalitarianism and pacifism, in part because their plight was taken up by Leo Tolstoy, and in part because Lenin's secretary, Vladimir Bonch-Bruevich, an avowed atheist and Director of the Museum of Atheism from 1945-1955, helped this group immigrate to Canada. A most unusual aspect of this extraordinary story is that Bonch-Bruevich not only assisted the Doukhobors while they were in Russia but actually sailed with them in 1899 to Canada and spent a year collecting Doukhobor hymns and religious songs that were circulating in oral tradition. He published the efforts of his labors in 1909 as *The Doukhobor Book of Life* (*Zhivotnaya kniga dukhobortsev*) and the book has acquired near canonical status among them.

An extraordinary story requires a special borsch recipe, and I was fortunate to find just such a recipe posted by Michelle Barabonoff. I contacted the author for permission to include her recipe and received a speedy affirmative response with the proviso that I give credit to the author's mother—Lil Potapoff, and share the web address of the page on which the recipe was posted: http://flowingfree.org/. The ingredients used in **Lil's Doukhobor Borsch** and the basic cooking techniques are quite similar to other Doukhobor recipes I had seen, but Michelle's style of presenting it and her willingness to share demonstrate some of the core values of the community: generosity, mildness in attitude, simplicity in living, hard work, anti-ritualism, and pacifism (a value evidenced by the vegetarian cuisine of the Doukhobors).

"Old Ritualists" and othe nonconformist religious denominations are related to Eastern Orthodoxy and are ethnically Slavs. An important religious community deeply identified with Russia but ethnically non-Russian are the Mennonites. Mennonites were Anabaptists, originally stemming from Holland and Flanders, who settled in Prussia around the Vistula River and who accepted Catherine the Great's invitation to settle in the Volga region in 1768.

They were first-class farmers who lived in autonomous enclaves with their own schools and medical facilities and who prospered in their agricultural endeavors. They were pacifists, but since they were willing to do alternative service their relations to the government were positive. Success led to overpopulation and the creation of a landless group within the community of Mennonites which, in turn, led to immigration to areas of the world where land was to be had. "Russian" Mennonites began arriving in the U.S. and Canada in the 1870s.

The Russian Revolution, Civil War, and later Collectivization and the anti-*kulak* (prosperous farmer) campaign created deep suffering in the community; consequently, the arrival of Germans in WWII was seen as a relief. Many Mennonites, as *Volksdeutche* (ethnic Germans) who enjoyed a reprieve from collectivization and religious oppression under German occupation, fled in the footsteps of the German army and just ahead of the Soviet forces.

During their centuries-long sojourn in Russia Mennonites adopted many of the culinary practices of the neighboring Russians and Ukrainians. They also developed their own borsch tradition. I first encountered Mennonites and their borsch while working as a folklorist at the Elkhart Public Library in Indiana. Soon after I arrived in Elkhart, walking on crutches with a hip-length cast on my right leg, a result of a broken ankle caused by a skydiving accident, I crossed the street from the library to have lunch for the first time in a Mennonite restaurant. The restaurant was arranged cafeteria style, with small dark-brown wooden tables and chairs around the room and a long, centrally located, stainless-steel, glass-fronted steam table, behind which stood a small group of young ample-bodied women in petite white caps and blindingly white, starched aprons.

The steam table was a cornucopia of Mennonite dishes but my eyes were drawn to two in particular: a tray filled with stuffed cabbage and a large tray of soup labeled **Kommst Borscht**. I was a bit perplexed by the adjectival "kommst," which I knew to be in German the familiar form of "kommen" (arrive or come). But I took it as a sign of welcome, much needed and appreciated at a time when I was still dealing with my physical injury. Only later did I learn that, in Mennonite German, "Kommst" means cabbage.

The borsch looked familiar, although the color was a bit off from what I was used to. This soup was a bright reddish-orange, not the familiar deep red. But I did see squares of cabbage, potato, and tomatoes, and it had bright orange islands of fat floating on the surface—signaling by that its village heritage—so I ordered a bowl. One of the young women began to ladle a bowl and asked, "Will you be having bread with the soup?" "Please," I responded, happy to be back with a tradition that eats bread with soup.

Another young woman, seeing my crutches, picked up the tray with the borsch and followed me as I found an empty table. I began eating my first bowl of Mennonite borsch, and was surprised to learn that it had no beet flavor.

Most commonly, Mennonites have two varieties of borsch: **Kommst *Borscht* (Cabbage Borsch)** and *Zummah Borscht* (Summer Borsch). The first, which contains cabbage, vegetables, and tomatoes, is in many ways reminiscent of a Ukrainian or Russian borsch, but without beets; the second is a sorrel-and-beet-greens borsch, quite similar to Russian, Polish, and Ukrainian versions.

The absence of beets in Mennonite borsch makes it improbable that the dish was borrowed from their neighbors the Ukrainians. Lack of beets in borsch suggests that Mennonites who previously moved to the Volga from Prussia, surrounded by Poles and Lithuanians, most likely initially learned to cook borsch with "cow parsnip" (*Heracleum*) instead of beets and later substituted cabbage for this plant. This supposition is bolstered by the presence of another type of Mennonite borsch, **Sauerkraut Soup (Zhure Kommstborscht)**, which in its ingredients is in no way different from Russian "schi." This leads me to conclude that Mennonite borsch became part of the cuisine of this group when it was viewed as a sub-type of schi, as evidenced by the entry for that dish in Vladimir Dal's famed dictionary. In short, it is likely that Mennonites brought their versions of schi/borsch to the Volga region from their Prussian area of settlement and did not borrow the dish from their neighbors in the South.

By now it should be obvious that borsch, being an integral and long-standing element of Central European food culture, is therefore intertwined with the religions of the region's inhabitants. On the simplest level it reflects the dietary laws and strictures of differing religious traditions and is part of the ritual celebration of religious holidays or life events. For example, in all my research I encountered no Jewish borsch recipe that contained pork, and the mixing of dairy products, such as sour cream, with meat-based borsch broth appears to have been confined to urban and largely secular Jews.

Sometimes, as in the case of the Doukhobors, cooking practices directly reflect central tenets of a faith, such as non-violence. At different times religious communities become propagators of borsch in new geographic areas, as was the case of Mennonites and East European Jews in America.

Sometimes, foodways become can even become the carriers of the very idea of belonging to a religious community. It would be just as hard for a Russian Orthodox practitioner to imagine Easter without the traditional *kulich* (sweet Easter bread) as it would be for a Jew to imagine a Passover *seder* (feast) without matzo. Within the secular setting of the International Center of Indianapolis I can recall the arrival of my wife's and my favorite Board member and stalwart volunteer, Anna Hylton, with the necessary ingredients for a Lithuanian **Šaltibarščiai** for a luncheon treat. Anna worked her magic in the spacious kitchen of the Holliday mansion, where the Center was housed, and when the borsch was ready the three of us would enjoy of that radiantly pink and tart nectar which was so cool and refreshing in the un-air-conditioned environment of a hot, humid Indiana summer day.

I am suggesting that borsch, because of the complexity of its history, evolution, and methods of preparation, lends itself perfectly to be the antithesis of the "food as fuel culture" and not only has had, but continues to have, an important role as a signifier of the special and sacred.

5. RUSSIAN COOKBOOKS - *MEDIEVAL TIMES TO THE EMPIRE'S FALL*

"But best of all, my Benefactor, is borsch made out of beets Ukrainian style, with ham and sausages. It's served with sour cream and fresh parsley with dill."
Anton Chekhov, "The Siren" 1887

The Russian cooking tradition can be divided into four major historical phases: Medieval, Imperial, Soviet, and Federal (*Rossiyskiy*). The Medieval period is normally viewed as the one preceding Peter the Great, towards the end of the 17th century. The Imperial period lasted from Peter to the fall of the Romanovs in 1917. The Soviet period ranged from 1922 to 1991, and the Federal phase followed the Soviet period. This chapter focuses on the first two periods; the others appear in the next.

The first Russian book with significant references to cooking is *Domostroy*—a compendium of moral principles, practical husbandry, and culinary advice, written in 1547. *Domostroy* served to create a pattern for Russian cookbooks that was followed in all major works on cookery well into the 20th century. It established the custom of going beyond the craft, or art, of cooking to include more general advice for living. This enhanced scope created a tradition of cookbooks of encyclopedic length. *Domostroy* is also a major early Russian written exemplar of Lenten and non-Lenten foods and of dishes associated with specific saints' days. An additional characteristic of *Domostroy* is that all foods in it are traditional foods of the area, without obvious imports.

The reforms of Peter the Great not only brought administrative, scientific, educational, and military innovations but also deeply affected Russia's food culture. According to legend, Peter I introduced potatoes to Russia. While that cannot be proven, it is unquestionable that the opening of close communication with the West and the wholesale adaption of Western cultural habits by members of the Russian upper class shifted Russian cookery from an evolution of its medieval foodways to a seeming wholesale substitution of new dishes and techniques. In many ways Peter's reforms created a schism between the traditional foodways connected to religious life as reflected in *Domostroy* and the new cuisine brought from abroad.

Creating secular cookbooks became a social necessity. Foreign dishes were socially *de rigeur*, but only the wealthiest nobility could afford to hire a foreign cook, and cookbooks became an important way to show the serf-cooks how to prepare the new dishes. The fashion created a slew of publications featuring French, Dutch, and German dishes. There was some resistance to the innovations, however. Some authors, like Sergey Drukovtsev, attempted to chart a middle course. His *Short Kitchen Notes* (1779) presented both foreign and native foods. While his book is very short, comprised of 44 pages, mostly a list of dishes, it is considered to be the oldest book printed in Russia that is a cookbook in the modern sense. His second cookbook, *Soldier's Cookery,* published in 1786, continued the notion of a native cuisine.

But the influence of non-Russian cookery among the elite was so pervasive that in 1795 Vasily Alekseevich Levshin wrote: "It is impossible now to present the complete description of the Russian kitchen, and one must be contented with only that which can be gathered from memory, for the history of the Russian kitchen was never written down." Despite this dire statement Levshin managed to include a substantial section on Russian cooking in his *Dictionary of the Russian Kitchen* (1795-1796), a compendium of different cooking styles and traditions. Furthermore, in 1816, when the War of 1812 made national cooking a sudden patriotic concern, he published *Russian Kitchen,* which is considered to be the first cookbook of "purely" Russian cuisine. Levshin's book includes all the dishes mentioned in *Short Kitchen Notes* and expands on them, giving a better idea of how they were prepared.

In contrast to the final quarter of the 18th century, with its manuals and books that reflected foreign traditions, several books published in the 19th century focused on Russian cooking alone. Among the most notable were those written by Ekaterina Alekseevna Avdeeva, which include *Handbook of the Experienced Russian Mistress* and *The Pocket Cookbook,* both published in 1842. Both books continued to be published in new editions from 1842 to 1877.

Avdeeva was a true pioneer. She was the first Russian writer to include observational data in her reminiscences and writing the first ethnography of Siberia, and she was the first person to collect folktales directly from oral tradition for publication. In a sense Avdeeva can be viewed as a food writer who helped to rediscover the traditional national cuisine that has continued to evolve separately from the elite cookery of the capital. Inclusion of three borsch recipes ("Little Russian" Borsch, **Celery Borsch**, and Lenten Fish Borsch) reminded cooks to look toward their own heritage. She was also a pioneer in expanding the notion of "Russian" cooking, by including dishes attributed to ethnicities other than Slavic, such as her recipe for fish prepared in the "Jewish Manner."

It is interesting that Avdeeva's borsch recipes are among only a handful published in the 18th and beginnings of the 19th century. It appears that borsch was such a common dish that no one bothered to write it down because every serf cook would know how to make it.

In *All the Happy Endings: a study of the Domestic Novel in America, the women who wrote it, the women who rea*d *it, in the nineteenth century*, a book by Helen Waite-Pakashvily, published in 1956, the author posits that women writers, often forced to toil after disasters suffered as a result of encounters with men, created in their works a subtle but powerful resistance to 19th-century patriarchy. In her view the domestic novels of the 19th- century were perhaps as significant and powerful as the political actions of the Suffragette Movement, though much more subtle in their affect.

Similarly, taking advantage of the opportunities that cooking and writing offered, a number of extraordinary women helped define their countries' national cuisine. An early example of this was *Mrs. Beeton's Book of Household Management* (1861), by Isabella Beeton, for England. Later came *The Boston Cooking-School Cook Book* (1896), by Fannie Farmer, an American. Still later, for Italy, came *The Talisman of*

Happinness (1929), by Ada Boni. In Russia the role fell to Elena Molokhovets and her *A Gift to Young Housewives* (1861).

Without a doubt the single most influential Russian food writer of the 19th century, and into the 20th, was Elena Ivanovna Molokhovets (née Burman). It is impossible to write about cooking in Russia, particularly in any historical sense, without mention of Russia's most popular culinary writer of the 19th century, whose seminal work went through 29 editions between 1861 and the Russian Revolution, and sold some 300,000 copies. It still reverberates in today's world of Russian cookery. And yet relatively little is known about the woman who has become the standard bearer of classical Russian cuisine.

The bare facts of her life are quite accessible, although her biography has not yet been written. Much of her life has been subject to sometimes cruel satire, mists of legend, derisive remarks, and plain lack of information. For a long time the date of her death was unknown, and even today the circumstances of it are vague. She bore 10 children and outlived eight of them, as well as her husband. Almost totally ignored during the Soviet period of history, she has become, in post-Soviet Russia, a cottage industry. Today one can find not only a slew of reprints of her books but even adaptations of her dishes for microwave cooking

We know the basics. Elena Burman was born to a local official in the city of Arkhangelsk in 1831; she lost her parents at an early age. With the help of her grandmother she matriculated at the Smolny Institute for Noble Maidens, graduating in 1848. She returned to Arkhangelsk, met and married the architect Franz Molokhovets, and the couple moved to the city of Kursk. In 1861 she first published her book of 1,500 recipes, which almost immediately became popular. In 1866 the family moved to St. Petersburg. Her husband died in 1899 and, on December 15, 1918, Elena died in Petrograd (Soviet St. Petersburg).

Her work grew from 1,500 recipes to more than 4,000. She also published a few other, less successful, cookbooks as well as a whole library of mystical, moralizing, and nationalistic tracts. Elena was an ardent monarchist and her haughty attitude toward servants and people of lower classes earned her the criticism of progressives and radicals. Her attitude is perhaps best exemplified by a quote, attributed to her but not found in any of her writings: "If you have twenty unexpected guests arrive, just go downstairs, pick a couple of hams that are hanging there, some eggs and a pound of butter...." Attitudinally, however, the quote is probably accurate.

Her shortcomings as a visibly compassionate being do not diminish her accomplishments as the standard-setter of Russian cuisine. Ever since the late 19th century any serious Russian cookbook has inevitably been judged and compared to *A Gift to Young Housewives*. One could even suggest that, as Russian cuisine evolved internationally, it included two major lineages: the French, initially established by Marie-Antoine (Antonin) Carême and then Auguste Escoffier, and the Russian lineage of Elena Molokhovets.

The difference between the two is that Carême, whose knowledge of Russian cooking came from a short stint working in St. Petersburg, used the Russian dishes he made popular in France as an imported exoticism in French *haute cuisine*, while Molokhovets defined the normative Russian cuisine. This distinction is clearly seen in the borsch recipes offered by these two giants of culinary history.

Carême's recipe is quintessential Carême—totally "over the top." (In Russian the term is *pereborschit'*—literally, "over borsch."). An incredible concoction, in the 21st century his borsch has made the rounds of Russian Internet sites, to the amusement and derision of knowledgeable folks.

The Molokhovets recipes, on the other hand, are practical and restrained, though not plain dishes. The total number of borsch recipes in each of her cookbooks varies somewhat between editions. The 1901 edition that I have been working with has a total of thirteen: seven in the borsch section "Little Russian" i.e. Ukrainian, Polish, Ordinary, In a Different Manner, **Baked Beets and Wine Borsch**," Celery Borsch, and Borsch with Fresh Mushrooms) and an additional six in the "Lenten Soups" section. Some of the Lenten versions are meatless variants of the initial seven recipes; others include fish as the main ingredient (**Borsch with Fried Herring**, for example).

A Gift to Young Housewives is fascinating not only in the enormous number of recipes it presents, or in the fact that every aspect of cooking from choosing the best water source for boiling to proper service is discussed in detail, but also because it harkens back to *Domostroy* (but from a new and proto-feminist point of view). *Domostroy* was a book of instructions on how to be a good master and proprietor (*khozyain*), while *A Gift to Young Housewives* is a handbook on how to become an excellent "mistress" (*khozyaika*) or head of a household. Joyce Toomre, in her wonderful translation of Molokhovets, indicates her struggle in deciding how to render the term), adopting the more easily understandable "housewives" despite the loss of the larger meaning implied in the original Russian.

As indicated earlier, among the exceptional women cookbook authors of the 19th century was the American Fannie Farmer. Her book, *The Boston Cooking-School Cook Book* (1896), a pioneering venture in her day, is still in print. Fannie Farmer is of particular interest because, unlike Isabella Beeton or Elena Molokhovets, who were housewives before they became household-management and cookbook authors, Fannie Farmer taught cooking and was particularly interested in the influences of nutrition on health. Her *Food and Cookery for the Sick and Convalescent* (1904) was a pioneering work, as were her lectures on the subject of diet and nutrition at Miss Farmer's School of Cookery and the Harvard Medical School. Nearly 100 years after her death Fannie Farmer still enjoys a reputation as a paragon of a clear, precise, organized, visually attractive, and nutritionally sound approach to food.

Russia's Fannie Farmer was Pelageya Pavlovna Aleksandra-Ignateva (1872-1953). Unfortunately, only the barest outlines of her life are currently available, and she never enjoyed the widespread popularity of Elena Molokhovets. But her impact on students of cooking was immense, through her classes (between 1894 and 1908 she taught over 6,000 students) and her book, *Practical Foundations of Culinary Arts* (1897), a copy of which nearly every professional Russian cook owns.

The book began as a series of 27 "Talks," published in the magazine, *Our Food*, in 1894. The "Talks" formed her first book, *A Guide to the Fundamentals of Culinary Arts*, published in 1897. In 1899 that book became (in a somewhat revised, corrected, and reorganized form) *Practical Foundations of the Art of Cooking*. Between 1899 and 1916 it was published in 11 editions. In 1927, during the period of the New Economic Policy (NEP), a time during which restrictions on publishing were loosened, an abridged 12th edition was self-published by the author.

Practical Foundations takes a departure from standard Western cookbook formats, such as that used by Molokhovets. It is not a collection of recipes divided into sections such as "Soups," "Meat," "Fish." The heart of the book is a guide to the techniques of preparing different foods. In that it is very similar to books like *Complete Kitchen Essentials* or *Le Cordon Bleu Cuisine Foundations* by Cordon Bleu. The guide for Poultry, for example, ranges from advice on how to pick the best domestic poultry or wild game in the market, to how to handle rooster combs. In all, 21 different steps in the process of poultry preparation are taught.

Unlike the Cordon Bleu books, however, *Practical Foundations* also contains many recipes, all of which are part of a series of Russian, French, and Lenten dinners. There are 30 Russian, 20 French, and 10 Lenten dinner menus suggested. Each dinner has a soup, entrée, and dessert. By presenting recipes for complete dinners, the book mimics a normal cooking school class and gives an experiential example of how to balance flavors, textures, and varieties of food for nutrition and enjoyment, not only within one dish but as part of a complete meal. For example, the first two borsch recipes for Ukrainian borsch prepared in St. Petersburg style and Ukrainian style appear in Dinner number 5. The recipe **"Little Russian" Borsch as it is Prepared in Petersburg** is quite different in its ingredients from the Ukrainian borsch. There is no cabbage in the Ukrainian recipe, and there is a variety of meats including duck or goose and smoked pork. In the St. Petersburg version no type of meat is specified. In addition to borsch, Dinner number 5 includes recipes for Boiled Chicken with White Sauce, Fluffy Rice, White Sauce, and Berry Jelly. The Lenten borsch recipe, Lenten Borsch with Mushrooms, is the first Lenten meals recipe; the menu also includes recipes for Fish Greek Style, and Sago (palm starch) in Wine.

An interesting and historically valuable part of the cookbook is an addition, written by the husband of Pelageya Pavlovna, related to meat. As an expert on meat production, his advice and cautions in regards to meat and meat handling before there was widespread refrigeration are valuable, but his charts showing the different regional styles of meat butchery are particularly interesting for understanding old terminology as it applies to various cuts of meat in various regions of Russia.

Pelageya Pavlovna is a transitional figure in Russian cookbook writing. She is the last of the giants of Russian culinary literature until the appearance of the culinary writings of William

Pokhlebkin in the latter part of the 20th century. She is also the first major Russian cookery writer who focuses solely on the technical and scientific aspects of cooking and nutrition and shies away from creating a universe of either patriarchal morality, like *Domostroy*, or the household kingdom of Elena Molokhovets. Her interests are not ideology but skill. The recipes are the most detailed and helpful that I have encountered, though not always technically perfect.

She is probably the perfect writer to serve as an end-point in the evolution of Russian cooking, and cookbooks, from the Medieval and Empire periods to the dawn of Soviet cookery. The culinary publications of the Soviet period that followed her work were similar in their adherence to high scientific and technical standards in terms of nutrition and preparation, but unlike Pelageya Pavlovna's individualistic work these were expressions of committee work and institutional and State priorities. Only beginning with the 1960s, when Pokhlebkin's popular writings first appeared, did the individual voice of a food writer begin to be heard again.

6. RUSSIAN COOKBOOKS - *SOVIET TO POST-SOVIET PERIODS*

In this book everything was important: the large format—a case of famed Monumentalism; the embossed cover—the embodiment of Stalinist Baroque; illustrations in strange colors—reminiscent of those colored black-and-white photographs which were customarily brought back from Black Sea resorts. And, of course, the content. Perhaps, this only happens to magic tales one reads in childhood: their plots eternally unified with childhood illustrations and the book cover.

Aleksandra Veselova, in the article, "A Book of Tasty and Healthy Food"

The more than 70 years of Soviet reality affected every aspect of life in Russia, as well as life in other Central and Eastern European countries. The outlines of political and economic changes that occurred are pretty well known. There is, however, much less knowledge of the fantastic cultural changes that transpired in an incredibly short time and under the most challenging circumstances imaginable.

It is therefore understandable that many who write about Soviet food history maintain that the first Soviet cookbook was *The Book of Tasty and Healthy Food*, published in 1952. This book met with immense popularity. An edition of 500,000 sold out in that first year, prompting the publisher to come out with a second edition of another 500,000 in 1953. In all, between 1952 and 1985 over 6.5 million copies were sold; virtually no household in the Soviet Union was without one.

The Book, as it was popularly called, was not the first major Soviet cookbook, however. That honor fell to a much lesser known but extremely important book called *Manual of Cookery*, produced in 1934 at the initiative of Anastas Mikoyan who, as Minister of Foreign Trade, curated both books. Shortly before the book came out, he asked the rhetorical question: "Do we have a cookbook which we can give to our cooks as a gift?" The reference to Molokhovets in this question is hard to ignore.

The *Manual of Cookery* is not an ambitious book in size or the number of recipes it contains. It is 276 pages long and contains only a few hundred recipes. Its intended reader was a cook for a public eating place, not the home cook. In general layout it is reminiscent of the Pelagia Pavlovna and Cordon Bleu cookbooks. The main part of the book is devoted to terminology, cooking equipment, techniques, and butcher charts; the second part has a few hundred recipes, organized according to types of foods (soups, entrees, vegetables, etc). The *Manual of Cookery* only has two borsch recipes and, like all other recipes in the book, the quantities for ingredients are expressed in grams (the Soviets replaced old Russian measures with the metric system as a sign of their commitment to internationalism), and the amount of ingredients were given on a per-serving basis as befits a cookbook destined for institutional use.

This book sets the pattern subsequently followed by most Soviet cookbooks: it is based on committee work and is not the product of an individual vision; it is written under the supervision of, or in coordination with, professional nutritionists (dietologists); recipes are simplified and standardized; and the quantities of ingredients are extremely precise and strictly adhered to.

As Anastas Mikoyan, who was tasked by the government with developing public eateries (restaurants, cafeterias, etc.), once remarked, to indicate the high quality of Soviet food: "Unlike the West where every seller tries to short-change the public, our recipes have the force of law behind them." The *Manual of Cookery* was almost a perfect expression of the ideological and political aspirations of the Soviet government. Its focus on institutional cooking fit perfectly within the political priority of industrialization and the development of high-quality institutional eateries, which were considered as liberators of women from kitchen drudgery.

1934 was a watershed year in Soviet life. It can be said that it was the year that marked the beginning of complete dominance of all institutions by the Party and was, therefore, the beginning of the

"Soviet" period. 1934 marked the end of the 1932-1933 famine. The Soviet Writer's Union was formed in 1932, but it was in 1934 that the First Soviet Writer's Congress was held and the principles of "Socialist Realism" and Party primacy in cultural life were publicly formulated and accepted. The appearance of the *Manual of Cookery* that year, therefore, is important as the harbinger of a new Soviet cuisine and a unified cultural program throughout the country.

Although the 1952 edition of *The Book of Tasty and Healthy Food*—a cookbook designed for family cookery—can rightly be considered the "canonical" one, it was by no means the first version. *The Book* was first published in 1939, shortly before the Soviet Union entered WWII; subsequent abridged editions were published in 1945, immediately after the war, as well as in 1947, 1948, and 1950. This book was also the personal project of Anastas Mikoyan, who championed its creation, curated it, and provided its first preface and who spearheaded the production of the earlier *Manual of Cookery*. The *Book* proved to be a cultural phenomenon of the first order.

Physically, the various editions are impressive; usually printed in a large format, hard-bound, on coated stock, with numerous illustrations (many of them in color, a rarity in Soviet publishing of the time), sewn pages, and numerous quotes from the leading political luminaries of the day, including Stalin and Beria (then chief of the secret police, NKVD—precursor of the KGB). The 1953 edition that I own holds, in its 400 pages, about 1,400 recipes, a number of articles, cooking technique tips, illustrations, and photographs; in short, it was a worthy Soviet response to Molokhovets and her *A Gift to Young Housewives*. The recipes are quite extensive and varied. Dishes from foreign cuisines are included, as well as Russian dishes. This cookbook promoted a new "modern" approach of "rational" nutrition. The article outlining nutritional requirements is entitled "Rational Nutrition" and was written by a scholar from the Academy of Sciences. Other articles in the book continue in this didactic vein, indicating "proper" choices for breakfast, lunch, and dinner; the sequence of dinner preparation; proper table settings; kitchen set-up; and kitchen and serving utensils.

Great care was taken to indicate the specific amounts of major nutrients found in various popular dishes. Sometimes, the nutritional guidelines ran counter to traditional practices. Such was the case in soups, where a specific point was made that soups need to be made daily so as not to lose their vitamin C content (serving a soup the day after preparation means up to a 50% loss of vitamin C), which runs counter to the tradition of eating many versions of borsch the day after preparation, to enhance its flavor. How closely the nutritional suggestions were followed is open to question. But the involvement of nutritionists in the book did give it prestige among the population.

Explicit government initiatives, such as encouragement of the greater use of processed foods, are reflected in the text. But by also appealing to the emotions, through color photographs of abundant and attractive displays of food items, the aesthetic aspects of food were brought out. The terms "eye candy," or the newly popular "food porn," can be used to describe these photographs of foodstuffs that few rank-and-file Soviet citizens actually had an opportunity to taste.

The "rational" industrialized approach to food is perhaps best exemplified by a quote from Mikoyan's introduction: "Today, all Soviet women demand factory-prepared food products so that their time is spent not only on household chores, but primarily on the job, on cultural endeavors, and on raising of their children."

What many who read the book were not aware of at the time, or even subsequently, is how deeply this book was affected by American industrialized agriculture and food practices. Mikoyan, as part of his duties as Minister of Foreign Trade, visited the United States for two months before WWII, fell in love with its food industry and, specifically, with American hamburger-making machines (hamburgers cooked on metal conveyer belts that pass between upper and lower banks of gas flames), a copy of which he purchased and brought to the Soviet Union.

Had it not been for World War II, which precluded the reassembly of the machine and its reproduction and dissemination across the Soviet Union, the worldwide reach of the "Big Mac"® could have been the "Comradeburger." I doubt that many in McDonald's management appreciate that the popularity of their chain in Soviet and post-Soviet Russia was, in part, eased by preceding Soviet food policies, in general, and Anastas Mikoyan, in particular.

The overall policies were to incentivize food consumption in public places, particularly at the work place. In many ways these initiatives succeeded. By the end of the 1960s most people in the Soviet

Union ate the bulk of their meals at work-connected cafeterias, and home cooking began to depend heavily on processed and semi-processed foods, particularly canned goods. I distinctly remember the family of a nuclear physicist in a campsite in Moscow cooking a mound of potatoes accompanied by a single can of Soviet-version SPAM for their family dinner, while my wife and I were frying filet mignon bought, for sandwich makings, at the Hard Currency Store.

In terms of cultural impact, the single most notable accomplishment of *The Book* was a successful definition of Soviet cuisine. By including a raft of dishes from a number of ethnic groups that were part of the population of the Soviet Union, without any self-conscious indication of their origin, a unified multicultural culinary universe was created.

In *The Book*, no single dish was wholly "authentic," because of the homogenizing effects of simplified techniques and spicing, so no cultural group could object to their cuisine being singled out for change. For example, the **Ukrainian Borsch** recipe in my 1953 edition lists about 10 ingredients, while a traditional "classical" Ukrainian borsch will have over 20 (although it must be admitted that if you read the preparations part of the recipe ingredients not listed in the ingredients list crop up and raise the overall number). The book had the imprimatur of the Ministry of Health, and any deviation from tradition could be explained as being a more "scientific" and "nutritionally sound" enhancement of the original dish.

One of the hallmarks of Soviet cuisine became its deep toleration for dishes that came out of a variety of cultures. In a real sense, Soviet cuisine could be called a multiethnic, if not international, cuisine. Food in this book became disassociated from its geographic origins and began to exist in an abstract "cultural space."

Of course, one could also say that "there is nothing new under the sun" since, already in the 1840s, Avdeeva had included Ukrainian and Georgian dishes as well as dishes from other ethnicities found in the Russian Empire. But this is precisely the distinction. In the Mikoyan book that ethnic differentiation is not made. Shashlyk is no longer Georgian; in this book it has become Soviet. In addition, Soviet cookbooks made culinary multiculturalism a mass phenomenon, and not just the province of the well-educated.

A cookbook consciously developed to reflect the latest ideas in government policy, and to be rational and scientific, also hearkened back to some very traditional practices. By that I mean the age-old practice of using food not only for sustenance but also as medicine. A whole section of the book is devoted solely to recipes that were deemed useful in the treatment of specific diseases. Two borsch recipes fall into that category: one, Vegetable Broth Borsch, was reputed to help with diseases of the liver and the other, **Borsch with Pickled Beets**, was for obesity and diabetes.

Much of the earliest Soviet thought, particularly in the 1920s, focused on public nutrition and the view of "food as fuel" and not as a way to "gladden the heart." In part, this was an attempt to live up to early feminist thinking of "unchaining" women from the stove. It was also strongly supported by Manuel Issakovich Pevsner who, as head of the Institute of Nutrition at the Medical Academy of Sciences, was actively promoting food as medicine and opposing the use of spices and "harmful" ingredients.

A significant aspect of *The Book of Tasty and Healthy Food* was its optimistic depiction of Soviet culinary reality. Some even go so far as to call it a classic example of governmental propaganda. Whether one agrees with that particular assessment or not, there is no doubt that the book served, at least, to feed the fantasies of children, who dreamed about a life that offered some dishes that never were part of their reality but looked so tempting in the book's colored photos. For those reasons I prefer to see *The Book* as a magic tale, despite its didactic intent of spreading "rational" cooking and eating.

A more nuanced view, than as direct propaganda, is to regard the book as a prime example of Socialist Realism in literature. It fully meets the four key principles demanded of Socialist Realism:

- Being relevant to the workers and understandable to them
- Presenting scenes of everyday life in terms of the ideal
- Being realistic in a representational sense
- Being partisan in promoting government policies

The Book is very deliberately orientated toward the family cook (all recipes are calculated for a family of five), and Mikoyan's personal insistence that the foods in the book needed to taste good. In fact, it was his direct intervention that resulted in a title beginning with the word "Tasty."

It is perhaps the combination of an ability to embrace the ever-shifting needs of the government in pursuit of its food policy, a willingness to combine the old with the new, and the unwavering optimism exuded from its pages that ensured the continued popularity of the cookbook. That combination of qualities also, perhaps, helps to explain the remarkable longevity of its champion, Anastas Mikoyan, at the highest levels of political power.

Mikoyan was the only early Bolshevik (from before 1917) who was never demoted, purged, or in any serious political trouble, even during the most intense periods of party "cleansing." He managed to retire and enjoy his family and the accomplishments of his many years of service. One wonders if identification with the most popular cookbook of the Soviet period had something to do with that.

Not much happened in 1955. Disneyland opened and also saw its millionth visitor that year; Ray Kroc inaugurated McDonald's; President Eisenhower sent the first advisers to South Vietnam; Israel killed 48 in Gaza; Churchill resigned; and the Warsaw Pact was founded, as a response to the inclusion of West Germany in NATO.

But in the Soviet Union 1955 was the year that the massive encyclopedic cookbook called *Cookery* (the title has also been translated as *Culinary*) was published. The first edition of 500,000 sold out within the year—a remarkable fate for a book designed for commercial cooks and not home use. In 1959 an abridged edition designed for home cooks was published and the print run of 500,000 sold out almost immediately. In 1992, one year after the collapse of the Soviet Union, the original 1955 edition was reprinted by the publisher "Resurrection" (*Voskresenie*). I purchased the "revised" and "expanded" 1999 fifth edition.

At first, I could not understand what was revised and what constituted expansion of the original *Cookery*. It seemed that an "expansion" could not have happened when I compared the page count of the original 1955 edition to mine, which was some six pages shorter. I was able to find a 1955 copy, however, and immediately understood what had happened. The 1999 reprint eliminated the first 112 pages of this book of more than 1,000 pages, substituting articles and adding new recipes. Original subject matter dealing with aspects of commercial cooking was eliminated and articles about the history of Russian cookery were substituted. A number of recipes for foods favored by Russian and Soviet heads of state were added. An interesting old recipe for **Lenten Borsch with Fish** (an unacknowledged borrowing from Avdeeva) is one of a whole number of such recipes.

Fortunately, this reprint kept the recipe section intact (including the borsch recipes), allowing the system of numbering the recipes to remain the same. I came to understand how a book in which the bulk of the material is a direct reprint, and with a shorter page count, could become "revised" and "enlarged."

Cookery can be, and I believe has been, viewed as a symbol of national (Soviet) identity on an institutional level. Its popularity after the collapse of the Soviet Union is a nostalgic yearning for a mythic time, not dissimilar to the nostalgia among many Romantics for the Holy Roman Empire, which was neither holy, Roman, nor an empire. One must keep in mind that *Cookery* evoked the time, not of the "horrible" 1980s that preceded the collapse of the country, nor the desperate decade right after the collapse; instead, it reflected in tone, format, pictures, and language, the 1950s—a time of remembered national pride, stability, and optimism in the future.

In format and style *Cookery* is a cross between *The Manual of Cookery* and *The Book of Tasty and Healthy Food*. On one hand there is an effort to promote the most modern and the aesthetic in cooking, and on the other hand the needs of institutional cooking are met. Perhaps there were fewer illustrations in *Cookery* than in *The Book*, and the extant photographs are of large industrial-sized cookery machines (no doubt the envy of small provincial food establishments). But the simplification of recipes and techniques, the simplification and standardization of flavor ranges, and a deliberate focus on presenting a multiethnic (Soviet, not just Russian) cuisine is virtually identical. *Cookery* includes a vast number of recipes (over 3,000). Most important, for institutional cooking all ingredients' amounts are given either, per serving, or for 100 servings.

From a cultural point of view, a special section entitled "The National Dishes of Allied Republics" marks a departure from the early Soviet policy of internationalism and supports the dictum attributed to Stalin: "Socialist in content, nationalist in form." In both *Manual of Cooking* and *The Book,* ethnic dishes are incorporated in the overall collection of recipes, whereas in *Cookery*, there is not only an overall growth of dishes seen as ethnic, but all major nationalities have their own recipe sections. Taking recipes for borsch as an example, the *Manual of Cooking* has a total of two recipes, *The Book* has eight, and *Cookery* has 30 (of which 16 are divided among the various "Borsch Belt" ethnicities).

The recipe for **Ukrainian Borsch** in the general sections of *The Book* and *Cookery* are different. The recipe for **Ukrainian Borsch** in the Ukrainian section of *Cookery*, on the other hand, is identical to the **Ukrainian Borsch** recipe in *The Book*. The contrast between the generic borsch found in *The Cookery* and its Ukrainian version is not dissimilar to the differences in Pelagia Ignatieva's "Little Russian" borsch recipes for Petersburg style and Ukrainian.

One can only speculate what prompted the difference in the recipes. My guess is that an indicator of how seriously Ukrainians regard borsch can be seen from the following joke:

"*Hey Cuz! Do you know what those damned Russians call our borsch?*"
"*What?*"
"*Schi!*"
"*There ought to be a law!*"

Interestingly enough, there are no Jewish borsch recipes in *Cookery*, despite the fact that borsch is an important element in Jewish culinary tradition and despite the existence of a Jewish Autonomous Oblast also known as Birobidzhan. The same silence greets the cuisines of Kalmyks, Chechens, and Crimean Tartars—all nationalities that were repressed and exiled in the post-war period.

In general, the high-water mark of Soviet cookbook publication runs from the latter part of the 1950s into the first half of the 1960s. This was also the time for an explosion of Soviet ethnic and foreign cookbooks written in Russian and minority languages. *Cookery* was translated and published in Ukrainian in 1956. The *Book of Tasty and Healthy Food* was also translated into the languages of member nationalities (and even into Czech). At the same time, cookbooks written in foreign languages were translated into Russian. Also during this period the first publication of a specifically Russian cookbook occurred (*Russian Cookery*, 1962); it combined recipes taken from *The Book* and from Molokhovets. Publication of ethnic cookbooks continued throughout the Soviet period, but large editions with print runs of 100-, 200-, and 300,000 were not repeated in the 1980s.

An example of ethnic cookbooks is the 450-page *Ukrainian Dishes*, in Ukrainian, published in 1957 in an edition of 100,000. The only earlier Ukrainian cookbook is *Dishes and Drinks in the Ukraine*

(1913), by Z. Klinovetska—now a classic of traditional Ukrainian national cuisine. As can be imagined, Klinovetska's *Dishes and Drinks in the Ukraine* has a number of borsch recipes. Of the ten recipes presented **Kiev (Kyiv) Borsch with Chicken** is interesting, not only because Kiev is and has been the historic capital of Ukraine but also because her version has chicken as a meat ingredient; normally chicken is associated with the borsch of Poltava, in Ukraine.

The 1957 *Ukrainian Dishes* became an instant standard in the Ukraine and in the Ukrainian community in the United States. To assist me with this project a family friend passed along her copy, which was given to her by her mother in New York City in 1958.

Ordinarily, the cookbooks of the different ethnic groups in the Soviet Union were first published in the official language of the Republic in question. Then they were translated into Russian. Availability in Russian accomplished three goals:

- it allowed speakers of Russian to become acquainted with the cuisine of an ethnic group
- it allowed spouses of a different ethnicity to provide for their partner the dishes of their beloved's youth
- it allowed non-speakers of the language of a cultural community to maintain a cultural identity through culinary practices

A number of ethnic cookbooks were also published in English. The motive for that is not clear. The most obvious motive could have been the possibility of earning hard currency from members of the diaspora community who had forgotten the language of their ancestors. In any case, my copy of *Byelorussian Cuisine,* (1979), which was originally written and published in Russian (1977), has three borsch recipes labeled as such; one recipe for *Kholodnik* (cold beet soup); and one recipe for green borsch called, *Schavelnik*. Curiously, borsch is classified as a modern Byelorussian dish and is not listed among traditional dishes. **Byelorussian Borshch with String Beans and Apples** is representative of the borsch recipes in this book. All three recipes are based on bone stock.

The collapse of the Soviet Union meant the collapse of this elaborate system of publications. Newly formed private publishers almost instantaneously began to produce cookbooks written following the collapse, and reprints of Soviet and old Russian classics. *1000 Antique Recipes* (1993) is one such book. It freely borrows from older cookbooks, particularly an unnamed 1905 book, unfortunately without any indication of what the book is, making further explorations impossible. It would have been nice to know that source because the recipe for **Onion Borsch** found in *1000 Antique Recipes* is unusual and would prompt further exploration for additional treasures.

In the newly independent republics, national cookbooks appeared almost immediately, as if to ensure that everyone would see the transformation to the present reality as complete and final: cookbook as a symbol of national identity. For example, the 1913 edition of Z. Klinovetska's book was reprinted in 1991, immediately after the dissolution of the U.S.S.R. and the independence of Ukraine.

The question of cookbooks in the post-Soviet Russian Federation lies outside the scope of this work. Suffice it to say, that food culture has blossomed. Classics have been reprinted numerous times, old cookbooks from the Soviet period have invaded the antique book market and fetch good prices (by Russian standards, where book prices have been historically inexpensive), and new books reflecting a variety of cuisines and techniques appear almost daily. New cookbooks extolling Soviet cuisine have appeared, as recently as 2013.

I need to briefly mention the first-class Russian food scholar and writer William Vasilyevich Pokhlyobkin, a veteran of WWII, a scholar of Scandinavia by profession, who turned to writing about food, in part, as an avocation and, in part, out of the need to earn a living after his access to Scandinavian research materials was restricted. In 1968 he published a short book about tea, which became the rage among the young, liberal urban youth and caused him to earn the disfavor of the government. As a consequence he experienced further difficulties in finding publishers for his work and was relegated to writing food articles and columns for newspapers and magazines.

Despite his problems and limitations in access to research materials, he continued writing until his death in 2000. It was only after the collapse of the Soviet Union that his books began to be published regularly. In all, he published over two dozen monographs on food and Scandinavian Studies. It is probably not an exaggeration to say that he was one the best known serious and prolific writers of Russian cooking during the Soviet period. Pokhlebkin, like Pelagya Povlovna, who was a transitional figure between old Russia and the Soviet collective, is also a transitional figure between the collectivist orthodoxy of the Soviet system and the individualist scholar practitioner that has begun to dominate the food writing in the post-Soviet time.

Pokhlebkin's **"Autumn-Winter" Turkey Borsch with Fettuccini** is remarkable for a number of reasons: the non-traditional use of turkey meat for the broth, the use of frozen meat which is usually avoided because that clouds the broth, and the inclusion of fettuccini as an ingredient. The recipe works very well, however, and can produce a remarkably good tasting borsch.

It is much too early to try to predict where the cooking of the peoples of the Russian Federation will head, but there is no question that food as the "gladdener of the heart" has won over the puritanical "food as fuel" approach

7. DIASPORA COOKBOOKS OF THE "BORSCH MIGRATION" - *COMMERCIAL PRESS BOOKS*

Recipes, like birds, ignore political boundaries. Just as the British empire still has a culinary pulse, beating in a curry in Scotland or in the mug of builder's tea with sugar and milk you are handed in some roadhouse on the Karakorum Highway; just as the Ottoman empire breathes phantom breaths in little cups of muddy coffee from Thessaloniki to Basra; so the faint outline of the Tsarist-Soviet imperium still glimmers in the collective steam off bowls of beetroot and cabbage in meat stock, and the soft sound of dollops of sour cream slipping into soup, from the Black Sea to the Sea of Japan and, in emigration, from Brooklyn to Berlin.
James Meek, "The story of borshch" *The Guardian*

Before embarking on a discussion of immigrant culture it would be good to review some of the terms as they are used in this work. *Immigrants* are persons who leave one country to settle in another. Immigrant culture is the distinct culture formed by such migrants in a new cultural environment. Immigrant culture lasts only as long as the first generation of migrants is dominant. The old culture seldom can be completely reproduced in a new environment, so immigrant culture is quite different from the host and usually from the immigrant's original culture. *Emigrants* are people who leave a country or culture area. Mennonites, for example, emigrated from Russia in 1899 and immigrated to Canada.

Ethnics are people who are united by significant culture traits, such as language, religion, customs, traditional practices and beliefs. Mennonites, who lived in Russia from the 18th century until 1899, were ethnically German, separated from their Slavic and Kalmyk neighbors by differences in language, faith, and many traditional practices. Usually, an ethnic culture is one that is a subgroup of an official or dominant culture. Ethnic cultures often form because of large-scale migration or the expansion of boundaries.

It is customary to regard the United States as a land of immigrants because of the massive migrations that occurred from the time of the Homestead Act of 1862 until anti-immigrant sentiment produced the Emergency Quota Act of 1921 and the beginning of migrant restrictions. It is probably more accurate to describe it as a land of ethnic cultures. Until very recently, when people from Latin America became the single largest cohort, the dominant group of immigrants came from the former Russian Empire, Soviet Union, and today's Russian Federation (i.e., Russia). The group included Poles, Jews, Russians, Ukrainians, Byelorussians, Lithuanians, Latvians, Estonians, Circassians, Carpatho-Rusyns, and a variety of nonconformist religious groups.

In all, the estimate is that about 20 million people emigrated from East-Central Europe to the U.S. between the middle of the 19th century and the 1990s. Although all these ethno-religious groups were divided by culture, custom, language, and religion, they shared at least one thing: knowledge and/or appreciation of borsch. This is why informally they can be called the "borsch" migration.

Cookbooks played an important role among some immigrants. Yevgeny Zamyatin, the Russian writer of the dystopian novel *We*, is reported to have remarked: *"Every immigrant family owns two books—one, a collection of Pushkin's writings and a copy of Molokhovets, and among the majority Molokhovets is the one most often read."*

This statement, while in all probability true, mostly serves to raise an important point. In a migration pattern as long and as complex as the more than 130-year odyssey from Eastern and Central Europe to the United States, many factors affected the transmission of cultural items and values. One important factor was class. Other factors include the degree of provincialism or sense of national identity found among a particular cohort; the question of language standardization and competence; and intent that motivated the migration.

Among many Catholic Lithuanians and Poles, for example, the journey to America was chiefly that of young men, just married, who left for America, found work, spent the next 30 years working and sending funds to their families, and then returned to their native land. This ideal, though more honored in its breach, was totally different from the intentions of Jews coming from the same areas, who were escaping pogroms and whose migration was permanent.

The Jewish immigrants, in some ways, had an advantage over others because they had their own language, Yiddish, that could transcend the local languages of their home settlements, so more readers could be reached. But they, like many of the others, began their life in America clustered in isolated communities organized around small villages or towns of origin. It is only over time that these clusters began to consolidate into larger entities.

I observed this process operating in the history of Jewish migrants to Cleveland, Ohio. At first, the two dozen or so synagogues were *shtetl* (village) oriented, often bearing their names. Over time, however, a consolidation occurred until only two major synagogues remained: one Conservative, which attracted East European Jews, and one Reform, favored by German Jews.

Despite the advantage that Yiddish offered in helping to foster ecumenicalism among Jewish immigrants, another important cultural element, the low rate of literacy among women, helped to slow publishing, particularly of cookbooks. With an overall literacy rate of 28 percent at the end of the 19th century, Jewish women were the most literate among the ethno-religious minorities in the Russian Empire, but that still meant that over 70 percent could not read. Not much use for a cookbook there.

The first Yiddish cookbook in America, *Lehr-bukh Vi Azoy Tsu Kokhen un Baken* [Textbook on How to Cook and Bake], was not published until 1901. Lack of Yiddish prevents me from discussing any books written in that language, but while I am confident that Yiddish cookbooks have been, and continue to be, part of the American Jewish experience I would be very surprised to learn that a book of the stature of Molokhovets, for example, became popular in the Yiddish-speaking immigrant communities. These communities were too small, provincial, and diverse to develop a "national" cookbook. Information here is limited to the English-language materials, which are compelling in their own right.

The earliest American-Jewish cookbook I found was *Jewish Cookery Book, on Principles of Economy, Adapted for Jewish Housekeepers, with the Addition of Many Useful Medicinal Recipes, and Other Valuable Information, Relative to Housekeeping and Domestic Management*, by Mrs. Esther Levy, published in Philadelphia in 1871. This book is reputed to be the earliest Jewish cookbook in the United States. Perhaps the most successful Jewish cookbook in the U.S. in the 19th century was *Aunt Babette's Cook Book: Foreign and Domestic Receipts for the Household; a Valuable Collection of Receipts and Hints for the Housewife,* by Bertha F. Kramer, published in 1889. Neither book has any borsch recipes, which indicates that its intended audience were German Jews who had no borsch tradition.

It is only in *The International Jewish Cookbook,* by Florence Kreisler Greenbaum, published in 1918, that one finds a recipe for **Borsh**). The publisher of Mrs. Greenbaum's book was the Bloch Publishing Company (founded 1854), the leader in publishing Reform Judaism texts and also the publisher of the non-kosher *Aunt Babette's Cook Book.* By 1918 the publisher saw its readership changing and reflecting the growth in importance of a more religiously conservative East European Jewish reader. *The International Jewish Cookbook* makes much of the fact that this is the "first" American kosher cookbook (an inaccurate claim) and it has a special section detailing proper koshering techniques.

The International Jewish Cookbook went through a number of editions. In 1941 the same Bloch Publishing Company brought out a substantially revised and expanded cookbook by Mildred Grosberg Bellin, called *The Jewish Cook Book*. This book stayed in print until 1983, when it was revised and published under the title of *The Original Jewish Cookbook,* a book still available today.

Jennie Grossinger was an extraordinary woman by any measure. Born in 1892 in Baligrod in today's Poland (in 1892 it was in Austria), she arrived in America with her family in 1899 and settled on the Lower East Side of Manhattan. Ten years later the family bought a large house and 100 acres in the Catskill Mountains, calling it Grossinger's Terrace Hill House. By 1972, when Jennie Grossinger died, the enterprise, which she oversaw and nurtured from its earliest daays, had grown to 35 buildings and 1,200 acres.

In 1958 her cookbook, *The Art of Jewish Cooking,* was first published by Random House. By 1969 the book had gone through 17 printings of the paperback version; the 1995 edition is still in print. Without a doubt, *The Art of Jewish Cooking* is the Jewish version of Julia Child's *Mastering the Art of French Cooking*—a classic that educated a whole generation of home cooks. Unlike *The Jewish Cookbook,* by

Mildred Grosberg Bellin, Grossinger's book makes no claim to internationalism and reflects more fully its Eastern European roots.

Her borsch recipes, for example, include Meat Borsch and **Cabbage Borsch**, neither of which is the purplish, watery broth that is often served cold and is associated in America with borsch, in general, and Jewish borsch in particular. While she offers one recipe for that cold borsch, she also has hot borsch recipes, with one being a meat and beets dish, while the other includes cabbage and tomatoes but no beets. That second recipe is particularly interesting because it is close to recipes of Mennonite borsch and manages to retain the sweet-sour taste while eschewing the use of beets. The inclusion of a range of recipes reflects a diverse Jewish audience.

Grossinger's book has a modern recipe format. Grossinger, unlike Greenbaum, includes a separate ingredients list with amounts given of each ingredient, and timing recommendations. It is not clear if this change is reflective of an assumed lack of cooking experience on the part of the reader, Grossinger's business experience—where costs are critical to profitability/economy—or because she wanted to ensure that readers could replicate the tastes found at the resort's dining table. I assume the latter is most probable. The absence of a green borsch recipe tends to support this assumption, since that soup is a staple in the Jewish kitchens of Poland and Ukraine. But "green" borsch is a spring dish, not the prime time for resort visitors. Of course, the answer to these questions could be as simple as that she was following contemporary American publishing standards.

Grossinger's intended audience is clear: Jewish women from the Ashkenazi immigration. These were the women of the ethnic generation, born in the U.S. and literate in English. Her purposes for publishing her book, however, could have been many. On one hand, it is a book for home cooks, with clearly written, uncomplicated recipes; on the other hand, it may also have served as a marketing tool for the Grossingers' resort—a souvenir, or fantasy of pleasant summer evenings in the Catskills.

Today the book market is rife with a wide variety of Jewish cookbooks intended for many different audiences and written in many different languages. I am sure that today's American Jew has adopted borscht as an expression of American Jewish cuisine and that it is equally popular among those whose heritage is rooted in Germany or Eastern Europe.

As the Zamyatin quip indicates, the first cookbook that immigrants possess is usually one that was brought from their native land. As the ethnic Russian experience also shows, by the re-publication of Molokohovets in Berlin in the 1920s, the next most likely new immigrant publication will be a reprint of a known classic in the native language of the immigrant. There is also the possibility of publishing a cookbook whose aim is to help the new immigrant in the country of his/her destination.

One such book is a small paperback printed in 1953 by the Ukrainian-émigré publishing house Hoverlia. The title, literally translated, means *The Ukrainian-English Female Cook* (*Ukrainsko-Angliska Kukharka*) but the publisher gave it the English title of *Ukrainian-English Cookbook*. The cookbook credits no author or compiler or even sponsoring agency. Its purpose was to help a recent immigrant (the post-WWII refugee) who has gotten a job as a domestic, probably as a cook, to prepare American dishes primarily, but it also contains recipes from the Ukraine.

The book is divided into three parts, with the first and most extensive part listing American dishes, their names (in both English and Ukrainian), and recipes for their preparation (in Ukrainian). The second section, entitled "Old Country Cook," contains traditional Ukrainian recipes. There are six recipes in the borsch section with five having the name "borsch" in the title. **Fresh Cabbage Borsch** is to me the most interesting recipe because it contains no beets and only uses beet kvas as a souring agent. The last section has various tips ranging from advice about rendering First Aid and home cures to how to wash hair and soften water.

It was from this book that I first learned about beet kvas, the fundamentally important role of kvas in the preparation of traditional borsch, and the startling, at the time, fact that originally borsch was the name of a plant which was in earlier times fermented. The author uses the term "borsch" to denote kvas, just like the Romanians who use the term *borş* for that purpose. It would be interesting to know who the author of the little Ukrainian-American cookbook was.

Normally one does not think of cookbooks in political terms but we see that from *Domostroy* onward cookbooks and politics are tightly intertwined. An interesting example of that is a reprint of Molokhovets, done in the late 1950s or early '60s in New York City by N.N. Martianov, a bookseller and publisher serving the post-

WWII ethnic Russian émigré community. Martianov's bookstore was located in the building next to the one in which we lived on Broadway and 141st Street in Manhattan. Mother owned a copy of this reprint.

The book is a hybrid, combining elements of the old and new; it is deeply rooted in pre-Revolutionary Russia and simultaneously clearly reflects the new American reality. The original text was copied by photographic means (it not clear which edition of the original was used), recipes were shifted around, some were eliminated, the original numbers given to recipes were also eliminated, and numerous illustrations (mostly black-and-white photographs) were added as fillers to keep to the original page count. To make it more useful in America, a table with old Russian measures, metric measures, and "new" American measures was added at the front of the book, but it contains no direct equivalent between the systems of measurement. There is, for example, no direct comparison between an American "cup" measurement and a Russian "glass." A table of contents for all recipes, and an index (the latter a rarity in Russian book publishing) were added along with a most useful Russian-English glossary of the names of ingredients.

While the text is a model of expedient and economical reproduction, care was taken with the physical appearance of the book. The copy I have is hard-bound, with an attractive deep-red cover with gold decoration and type. The paper is heavy-weight rag, ivory colored (after more than 60 years the pages have not yellowed at all), and the pages are sewn in. It is obviously meant to reflect its title and be a "gift" to a young housewife.

The fascinating aspect of this book is that the intended audience were children of the immigrants (from lands of the former Russian Empire to Europe) of the WWI generation who emigrated from Europe to America after WWII. These people knew Russian because they were educated in Russian schools created by the immigrant community in Europe; most of them were deeply hostile to anything Soviet and would not purchase anything produced in the Soviet Union. It is a bit ironic, therefore, that the vast majority of illustrations found in the Martianov edition are unattributed black-and-white copies of photos from the bestselling Soviet *Book of Tasty and Healthy Food* (1939).

In subsequent Russian diaspora cookbook history the cookbooks in English start with books written *by immigrants for* Americans (ethnic or the general reader). These are commercial ventures. English language cookbooks written for the ethnic community by fellow ethnics are predominantly limited to community or charity cookbook publications.

One exception to this is Lynn Visson's *The Complete Russian Cookbook: A Heritage Preserved* (also published as *The Russian Heritage Cookbook: A Culinary Heritage Preserved in 360 Authentic Recipes*) which is treasure trove of recipes current among Russia's elite émigrés in New York City. The author gives a wonderful glimpse of the milieu in the following description:

> *These women had another trait in common—a strange kind of dignity. It was the dignity of having survived and having retained a cultural and spiritual identity and integrity. They were always elegantly dressed for their long afternoons of tea and talk. In fact, they were perfectly dressed even when they went to the grocery store or the hairdresser' in rustling black silk dresses with a single strand of matched pearls and earrings or gold pendants and cameos, seamed stockings and bright red lipstick, with lacquered hair and tapered eyebrows, perfectly manicured hands playing with gold and white cigarette holders. The Russian maids who helped them serve—and there seemed to be an unlimited number of these women ready and willing to help bake cabbage pies and nut cakes or skim stocks and chop mushrooms—were small, rotund, middle-aged ladies with thick upper arms who wore sleeveless print dresses even in mid-winter as they spent days near a hot oven, padding back and forth to the kitchen in flat felt shoes and rumpled aprons, dirty-blond hair pulled back in tight buns from wide foreheads.*
>
> *I loved watching them cook, and our wonderful Austrian housekeeper could imitate any Russian dish by tasting it once or even from a description. ...*

Reading this I recalled Mother's first room in New York City rented from Ksenya Chizh, the widow of General Anton Denikin the Commander of the White Armies during the Civil War—Ksenya Chizh fit that description fully.

8. DIASPORA COOKBOOKS OF THE "BORSCH MIGRATION"- ADDRESSING DIFFERING CULTURAL NEEDS

"There are probably as many versions of borsch as there are Russians."
Irma Rombauer, *Joy of Cooking*

Of course, a book written in the language of the immigrant often dies with the generation that possesses that language; to survive, a book needs to reincarnate into the new language. This happened in stages for Molokhovets. In 1936 Sasha Kashevaroff, the daughter of a Russian Orthodox priest in Juneau, Alaska, published a short translation of 20 recipes found in *A Gift to the Young Housewives* and called it *Famous Russian Recipes*. A second edition was published in 1969; a third, revised, edition was published by Sasha's daughter, Margaret Calvin, in 1985.

Of the 20 recipes in this slender book, one is for borsch. Considering that the translator had more than 1,500 recipes to choose from, the inclusion of borsch helps to reinforce the connection between the image of Russian cooking and this dish. The borsch recipe and the book *Famous Russian Recipes* are an enigma. There are so many changes and adaptations to modern American cooking practices that one cannot even discover which of the Molokhovets recipes were used. The temptation is to see this booklet as a bad translation.

A more charitable interpretation is that in this book we are witnessing the complete adaptation and transformation of the original to local cultural conditions and practices. This intent is clearly stated by Margaret Calvin: "This book is essentially a product of Sitka, which has been home to its translator, artist and reviser and is the place of its publication." In that sense, despite its foreign origins, this book is as much an American community cookbook as those created by a church or temple committee.

This process of translation and adaptation is seen in yet another cookbook, *The Art of Russian Cuisine*, by Anne Volokh and Mavis Manus, published in 1985—almost 50 years after Sasha Kashevaroff's. Anne Volokh, who was born in Kiev during the Soviet period, was a food writer for the weekend edition of the governmental newspaper *Izvestia* for a number of years. The Volokhs emigrated to the U.S. in the 1970s as part of the Russian-Jewish migration during the Brezhnev Era. Both Anne and her husband, Vladimir, were ambitious and highly accomplished professionals whose dissatisfaction with reality in Soviet Russia and desire for greater opportunity drew them to the U.S. In 1983 Anne co-authored (with Mavis Manus) *The Art of Russian Cuisine*; in 1985 Anne created "Movieline Magazine," an online zine.

In the cookbook the author states (the book is written in Anne's voice) that her work is based on Molokhovets, Pokhlebkin, and a number of other Russian cookbooks. Volokh also informs the reader that Molokhovets was not re-published in the Soviet Union "…because of the fear that the abundance of foods and ingredients described in the book might have an unsettling effect on a populace experiencing permanent food shortages."

While this motive is possible, it is far more likely that Molokhovets was not re-published until the end of the Soviet era for two reasons:

- Cookbooks published by the Soviets since the 1930s not only fit their political or economic policy needs but also were reviewed by nutritionists to ensure maximum health benefits for those who used the books
- Because of Molokhovets' other writings, such as "Monarchism, Nationalism and Orthodoxy," in which her conservative monarchist and mystical Orthodox views find full expression

Without question, Anne Volokh's book is one of the more comprehensive Russian cookbooks published in English in the U.S. The solid foundation provided by Molokhovets, Pokhlebkin, and others, combined with Anne Volokh's experience in food writing and Mavis Manus' help in ensuring idiomatic English, created a genuine "American" Russian cookbook. This cookbook, with its solid foundation of 19th and 20th century cookery practices and dishes, ably attempts to reflect Russian taste preferences in light of available American ingredients. Through adaption or transformation of recipes this book, perhaps more than any other I am familiar with, makes Molokhovets directly a part of American culture.

In terms of borsch, Volokh does not seem to have used Molokhovets' recipes. Her recipes are confined to the Ukrainian varieties and do not present other regional exemplars found in the *Gift to Young Housewives*.

It would be impossible to end the consideration of Molokhovets in emigration without giving some attention to Joyce Toomre, a Slavics Ph.D. from Brown University, translator, and food historian. It is probably no exaggeration to say that Toomre, with her translation and adaption of Molokhovets' work in *Classic Russian Cooking, Elena Molokhovets' A Gift to Young Housewives* in 1992, not only brought Elena Molokhovets directly to the attention of the English-speaking reader and cook, but also helped to resurrect Molokhovets by making her the subject of serious academic study.

Molokhovets' writing was treated dismissively, even by her, both during her lifetime and during the Soviet period. It was Toomre who, for the first time, treated *A Gift to Young Housewives* as a cultural phenomenon of the first order. Just as Julia Child revolutionized the American kitchen, Molokhovets revolutionized the Russian kitchen by taking it out of the realm of the professional writer/cook of haute cuisine or the pursuer of the pre-Petrine Russian culinary "soul" and, instead, establishing a cuisine that combined Western, Eastern, and native influences into a cohesive whole. In that sense Molokhovets created Russian national cuisine just as Fanny Farmer did the American and Mrs. Beeton the British.

The parallels between Mrs. Beeton and Elena Molokhovets as writers are particularly remarkable. Both had their initial publication in the same year, 1861; both wrote their seminal work at a young age; both affected their national culture in a fundamental manner; and, both wrote guides to operating a household (not just cookbooks). Molokhovets outlived Mrs. Beeton but their impact on their respective cultures was equally defining.

Lynn Visson, an ethnic Russian New Yorker, graduate of Radcliffe, with a Ph.D. from Harvard, approached the problem of preserving and publicizing Russian classical cooking not by translating and adapting recipes from cookbooks but by collecting the recipes from Russian immigrants in New York. Her father, Vladimir Visson, was the director of exhibitions at the Wildenstein Gallery in New York City from 1943 to 1974. As a result, Lynn Visson had access to the elite of the Russian émigré society, as well as American society.

The result was the publication of her first cookbook, *The Complete Russian Cookbook,* in hardcover by Ardis Press in 1982. Lynn Visson was fortunate to have Barbara Norman, the author of *The Russian Cookbook,* write the foreword. The same year Ardis published Visson's book in paperback under the title of *The Russian Heritage Cookbook: A Culinary Heritage Preserved in 360 Authentic Recipes.* The book was published under the same title in 1998 by Casa Dana in California, and in a revised edition in 2009 by Overlook Press, who bought some titles and the name of Ardis Press. Of interest is the commentary on culture and life in the Soviet Union and post-Soviet Russia between the 1982 and 2009 editions, since Lynn Visson served as an interpreter at the UN for over three decades, married a Russian dissident of the 1960s, and has maintained close ties to the country to this day.

In 2008 the Moscow publishing house of R. Valent, which specializes in textbooks on translation and interpreting, produced a condensed Russian-language version entitled *200 bliud russkogo zarubezhia* (200 Dishes of the Russian Emigration).

In terms of borsch *The Complete Russian Cookbook* has 11 recipes with the term borsch in the title and 2 recipes that are called cold beets soups and are equivalents of the Polish *Chłodnik* and Russian *Svekolnik.* Each of the recipes is attributed to a specific individual. and I found the **Lenten Borshch II** recipe shared by Sophia Nabokov, the cousin of the writer Vladimir Nabokov and an assistant to George Balanchine, quite tasty.

One does not associate borsch with American country music, but the well-known song *That Wonderful Someone,* made famous by Patsy Cline on her Decca debut album *Patsy Cline,* in 1957, was written by Gertrude Berg. Born in Harlem (the major enclave of Jews escaping the overcrowded tenements of the Lower East Side of

Manhattan) in 1898, as Tilly Edelstein, Gertrude Berg became famous as the creator and actor in the comedy series *The Rise of the Goldbergs*, usually known as *The Goldbergs*. The story of the show was one of immigrants adjusting to American life.

The show, which began as a radio drama in 1929 and then successfully migrated to television in 1949, ran until 1955, and at the time was only eclipsed in its popularity by the *Amos and Andy Show*. It is not clear how deeply McCarthyism and the anti-Russian hysteria of the time affected Gertrude Berg personally, but her co-star on the show was black-listed and had to leave it shortly before it was cancelled. Despite the political troubles Gertrude won the first Emmy awarded to a woman leading actor, and then a Tony for her appearance in the Broadway show *Majority of One*—a show dealing with racial prejudice and hatred engendered by war.

In 1955, using the name Molly Goldberg (the show's heroine) she co-authored with Myra Waldo, a prolific cookbook and travel writer, the *Molly Goldberg Jewish Cookbook*. The cookbook is in a league of its own since it is written in the voice of a fictional character. Not any different than if we had a cookbook entitled *100 Favorite Recipes of the Count Monte Cristo*. Although the narrative text and commentary are probably the work of Gertrude Berg, in a clever way Myra Waldo indicates that she is the primary writer of the book by confiding to the reader in her introduction that she was observing and writing as Molly cooked the dishes.

The recipes in the book are for classical East European Ashkenazi foods and include four for red borsch and one for green borsch i.e, *Schav*. All four borsch recipes, Cold Borscht, Hot Meat Borscht, Fish Borscht and **Passover Russell Borscht (Fermented Beets)** are well written, substantial, and good; with the fish and Passover soups being most unusual. In fact, I have not previously encountered either type of borsch in any other Jewish cookbook, and I never have observed borsch as part of a Passover meal.

What makes Passover Borscht particularly fascinating is that it calls for *russell*, a term for which I have not been able to find a culinary definition outside of this book. *Russell* is the familiar beet kvas. Since it is made by fermenting beets, it appears to contradict the laws of Kashrut, which are quite strict in insisting on the requirements for "unleavened" food ingredients. Also fascinating is the information that in the 1950s one could purchase ready-made *russell* in stores.

The book, while featuring classical Eastern European Jewish cooking, was intentionally aimed at a non-Jewish readership, as is indicated in Myra Waldo's introduction. What is not clear is whether this was motivated by a desire for Jewish cultural outreach to a non-Jewish dominant culture, pure marketing strategy, or reflected the need to downplay cultural and religious differences at a time of strong anti-Semitism and fear of Eastern Europeans. I do know that sometimes the book was given to non-Jewish brides who married Jewish men.

Immigrant or ethnic cookbook publication in a language other than the author's native language immediately raises the question of the author's motivation and who the intended reader is. While it is logical to conclude that both *The Jewish Cook Book* and *The Art of Jewish Cooking* were intended to serve the needs of the English-speaking ethnically Jewish housewife (English, in effect, becoming a substitute for Yiddish as a common language) motivations are more difficult to establish for books of other groups.

Sasha Kashevaroff's book, for example, contains too few recipes to be a useful guide to Russian cooking for the aspiring cook who doesn't speak Russian. As revised by her daughter, its scope is limited to members of the Sitka community and those who may visit Sitka and want a souvenir.

Anne Volokh's book, on the other hand, could easily serve as a text book to develop full competence in the classic Russian cuisine as defined by Molokhovets and extended by Pokhlebkin. Anne Volokh's intent was to reach the American reader/cook.

The intent of Toomre's work is clearly academic, though deeply suffused by love for the author and the cuisine. My own copy of her book came to me from my sister, who left no signs that she had ever used the book as a cooking guide—making it more of symbolic possession than a practical guide.

Sometimes the reader is "accidental" and may not fit the most likely audience of the cookbook's writer. Most likely such is the case of my ownership of *The Art of Russian Cooking*, by Nancy Phelan, featuring the cooking of Nina Nicolaieff. I purchased my first copy in the mid-1970s, while attending Indiana University, from an itinerant bookseller who came each summer during the intensive summer

Russian immersion program and held an auction of a wide variety of Russian books—mostly academic studies.

I bought the book because I liked Nina's recipe for marinated vegetables—particularly good for grape tomatoes—and could not remember how Mother prepared them. Cool, tart marinated grape tomatoes on a hot Indiana day were a refreshing treat. Over time I discovered that most recipes in this book yielded dishes that tasted very much like Mother's, and the book became a mainstay in our home.

Nina stayed with me after the divorce from my first wife. My second wife, Gail, has profited from Nina's recipes and the growth of my cooking skills. Nina not only affected my cooking but I also have used her convention to transliterate the word "borsch," as the most accurate transliteration of the original Russian into English.

At first, my approach to the book was quite direct and naïve. I learned the recipes I liked and incorporated them into my own repertoire. It is only after I began to think about the book's role in the sphere of émigré cookbooks that I began to appreciate the subtlety of the book and, perhaps, to understand the author's intent. Nina Nicolaieff was a home cook born in Russia who, after WWII, emigrated to Australia. All her recipes are well-articulated Russian recipes, but if one looks closely it becomes obvious that the intended reader for this book is not someone from the Russian foodways tradition, but rather an English-speaking Westerner.

That recognition came to me as I considered her suggestions for breakfast foods: toast, tea or coffee, eggs, hot cereal, cream cheese, and yogurt. All of these dishes could be served in a Russian household at breakfast and therefore they do not call attention to themselves, but if one considers what many Russians would actually eat for breakfast this menu is clearly more American or Australian than Russian.

Whenever I visited my parents in California, Dad and I would have breakfast together. It was a wonderful morning ritual that included California sunshine, the morning paper, coffee, cold cuts, tomatoes, scallions, and bread. I would also go into the yard and pick a few oranges and an avocado from their trees. Occasionally, Dad would make scrambled eggs and I would inevitably tease him, telling him that he was becoming Americanized and forgetting his roots. A recent quick tour of Russian Internet sites yielded the consensus that a good breakfast consists of hot buckwheat cooked in milk, fried fish, tea, and either sausage sandwiches or fried cottage cheese patties (*syrniki*). I distinctly remember the outrage of my American students, one morning in Moscow, when we were served frankfurters, hard-boiled eggs, untoasted rye bread, and butter for breakfast.

Once one becomes sensitized to the fact that the menu choices are not meant to reflect Russian customs, the absence of certain dishes becomes obvious. In Nina's book there is no recipe for *pokhlebka*—a type of vegetable soup, or *vzvar*—a kind of stewed fruit dish, or brains—our grandmother's favorite, for example. Other dishes that have entered the Russian cultural space since our grandparents left their native soil, and which came to Russia from the West, are, however, included in this book. Casseroles, which were invented in 1866 by Elmire Jolicoeur in Berlin, New Hampshire, have become, since the Revolution, a Russian staple but were so foreign to my own experience that I did not even notice the recipes for them in *Cooking with Nina* until I examined it very closely for this work.

The subtlety of the approach to presenting Russian fare in a manner that would stay true to how Russians do things but also be quite compatible with Australian habits forced me to think deeper about possible motives for the book's writing. Looking at my own fondness for the book, its seeming simplicity and artlessness, and years of living with this book I realized that what I had in my possession is a delightful portrait of Nina—a talented, warm, and nurturing woman. It would not be an exaggeration to say that Nina became a surrogate mother, teaching me the preparation of familiar dishes and passing along cooking techniques. In all, *Cooking with Nina* has four borsch recipes, and besides the **Flotskij borsch** I have enjoyed her **Moscow Borsch** frequently.

The earliest English-language cookbook of Russian food published in America was written by a Russian, Nina Nikolaevna Selivanova, and was aimed at American readers. This was *Dining and Wining in Old Russia*, published by Dutton in 1933. Little could be established about the author except that she was of noble heritage, emigrated after the Revolution and was the author of *Russia's Women (Pioneers of the Woman's Movement)* (1923), *The World of Roerich*(1924) and two translations. I have not seen the book itself and therefore cannot comment on its contents, but I would be surprised if it did not have a borsch recipe.

The next book was the 1936 translation of 20 Molokhovets recipes by Sasha Kashevaroff. The limited number of recipes and publication in Sitka, Alaska, made this primarily a book of local interest. *Betty Grant's Russian Cook Book: Recipes of Many of the Most Popular and Famous Russian Dishes as Prepared by Betty Grant* was published in 1941 in Richmond, Virginia. In 1946 the same publisher produced, virtually identical book under the title *Samovar: A Russian Cookbook,* this time listing the author as Elizavetta Dmitrovna, a Russian immigrant from China, married to an American government official stationed there before WWII.

My used copy of *Betty Grant's Russian Cookbook* came with a handful of "surprises." In addition to the expected check-marks denoting favored dishes, there is a handwritten recipe for "Madam Yusupoff's Paté" (possibly a recipe from Princess Irina Yusupoff) and two magazine cut-outs with Russian recipes. One, dated 1946, is from "Harper's Bazaar." The other is from a 1947 edition of "Vogue," has, among other recipes, one for vegetable borsch. The author of the book, Elizavetta Dmitrovna (aka Betty Grant), was an immigrant Russian who lived in Harbin and Shanghai, China, before WWII. She is a representative of the Russian immigrant wave that came to America from China and the Philippines, the so-called "Chinese Immigration." Elizavetta uses the French transcription for borsch (*bortch*) and schi (*stchee*), which signals that she was most likely of the Russian upper classes by birth. The book's three borsch recipes range from a complex Ukrainian version to one, based on canned ingredients, that the author calls "Quick Borsch."

While her contributions to the dissemination of borsch recipes is significant (she even gives directions on how to make kvas), it is her inclusion of a recipe for a dish called *hóngtāng* (**Red Soup**) that makes her work unique. Red Soup comes from Harbin, China, and is a regional variant of the Chinese borsch tradition, mostly centered in Shanghai and Hong King. Most often "Red Soup" is made with red cabbage, although not in the recipe given by Elizavetta Dmirtovna. Harbin, the capital and largest city of Heilongjiang Province in Northeast China, was founded by Russia in 1898 and remained an important settlement of Russian merchants and immigrants until after WWII. Today it still enjoys an important role as a trading center with Russia.

There is no evidence that this book, in either edition, found a wide readership, thus making *How to Cook and Eat in Russian* (1947), by Princess Alexandra Kropotkin, initially published by G.P. Putnam's Sons, the first post-war Russian cookbook more widely known on Russian cooking. This we can surmise by the fact that the book was republished in 1964 by Charles Scribner's Sons and published yet again in 1993 and 1997 by Hippocrene Books, a publisher specializing in folklore, dictionaries, and cookbooks. More than 60 years after initial publication, it is still in print. An out-of-print 2003 bilingual edition, edited by Evgeny Steiner, was also produced by Hippocrene Books.

Princess Alexandra was ethnically Russian, born in London, lived a good portion of her life in America, and married an American. Her father was the famous anarchist Prince Peter Kropotkin. The success of her cookbook can be explained by her presence on the American literary scene with her translations of *War and Peace*, *The Brothers Karamazov*, and *Crime and Punishment*, as well as her numerous lectures, and articles published in magazines such as *Life*.

The intended reader for her cookbook is clearly an American, as the author provides some basic information about Russian culture in addition to nearly 300 very good recipes. A clear indicator of the intended audience is that the book's foreword was written by Craig Clairborne, a contributor to *Gourmet* magazine and food editor for the *New York Times* for many years.

There are three borsch recipes given in the book. The author very deliberately chooses a range of soups that are very hearty, as in her Ukrainian Borsch, to an elegant but efficient **Quick Borsch**.

Some purposes of the book are made clear: it was meant to acquaint the American reader with Russian culture and people, and to humanize a little-known country with which relations were worsening after a highly positive period during WWII. Perhaps another purpose was to give a more "real" dimension of people in the novels that the princess translated; yet another possibility was perhaps to share the author's obvious knowledge of and love for cooking. Whatever the specific motives, the book has become a classic in presenting Russian cuisine to American readers.

Princess Alexandra's book was a pioneering effort, to be followed by a number of cookbooks that reflected the changing face of Russian emigration in the U.S. In 1961 a cookbook written by

Kyra Petrovskaya, an émigré from the Soviet Union, was published by Prentice-Hall. Initially titled *Kyra's Secrets of Russian Cooking,* the book was later renamed *Russian Cookbook* and published by Dover in 1992. Kyra wrote: *"But this book is not for my Russian friends, who know how to prepare Russian food. This book is for my other friends, who are used to short cuts and who utilize these short cuts with great intelligence."*

Kyra Petrovskaya's story is another extraordinary one. Born in 1918 in the Crimea, along the Black Sea coast, she lost the male members of her family during the Revolution and Civil War and spent her childhood in Leningrad, raised by her mother and grandmother. An actress and singer by training, she was drafted into the Soviet Army during WWII and served as an officer, a sharpshooter, and nurse during the Siege of Leningrad. After WWII she went to Moscow, met and married an American diplomat, and emigrated to the United States. In the U.S. she became a housewife, singer, speaker, and writer, and in 1959 published her memoir. In 1960 her first novel came out, followed in 1961 by *Kyra's Secrets of Russian Cooking.* Next came a career in Hollywood, then another marriage, and more writing and lecturing. In all, she has published over a dozen books, appeared in a couple of films (Soviet and American), and was a lecturer for Viking Lines. In 2012, a little over 90 years old, she was present on the Internet, with a wonderful website, and is active on Facebook.

Her cookbook has some 200 recipes, and Kyra makes the point that the dishes in the book are Russian and that she excluded French and German dishes that have been part of Russian culinary tradition since the 18th century. Two of her recipes are for borsch: one is for a Ukrainian, the other one she names **Russian Borsch**.

Since the publication of Princess Alexandra's and Kyra's books, the field of Russian cookbooks in English has expanded exponentially. In 2012, amazon.com listed 84 titles for the search term "Russian cookbooks English"; even if one allows for duplicate editions, more than 50 different Russian cookbooks are available.

Books such as Alexandra Kropotkin's, Kyra Petrovskaya's, the popular cookbook by Darra Goldstein (a scholar of Russian and author of *A Taste of Russia*), or the academic work of Joyce Toomre all have at least two purposes. One is the stated public purpose of providing information to the public; the other, a much more personal one of enhancing the literary or academic aspirations of the authors and/or allowing for personal reminiscences.

There is little doubt that Alexandra Kropokin's book was part of her overall literary output. The same is true with Kyra Petrovkaya's book, which came out a year after her memoir found success. Darra Goldstein is also explicit in stating her personal aims: *My interest in Russian cuisine stems from two sources. As a student of literature, I was eager to satisfy my curiosity about the preparation of foods described in Russian novels and short stories. More deeply rooted in me, however, were memories from childhood—the dishes I first tasted from my grandmother's spoon.* That aspect of cookbook writing becomes more prevalent as the number of cookbooks increases.

The phenomenon of commercial cookbook publishing as it relates to a diaspora community is quite complex. Initial publications are usually aimed at members of that community in that community's language and imitate the known classics. Subsequent publications in the language of the new culture can be directed to the diaspora community, as in the case of the Jewish or Mennonite communities, or at the general reader of the dominant culture, as with books created by Slavic Russians. Arguably, there is no English-language Slavic-Russian cookbook published by a commercial press that is aimed primarily at members of Russian ethnic communities. There is, however, another whole category of cookbooks that further complicate foodways literature as it affects a diaspora group and its host culture. That is the non-commercial, ethnic, or charity cookbook, which is examined in the next chapter.

9. DIASPORA COOKBOOKS OF THE "BORSCH MIGRATION"- *CHARITY OR COMMUNITY COOKBOOKS*

"A close reading of the humble literature of Jewish cookbooks can reveal how the malleable medium of food shapes social life and cultural values. Unlike other material manifestations of social life, which can be built and left to stand, food is perishable, ephemeral, constantly renewed by women in their kitchens. Preparing food and eating it are daily affairs. Cookbooks, though not direct indications of what people ate, nevertheless represent Jewish cuisine and social life in ways that illuminate changing notions of Jewish womanhood and the Jewish home in the United States."

Barbara Kirshenblatt-Gimblet,"Kitchen Judaism"

The genre of the so-called "charity" or community cookbooks is of particular interest to cultural historians and anthropologists. These books are a modern phenomenon. Not counting handwritten family or small-group recipe collections, printed cookbooks whose aim was to promote a specific cause and raise funds for it became popular in the U.S. after the Civil War. It's not my purpose to delve into the history of these books either in general terms, or as it applies to the various ethnicities that emerged from the Russian Empire or the Soviet Union, although this is a fascinating, vast and complex field. In terms of Jewish cookbooks alone the question arises: How, and why, did Mrs. Simon Kander's, *The Settlement Cook Book: Containing Many Recipes Used In Settlement Cooking Classes,* originally published in 1901, sell, by 1991, over two million copies?

The sheer number of ethnic cookbooks can be easily illustrated with the example found among the groups of Germans from Russia. In the period between 1890 and WWI, the largest cohort of Germans from Russia immigrated to the United States. Many settled in Kansas and North Dakota. The estimate is that today there are approximately one million descendants of these immigrants, mostly concentrated in the Midwest. The University of North Dakota's library's online listing of cookbooks for the groups contains more than 100 different books. A search of the library's database for borsch recipes yields 90 examples, culled from 52 different cookbooks. The website also warns users that the online materials do not constitute the whole collection. In short, if a relatively small migrant group has this many books, the overall numbers must be quite impressive.

If one takes a larger group, such as the Jewish migrants from East-Central Europe, the number of community cookbooks becomes even higher. In its collection of Jewish books the New York Public Library has 700 cookbooks, most of them community books.

My interest in these books began in the late 1970s when I had the opportunity to do folklore research in Cleveland, Ohio. In preparing an exhibition of the history of Russian ethnics in Cleveland I made the decision to work with members of the overall community who identified themselves as Russians. In earlier work I was involved in attempting to define ethnicity, specifically Russian ethnicity, and tried to understand the whole range of issues associated with the term "Russian." Keenly aware of the problems in trying to define that term abstractly I wanted to have members of the community define themselves. The idea was modest: to try to make sense once the materials were gathered, and not to try to predefine someone else's reality. In hindsight I realize that, at the time, I was grappling with the concepts of Russia and Russian as a cultural space/affiliation and not as the country of a single ethnic group.

The decision to allow people to self-identify offered an opportunity to include individuals and ethnic groups who saw themselves as Russians in the American context, but who would not be classified as such by more traditional methodologies. My approach yielded a wider range of observed cultural practices and a more inclusive description of Russian ethnicity in America. As a direct result of this choice I was able to include the traditions of Carpatho-

Rusyns (Lemkos) and Russian Jews without any need for hyphenated terms or long-winded explanations.

The first community cookbook I purchased was *Just a Pinch of Russian*, the 1974 edition of a book originally published in 1972 by St. Michael's Orthodox Church. The congregation was mostly comprised of Lemkos (Carpatho-Rusyns), who despite their origin on the Polish side of the Carpathian Mountains saw themselves as Russians.

Around the same time the American Folklore Society held its annual meeting in Los Angeles, California. I went, in part as an aspiring folklore scholar, in part so that I could visit with family living in Fullerton, California. The most notable memory of that gathering was a side trip that a group of us took to The Holy Virgin Mary Russian Orthodox Cathedral in Los Angeles. For someone used to Russian Orthodox architecture this church seemed unremarkable. It is a nice whitewashed church, rendered in the Pskov architectural style, with nothing seemingly extraordinary about the building. Next to the main entrance there was, as is so often the case in an ethnic Russian community, a birch tree.

This church is quite extraordinary. Not only is it one of the earliest Russian Churches built in the U.S. after the Russian Revolution, but the church building served as a set piece in the 1932 MGM movie, *Rasputin and the Empress*, and was made available to the congregation by the movie's art director. As far as I know, this is the only Orthodox Church that starred in a movie before it became the heart of a congregation. There I purchased my second community cookbook, *Joys of Ethnic Cooking*, which was in its third printing in 1979.

These two books share a number of similarities even though they originated within two distinctly different congregations. The Cleveland congregation was predominantly Lemko and, therefore, relatively homogenous. The Los Angeles congregation, while rooted in the Russian community of the 1920s, was more diverse in its ethnic composition, as evidenced by the names of contributors to the book and the dishes shared: *Miso* soup (Japanese), Pastitso (Greek), or Eggplant Parmigiana-Melanzana al Parmiagiano (Italian). Both books were successful, since the copies I own are from the third printing. Each book has a cover design done by members of the congregation. Both books also have a number of borsch recipes. Physically, there are also similarities: both have plastic comb bindings and are close in total page count.

A difference between the two books is that a *Pinch of Russian* adds a range of categories absent from *Joys of Ethnic Cooking*, which include recipes by famous people, quantity cooking, household hints, refrigerator hints, and most important, Christmas and Easter dishes. In the *Pinch of Russian* the sections on the holidays have short descriptions of relevant traditions, followed by recipes; the Christmas section includes a Christmas carol, and the Easter section, a description of how to make batik-decorated Easter eggs. One of the recipes is for **Borsch (No Meat)**, a time-honored traditional part of the Lemko *Sviata Vecheria* (Holy Supper) or Polish *Wigilia* (Christmas Eve dinner).

In all, *Just a Pinch of Russian* has five different borsch recipes, although the index list, only three. Of those the **Old Country Borsch** recipe is typical.

Both cookbooks are expressions of the two congregations and their dominant ethnic identities, but the California church emphasizes its ethnic diversity and the Ohio church emphasizes its traditions. On a pragmatic level the publication of each book helped raise funds for the operation of the church while simultaneously helping to define the group.

Joys of Ethnic Cooking, true to its more cosmopolitan membership, offers a wider range of borsch recipes. On one hand, we have a recipe for **Sara's Borsch**, a pretty standard recipe for the Russian ethnic community in the U.S., on the other, we see **Matushka Gizetti's Borsht,** which is quite a departure from traditional borsch recipes. Interestingly enough even the transliteration of the term "borsch" differs.

Recipes of San Francisco Russian Molokans (1973) is a compendium of mostly Russian and some non-Russian recipes of a small religious community that initially migrated to the U. S. in 1905, but had a larger influx of migrants in the post-WWII era. Most Molokans settled on the West Coast, particularly in the Boyle Heights area of Hollywood with a smaller group in San Francisco, a traditional city of settlement for Russian immigrants. Today, it is estimated that there are approximately 25,000 Molokans in the United States, with some 5,000 expressing a strong sense of ethnic identity. Their nickname—"Molokans" (Milk Drinkers) stems from a religious tradition of drinking milk during Lenten periods when animal products are banned for Orthodox Russians.

The cookbook is typical, in most respects, of other community cookbooks, although it appears to have been published by the community itself and not by one of the community cookbook publishers. Like most community cookbooks it met success, and my copy is the third edition of 1988. There are ten borsch recipes in it with **Posnee [Lenten] Borsch (Vegetarian)** and **Borsch For a Large Church Dinner** of particular interest because the first includes milk products in a Lenten dish and eschews beets (like many Molakan borsch recipes), while the second recipe is a wonderful example of quantity borsch cooking.

Indy Cooks International, brought into existence in 1984 under the able leadership of Sidonie and Werner Stolz of the Swiss Club (at that time a member group of the International Center of Indianapolis), contains some 400 recipes contributed by 46 different ethnic organizations. It is a different kind of community book. Both *Joys of Ethnic Cooking* and *Just a Pinch of Russian* were organized to support a single ethnic orientation. *Indy Cooks International,* on the other hand, is a cookbook that helped establish a multiethnic association—The Nationalities Council of Indiana. The Council began as a committee of the International Center of Indianapolis but broke away from it and became a rarity, in that it became a successful, grass-roots initiated, multiethnic organization.

Much of the credit for that can be attributed to the effective creation of a Nationalities Council cookbook: *Indy Cooks International.* This was the first major Council-generated project that benefited the Council itself, and fostered the growth of cooperation among leaders of various groups. The cookbook was an idea born while I was the Director of the International Center, an idea that I supported with great enthusiasm, contributing a borsch recipe and a foreword.

At the time, I had just begun my involvement with borsch, and the recipe is evidence of how little I knew about borsch preparation. I tried to create a version of Poltava borsch in honor of our maternal grandmother but the recipe I generated is so convoluted and inaccurate in terms of an actual Poltava borsch that I blush on the rare occasions that I reread the recipe. One good result of this effort is that it illustrates how forgiving borsch is. The prime taster of my cooking was willing to marry me even after tasting this creation.

Physically, *Indy Cooks International* fits the standard format of community cookbooks with a plastic comb binding, illustrations donated by members of the community, and the division of recipes into different categories. Because the book was not published through Cookbook Publishers (or a similar publishing enterprise) but by the Council itself, it had greater format flexibility than others of its ilk. The recipes, for example, are not divided according to standard cookbook categories but, rather, according to ethnicity; the book's two borsch recipes are in its "Ukraine" section. To spare myself embarrassment the **Vegetarian Borsch** recipe which was donated by the Ukrainian-American Cultural Society is offered as a sample recipe for this book. It is interesting that this dish is called vegetarian instead of Lenten, although the text preceding the recipe explicitly states that the borsch is served on fast days.

A particularly fascinating charity cookbook is *The War-Time Edition Russian Cook Book for American Homes,* published in 1943 by the Russian War Relief Fund. The aim of the Russian War Relief was to establish a direct line of communication between ordinary Americans and Russians. The technique currently known as targeted assistance was the prime principle of the organization, and was expressed in programs supplying clothing, emergency kits, and medical supplies to needy Russians. Individual packages were sent from a specific American to an individual Russian. A postcard was enclosed in each package in hopes that the recipient would use it to contact the donor. We know that Dr. Helen Sorokin, one of the book's notable contributors, received at least one such postcard from a woman who underwent the siege of Leningrad. In all, between 1943 and 1944 over $17 million was raised by the organization to help Russian families.

The unusualness of this book calls for closer examination. *The War-Time Edition Russian Cook Book for American Homes* looks quite different from the vast majority of community cookbooks. The cover, a tri-color design that depicts a smiling couple walking arm-in-arm with a basket of produce and a war ration coupon book in hand, is the work of Lucille Corcos (1908-1973), a well-known artist and illustrator of the time. Trained at the Art Students League, Corcos is considered to be a "modern primitivist" painter. She was also an illustrator of magazines (*Vanity Fair, Fortune*) and books (Deems Taylor's *A Treasury of Gilbert and Sullivan*) and *Grimms's Fairy Tales*. Virtually in all other cases community cookbooks have designs donated by nonprofessional cover designers and consequently do not have the same aesthetic and emotional impact as this book. I bought my copy on the strength of the thumbnail picture of the cover, and it is the only cookbook that I have mounted in a shadow box.

The professional dimensions of the book extend to the editorial board, which consisted of professional food writers that included college professors, editors at *Esquire*, *PM*, *American Home*, *McCall's* and *Good Housekeeping*, and authors of books and articles on food, nutrition, and drink. This "blue ribbon" editorial board created a superbly edited book. While most community cookbooks do well to have a decent proofreader, this book unifies the disparate voices of recipe donors into a single voice. In doing so it models the traditional motto of the United States, *E pluribus unum* ("Out of many, one"), which was used from 1782 until 1956, when it was officially replaced by "In God We Trust."

To achieve a consistent style must have been a challenge, given the breadth of contributors to the volume: Russians, Americans, Ukrainians, Georgians, Circassians (Adyghe people), Sephardic and Ashkenazi Jews, corporations, estates of passed notables, and Russian War Relief committees from around the United States. Among the contributors are James Beard, considered the pioneer of American haute cuisine; the vodka company Ste. Pierre Smirnoff Fils; Mrs. Dexter Perkins, Editor, *Fanny Farmer Cookbook*; the estate of Prince George Matchabelli; the opera bass, Alexander Kipnis; the restaurant Casino Russe, New York; Helena, Baroness de Polenzska; Daniel P. Woolley, Commissioner of Markets, New York City; Prince George Chavchavadze; Prince Koudasheff; and a host of less notable people. The simplicity and clarity of language, the economical style of exposition found in the borsch recipes, carry throughout the book and resonate with the simplicity of the book's design and illustrations.

There are three recipes for red meatless borsch, one for borsch with meat, and one for green borsch which is titled "Shav." In the short section introduction an opinion is offered that borsch, and other Russian soups, will provide good nutrition while using the minimum number of war ration points. **Borshch** (with meat stock) and **Meatless Borshch** are the two contributions shared.

Two names of contributors to the book struck my interest: Fatima Natirboff and Mrs. Pitirim Sorokin. While the name of Fatima Natirboff drew my attention because it is a Muslim name and unexpected in a book reflecting the Russian community, the name of

Mrs. Pitirim Sorokin raised my curiosity because the name "Pitirim" is a quintessential Russian name, while "Sorokin," in English, means "related to a magpie"—a colorful name.

Fatima Khanim and her husband Kuchuk Natirboff, both Adyghe (Circcasian—an ethnic group in the Caucasus Mountains), emigrated from Novorossisk, Russia, to Istanbul, Turkey, in 1919. Soon after arriving Fatima persuaded one of the sultans to allow the Circassians to use a palace to house refugees who had no other domicile. Over 100 fellow refugees eventually inhabited the so-called "Circassian Home," to which the naval flag officer Admiral Mark L. Bristol, the U.S. High Commissioner for Turkey, was invited.

Admiral Bristol found the Circassians to be admirable people and petitioned the State Department to allow them to come to the U.S. as a group. That permission was granted. Although the majority of the Circassians did not accept the proffered invitation, as they expected the imminent collapse of the Bolsheviks, the Natirboffs and a few other Circassians decided to go to the U.S. Those first Circassian families arrived on Ellis Island on August 1, 1923. They were welcomed by the Russian Immigrant Society, given rooms in a cheap hotel, and then offered jobs in Stamford, Connecticut, at a lock factory.

In 1925 Fatima's husband died, leaving her with four children to support. She began to earn a living by sewing and, after a few years of working 16- and 18-hour days, established a clientele among New York's elite. As she became well-known she continued to help immigrant Circassians and to sponsor scores to the U.S. In short, she became a force in the Russian and Circassian immigrant communities, as well as being associated with New York's elite. Her contribution to the cookbook was a continuation of her overall public work.

Born in Russia, Dr. Elena Sorokin (née Baratynskaya, 1894-1975) was the wife of Pitirim Sorokin, a member of the Kerensky government and an anti-Communist who was condemned to death several times, the last time by Lenin himself. Instead of being executed, however, he and his wife were expelled from the Soviet Union and immigrated to the U.S. in 1923. Initially, both of them taught at the University of Minnesota; then he was recruited by Harvard (1930) and asked to form their Sociology Department.

Pitirim Sorokin, who wrote extensively on structures of society, developed a theory of social regeneration based on altruism. His views were most exhaustively developed in his books *Altruistic Love: A Study of American Good Neighbors and Christian Saints*, and *Explorations in Altruistic Love and Behavior (symposium)*, in which he explored the idea of a "community of altruism." After Russia was attacked by the Nazis he joined his wife in the work of Russian War Relief, Inc.

While doing research for this chapter I came across an article in the *Harvard Crimson* (student paper) for February 13, 1968, which announced his death. The article made particular note of Professor Sorokin's talk at a 1966 Harvard "Speak Out" sharply criticizing American foreign policy. The article also pointed out that Pitirim Sorokin's Harvard Research Center in Creative Altruism, which he started in 1949, attracted a large degree of derision. I could not help but reflect that it was possible that I could have crossed paths with Professor Sorokin on the way to Widener Library and been totally unaware of him. Also had I attended the "Speak Out" I would have probably been highly critical of his presentation, given my political views of the time. Today, on the other hand, I hold him up as an exemplar of clear and humane thinking.

The "community of altruism" that this cookbook so well illustrates echoes the early charity cookbooks published in support of the suffragette movement in that *The War-Time Edition Russian Cook Book for American Homes* was a national effort to support the idea of personal international assistance, just as the suffragette books were a national effort to support the idea of greater female equality. Unfortunately, however, that concept of community did not last. As early as 1943 the FBI declared the cookbook's parent organization, Russian War Relief, a Communist front (the "evidence" was based exclusively on anonymous denunciations and innuendos) and the organization never had an opportunity to morph from war relief to reconstruction assistance. Russian War Relief, the organization, ceased to exist by late 1945 and a wide variety of people who had joined in this community of altruism during the war were later accused of Communist sympathies or outright Communism.

It is not the purpose of this work to examine the cultural politics in post-World War II America or the Soviet Union or to try to decide the reasons for these politics. It is enough to indicate that in

1946, when talk began about a Cold War between these two powers, periods of cultural repression and insistence on orthodoxy began in both countries. In the Soviet Union it was called Zhdanovschina (named after the Communist Party's Secretary of the Central Committee, Andrei Zhdanov), and in the United States the period is loosely called McCarthyism. In both countries the intent was to stifle liberal and progressive initiatives and to assert a conservative control over forms of cultural expression. In real terms this conservative bent resulted in America supporting the attempts of its Western s allies to reimpose colonialism in Asia, Africa, and the Middle East, with consequences of that policy reverberating to this day.

The brief discussion of some of the community cookbooks in my possession shows that community cookbooks vary significantly in motives for their creation and also what constitutes a community, which publishes the book. The motives can be as simple and direct as raising funds for a local church or school, for a national or international cause, or to help solidify a sense of group identity, as was the case with *Indy Cooks International*. But even within a single category differences can be observed. Both *Just a Pinch of Russian* and *Joys of Ethnic Cooking* illustrate that within the category of single congregation cookbooks aims differ—one book celebrates ethnic tradition; the other, ethnic diversity. *The War-Time Edition Russian Cook Book for American Homes* stands out among this genre not only in the professional level of its execution, but because it successfully melds an incredibly diverse assortment of people from distinctly different cultural and social strata and interests into a community motivated by a purely altruistic idea.

While in this chapter I limited myself to community books that either reflect or are the product of the ethnicities that came out of the Russian politico-cultural space, in the next chapter I delve briefly into cookbooks that contain borsch recipes but are (in most cases) the product of non-Russian culture and therefore indicate the acceptance of borsch as an international dish.

10. BORSCH GOES INTERNATIONAL

...a year before Yuri Gagarin's flight [1961] they sent up a test rocket. The mission was to test communication with the spaceship. They launched the famed manikin "Ivan Ivanych" broadcasting a tape recording. The question became: What should the broadcast from space be? In the end, during the flight a borsch recipe was transmitted. So, the first transmission that American intelligence intercepted was a recipe for borsch.

Anna Vygolova "Americans Receive the Recipe for Russian Borsch from Space"

History has a funny sense of humor. In August of 1968 the Beatles recorded "Back in the USSR." The song, a parody of the Beach Boys sound, Chuck Berry's "Back in the USA," and a nod to Hoagy Carmichael's "Georgia on My Mind," was part of their immensely popular (and banned in the USSR) *The Beatles*, best known as the *White Album*.

In 2003 there were no more Beatles, there was no longer a Soviet Union, and both Georgia and Ukraine—two constituent republics of the USSR—were wholly independent nations. In May of 2003 Paul McCartney, the author of the song (which he wrote while studying Transcendental Meditation in India), performed it in Moscow to a totally packed Red Square with smiling ex-KGB agent and President of the Russian Federation, Vladimir Putin, in attendance. The crowd roared its approval and sang along when McCartney began singing "Back in the USSR"; portraits of Stalin flashed on the screens behind him, and Putin grinned. History, indeed, has a funny sense of humor.

In 1969 Time-Life Books published, as part of its *Foods of the World* series, the book *Russian Cooking*, written by Helen and George Papashvily, with photography by Eliot Elisofon and Richard Jeffery. *Russian Cooking* is a gorgeous book. It is a large, hard-cover, coated-paper volume filled with great photography. The book originally came in a hard slipcase that held both the large picture-and-narrative tome and a smaller book of recipes. The large book could serve as a pristine feast for the eyes while you could prepare a gastronomic feast, using the recipe book.

Without question, four decades later the photographs are the main attraction of the work, speaking to a time and reality long gone. Most of the book describes the regional cuisines found in the then-USSR. Today, of course, most of the cultural regions presented are independent nations: Uzbekistan, Ukraine, Georgia, Estonia, Lithuania, and Latvia. Presciently, however, the book's title, *Russian Cooking*, approaches the question of Russian cuisine from the point of view of a cultural area rather than the more transient geopolitical realities. History justifies that approach, since Uzbek pilaf, Georgian *shashlyk*, Ukrainian borsch, and Estonian herring salad are as much a part of Russian cookery and identity as *schi* (Russian cabbage soup) or *priannik* (Russian gingerbread cookies).

George Papashvily, born in Georgia (that is what recalls the Beatles' lyrics: "…and Georgia's always on my mi-mi-mi-mi-mi-mi-mi-mi-mind"), was a 1920s émigré from Russia who operated a Russian restaurant in California for a while and later became a recognized sculptor and writer. His life story is akin to a magic tale: born in 1898 in a small village, he was trained as a sword maker and decorative leather worker, served as a sniper in the Russian army during WWI, emigrated to the U.S. in 1923, established a restaurant, married an American (Helen Waite-Pakashvily), moved to New York, bought a farm in Bucks County, Pennsylvania, and in the 1940s began publishing writing done with his wife.

Russian Cooking came toward the end of their collaborative effort and involved a grand tour of the Soviet Union in the 1960s to gather materials for the book—a voyage of rediscovery for George and of discovery for Helen. The book includes two borsch recipes, one for the so-called Moscow borsch, the other a version of Ukrainian borsch.

The recipe for ***Borshch ukrainsky (Ukrainian Style Beet Soup)***, while delicious, is unusual, since Ukrainian (non-Jewish) meat-based borsch recipes call for pork to be part of the meat broth and, most important, call for a ground mixture of bacon/fatback and garlic to be added as the final seasoning. I don't know why the pork and bacon are left out of this recipe. Most likely this was a marketing decision on the part of Time-Life, to have a Ukrainian borsch recipe that would be acceptable to American Jewish readers of Russian descent. This small adjustment of ingredients to a traditional recipe is a perfect example of *glocalization* (adjustment of a phenomenon to local conditions), decades before the term was coined.

In the mid-1970s, *Russian Cooking* was popular among graduate students in Slavics and Russian Studies at Indiana University, Bloomington. Quite a number of us owned a copy and, over time, we all developed a reputation for executing a particular dish well. At the time, because I still disliked borsch and had not yet become an aficionado, my specialty became spring-chicken *tabaka* (a Georgian dish), which made me part of the process of expanding understanding of Russian cooking to include dishes of other cultural groups.

The points made above are to introduce consideration of borsch as it is reflected in cultures other than those that are part of the European "Borsch Belt." The first known re-creation of borsch in Western Europe was by Marie-Antoine Carême, and while it is currently fashionable to deride his most extreme borsch recipe, in many ways that recipe is not very different from a number of other recipes of that time. Carême did what Charles Garnier did in his design of the *Maison Russe* (Russian House) for the Paris Exhibition of 1889, which combined as many stereotypical details of Russian architecture into one building as was possible, creating, in essence, a cartoon or fantasy made up of "Russian" elements. Both Carême and Garnier focused on the exotic features of Russian cultural expression ("exotic" in French terms) but maintained acceptability among their

French compatriots by adhering to French cultural norms.

The Carême borsch tradition was passed on to his disciples and became most closely associated with Auguste Escoffier who, in turn, passed it on to a host of French-trained international chefs who specialized in cooking for the wealthy. With Escoffier and his followers the most extreme aspects of Carême's interpretation were muted, but the dish still symbolized something a bit unusual and foreign. Escoffier particularly loved borsch for its red color and it is this characteristic that often interested him in including the dish in his table settings. Offering of a number of recipes in his *Ma Cuisine* of 1934 virtually guaranteed that the soup would be viewed as a normal part of French haute cuisine. The **Potage Bortsch** (Borscht Soup) recipe published in *The Escoffier Cookbook and Guide to the Fine Art of Cookery* (1989) is typical for his borsch recipes. As can be seen from the publication of cookbooks by Mary Henderson, who borrowed his recipe for her *Potage borshch Polanais*, and Louis P. De Gouy, that acceptance of borsch as a standard Western dish was indeed established, both in Continental diplomatic and American haute cuisine, respectively.

Of course, while haute cuisine is an important indicator of a food's acceptance in a culture that sort of cooking affects only the elite. To become truly integrated within a society the dish also needs to enter the repertoire of the average home cook. We have the evidence that in Britain borsch has entered the naval sphere, which is an indicator of wider acceptance. Recent demographic realities, such as the ever-increasing numbers of Russian and particularly Polish expatriates in England and Ireland, are ensuring that the borsch tradition will continue to be an important part of the respective restaurant cultures.

The Joy of Cooking: a Compilation of Reliable Recipes with a Casual Culinary Chat is the full original title of Irma von Starkloff Rombauer's cookbook that became known as *The Joy of Cooking*. The book arose out of Rombauer's need to support herself and her children after her husband committed suicide. She responded to that challenge by collecting recipes from her friends and self-publishing *Joy of Cooking* (1931). The book was subsequently published by Bobs-

Merrill from 1936 until 1997, and since then by Simon and Shuster.

The story is one of phenomenal success. While initially the book sold slowly, by the 1940s it was a best seller, with over 16 million copies sold to date. An important element in Rombauer's success was that, unlike standard cookbooks that, at least since 1896 and Fannie Farmer's *The Boston Cooking-School Cookbook,* presented recipes in the format of title, list of ingredients, cooking sequence, Rombauer's book presented the recipes as a chatty narrative with ingredients embedded in the text, in boldface type to make them more visible. It is this warm and casual tone that must have helped young cooks overcome their fear of trying new dishes and helped ensure the book's success.

Joy of Cooking, at least from the 1964 edition on, has had three borsch recipes. Two of them are for a "blender" borsch such as **Blender Borsch II**, and in the 75th anniversary edition a third recipe was added, made from canned ingredients. While Rombauer's original way of presenting recipes was changed over the years to the more common manner, much of the chatty nature of her writing has been retained within the cooking instructions or as asides. One that immediately comes to mind is, "I like your *soup du jour,* but I can't understand why it's different every day."

A review of cookbooks at our local library shows that major cookbooks aimed at the general reader range from McCall's, Craig Claiborne's *The New York Times Cookbook,* to Mark Bittman's *How to Cook Everything,* all of which contain at least one borsch recipe. My own cooking teacher, the 1966 edition of *The Women's Day Encyclopedia of Cookery,* which was an A&P supermarket give-away, had a whole number of borsch recipes listed in a variety of categories. I was surprised to note, however, none of the Martha Stewart cookbooks that I reviewed had a borsch recipe. This was a surprise since Martha Stewart is an ethnic Pole from Nutley, New Jersey.

A recipe for a dish intended for an average cook is an obvious indicator that the dish is becoming part of that culture. The large number of cookbooks offering recipes for borsch shows that this phenomenon is not a fluke or simply a trendy item at a particular time. The inclusion of **Russian Cabbage Borscht** as one of two borsch recipes in a book such as Molly Katzen's *The Moosewood Cookbook*, initially published in 1977 for the rising vegetarian community, is further proof of widespread acceptance. Even more proof is provided by the inclusion of borsch in the charity cookbooks of expatriate communities.

My wife and I have led peripatetic lives, and since both of us are interested in other cultures and food, we have accumulated and share a number of cookbooks from our varied sojourns. Some of these books include borsch recipes.

The oldest of these (1957) is from Geneva, Switzerland, and was published by, and for the benefit of, the United Nations Nursery School. *Could I Have Your Recipe? An International Cookbook* is a fascinating book and historical artifact. The preface, written by some anonymous "husband," is painful to read some 50 years later; in the space of a few paragraphs one finds such antiquated notions as "little woman," referencing wives, or turns of phrase such as "their women," again referencing spouses. Also it is interesting that in a book of some 270 pages, published as part of a United Nations school in Geneva, there is not a single recipe from one of the permanent Security Council members: Russia (then the USSR).

The single borsch recipe (**Barszcz**) is from Poland, and the beet soup **Cholodnik** (also known as *Svekolnik* in Russian) is not attributed to a Slavic nation but to France. The book is a rarity in community cookbooks in being bilingual; sections are in French, making it truly international. *Could I Have Your Recipe? An International Cookbook* is obviously and intentionally designed to welcome expatriates in Geneva to the community of expats involved in the UN school. Since nearly everyone associated with the group represented a distinct nationality, this indeed is an international cookbook.

Similar in some ways, but also totally different, is the *Cook Book-Libro de Cocina* published by the American Women's Literary Club of Lima, Peru. Unlike the Geneva book, which reflects an international community, the *Cook Book-Libro de Cocina* is an American effort supporting women in Lima's American expatriate community. It is a rare example among community cookbooks in that it is completely bilingual, with recipes in the primary language of the group (English) and that of the host country (Spanish). The **Borsch** recipe in this book is found in Chapter 15, "World-Wide Cooking." There is no way to determine the exact nature of the relationship between the Lima cookbook and Molokhovets, but the similarity in the recipe for borsch is striking, and probably not accidental.

An example of a local cookbook that expresses a sophisticated and wide-ranging interest in differing cultures is that produced by the women's guild of the Indianapolis Museum of Art, *Indianapolis Collects & Cooks*. This book has a "different" borsch recipe. The Indianapolis Art League's **Borscht with Sour Cream** is clearly based on the second blender recipe in the 1964 edition of *Joy of Cooking*, but includes some twists that help demonstrate how a dish adapts to local conditions/needs. I always smile when reading the recipe because it is the only one I have encountered that makes an alcoholic drink out of a traditional soup.

Indianapolis produced another interesting community cookbook. This is *101 Recipes of Old Russia*, published in 1982 by the Christ the Saviour [sic] Orthodox Church. This modest tome of 60 typewritten pages was the effort of Father Stephen Wallstead and his spouse. What makes this book unusual is that Father Stephen was an American convert to Eastern Orthodoxy from Roman Catholicism, and virtually all the members of the parish were also American converts. They, however, embraced Russian culture in addition to the Orthodox faith The cookbook was one instance of that; their participation in the annual International Festival and presentation of the Russian culture booth at that Festival was another. The recipe for **Borscht** in this cookbook is very modern, with the almost exclusive use of canned vegetables.

Few Americans know the historic connection between Russia and Hawaii, which began as early as the 1790s. The first Christian Easter liturgy was celebrated by Russians in Hawaii around that time. In 1815 the first Orthodox church was built by Russians on the island of Kauai; three forts were also built there at that time. Fort Elisabeth, the largest of the three, is a state landmark today.

For a while the Russians thought of colonizing Hawaii,

envisioning it as a reliable resupply point for the Russian-American Company and settlements in Alaska (particularly Sitka) and California (Fort Ross), but these efforts at colonization were unsuccessful because they were opposed by the British and the Americans, who had greater influence with King Kamehameha I. A Russian blockhouse, however, was built in Honolulu in 1816 on land given to the Russian-American Company.

Despite abandoning their colonizing ideas after the Russian Imperial Decree (*Ukaz*) of 1821 was countered by the Monroe Doctrine, the Russians continued to maintain contact with the Hawaiian rulers. As late as 1882 the Hawaiians sent diplomats to Russia, and in 1884 a Russian embassy was established in Honolulu. Only in 1900 was the Russian ambassador recalled and embassy closed. It is therefore not surprising, although it is unexpected, that a cookbook published by the Daughters of Hawaii would include a **Borsch** recipe.

The presence of borsch recipes in American community cookbooks that are not associated with any specific ethnicity seems like a solid indicator that the soup has become part of the overall culture. We can also observe that borsch in America, both in the general population and in ethnic enclaves, has undergone changes that ethnic recipes undergo as they become Americanized. A list of these changes is given in Mark H. Zanger's *The American Ethnic Cookbook for Students* (2001):

1. *What Chef Louis Szamarathy [Szathmáry] has called the "passion for ease of preparation"—reduction of cooking time and complexity of preparation*
2. *Pre-portioning into portable and hand-size forms like sandwiches, pasties, or cookies*
3. *Combining ingredients into one-pot dinners.*
4. *Use of labor-saving machines*
5. *Substitution of baking powder for yeast, and increased sugar in baked goods*
6. *Increased amount of meat, especially beef, and substitution of beef for other meats*
7. *Substitution of American foodstuffs, specifically corn, chili peppers, beans, and squash*
8. *Increased use of tomatoes and substitution of canned tomatoes for other acidic ingredients such as vinegar, lemons, or yogurt in sauces, soups, and stews*
9. *Increased use of potatoes and substitution of potatoes for other carbohydrate foods*
10. *Substitution of canned or otherwise packaged foods for whole-food ingredients.*

I was happy to discover this concise list for two main reasons:

one, it conforms closely to my own experience and observations, and helps to briefly explain the process of an ethnic food adapting to American reality; two, it was great to find a reference to Chef Louis Szathmáry, a Hungarian chef from Chicago, whom I met while doing work with Hungarians in New Jersey.

Chef Louis, as everyone called him, emigrated from Hungary to the U.S. in 1951. Arriving in this country with a suitcase full of books, a dollar and change in his pocket, and one suit, he became over time a very successful restaurateur, writer (of cookbooks and poetry), and collector. Donations of books to different universities and organizations number well over 300,000 items. My wife and I had the good fortune to be his guests at his The Bakery restaurant in Chicago and enjoyed a dish I still remember more than 30 years later—Duck in Sour Cherry Sauce. He also gave me an autographed copy of *The Bakery Restaurant Cookbook* (1981), which taught me how to make a delicious leg of lamb. More importantly, Chef Louis's willingness to share his recipes and tricks of the trade and his directly expressed belief that good cooking lies not in "magic" recipes but in talent and years of practice, helped form my own approach toward cooking and life.

Chef Louis's point about "passion for ease of preparation" was illustrated one time when I was videotaping a Chilean woman making empanadas. As she was showing her technique for rolling out the dough, her daughter returned from school and, seeing her mother at work, opened a cabinet, took out a pasta-making machine, and said, "Mommy, why aren't you using this? You always do." I found the incident quite humorous, but my hostess was visibly embarrassed and asked that I stop taping. It would be unrealistic to expect recipes and techniques not to change under new and differing conditions. The borsch that I ate in Ho Chi Minh City was very much a borsch in taste and in the ingredients used, but the cut of the vegetables and meat was very Vietnamese. So, cultural accommodations are necessary and inevitable and do not make a dish "inauthentic."

One caution I would suggest in considering Zanger's list is that some of the characteristics apply not only to the process of Americanization of borsch but sometimes occur in the country of origin as social and economic conditions change. The change from kvas to tomatoes as the main supplier of acidity in borsch, for example, is observed in recipes from the 19th century on in Russia, Ukraine, and other countries of the "Borsch Belt." The same is true in the substitution of potatoes for turnips as one of the main vegetables. That being said, the characteristics listed are very important in understanding the process of the evolution of an ethnic dish as it enters the dominant culture. In Chapter 12 I share my observation of a changing borsch tradition as practiced by the excellent Kalmyk cook, Matza Andreyev.

11. BORSCH IN THE AGE OF THE INTERNET

"krysia ♀   Mar 1, 10, 19:24   Reply / Quote #45
The person who posted this almost 2 years ago died from eating moldy,
fermented oatmeal soup. Good luck to you."

No author or publisher likes receiving potentially significant information at the last minute. Such "gifts" can upset the architecture of the book and wreak havoc on production schedules. But, fortunately, we live in the age of computers and the Internet. As this book was going through its final edit and rewrite, my brother Al sent me a copy of a handwritten borsch recipe from Allen Ginsberg that initially appeared as a sales item on eBay. **Alan Ginsberg's Cold Summer Borscht** bears no date, but since it went on sale with a number of other papers dated 1972, we can assume that the recipe was written down somewhere around that time.

This wonderful but potentially disruptive bit of added information serves to underline the theme of this chapter: the power of computers and the Internet to affect expressive culture. If we were to look at the probabilities involved in finding the recipe and having it land in my computer shortly before the book went into print, they would be astronomical.

I heard Allen Ginsberg read his poetry at Harvard my freshman year, saw him later eating a Waldorf Salad at the Waldorf Cafeteria in Harvard Square, memorized the first couple of pages of "Howl" when recuperating from surgery while in the Army, and puzzled over his translation from the Japanese (a language he did not know) of the Heart Sutra. My brother found the recipe on a British website dedicated to the work of Allen Ginsberg. Individuals associated with this website found the original eBay offering, authenticated the recipe, and posted it as part of their website archives. Al found it there and sent me the URL. I investigated the sequence of events and chain of custody for the manuscript and decided to include it in this book. In all, a few days' work—and the book has become richer and more intriguing.

Al Gore (not my brother), whom I knew casually in our student days and whom I once beat in a 9-ball pool game (a surprise to both of us since he was a vastly superior player), in his most recent and very important book, *The Future: Six Drivers of Global Change*, developed the catchphrase, "Global Mind." By that he means the almost seamless connection between people, ideas, machines, and information that helps create a reality which is greater than the sum of its parts.

The "Global Mind" is a product of the personal computer and the Internet. I consider myself fortunate in the opportunities I had in observing the development and growth of the personal computer and the Internet from the beginning, and the continuing evolution of the "Global Mind"—first at Harvard, with the hijinks on the top floor of Dunster House where some managed to penetrate the NORAD telephone system, then in Mt. Kisco, New York, with an IBMer who nightly used the precursor of Arpanet to communicate with colleagues at Stanford, helping my friend Tom build his MITS Altair 8800 kit, afterwards going to the IU Computer Labs to play the then newly developed Star Trek game on the University's mainframe, and dreaming of a day when computer games would have images associated with actions. In the early 1980s I purchased a Commodore 64 at Toys R Us, writing reports and even our wedding invitation on it. The potential of personal computing seemed apparent, exciting, and limitless.

But even I, who so enthusiastically embraced the reality and potential of personal computing, have come to a point where the pace of actual change outstrips the ability to predict the next developments, except at the most abstract level. To illustrate how far we've come, I cite my personal experience with two books. The first, *Folklore on Two Continents,* published in 1980, was a project at the Folklore Institute at IU, and a pioneer in team editing and "setting type" by means of an electronic Olivetti typewriter. More recently, in the summer of 2012, I published *A Kalmyk Sampler,* an international project that was initiated, planned, and executed using only computers and the Internet, and one in which the key collaborators never met face-to-face but knew each other only through the Internet.

Folklore on Two Continents was innovative for its time, and there is little question that without the use of the electronic typewriter it would not have been possible for a group of students to prepare the manuscript text as camera-ready copy in the time allotted. But outside of this important but narrow technological scope other factors were more critical to the success of the project. The book was addressed to and drew upon the support of a community of established and beginning scholars, and developed within a supportive institutional context; it depended on a large number of volunteers, and took nine times longer to develop than *A Kalmyk Sampler.* The *Kalmyk Sampler,* on the other hand, was created completely outside institutional settings and went from conception to publication in two months.

The World of Russian Borsch is also a creature of the computer and Internet age. There can be little doubt that were it not for that, the project would have been radically different. The book was written, edited, typeset, and published on a computer, and printed on a computer-controlled press. The Internet provided many necessary sources for research, and although I had amassed, over the years, a substantial library of print books dealing with cookery and containing a wide variety of borsch recipes, many of the more obscure or serendipitously important bits of information would not have come to this work without the existence of the "cloud" knowledge base.

But, again, these are important but technical issues. The most important cultural features that have occurred as part of the computer revolution in the 30 years since publication of *Folklore on Two Continents* are the significant changes in social relationships and interactions. By almost instantaneously creating associations and communities, new modes of social interaction have become part of global cultures. In terms of this book, a rich combination of websites, blogs, discussion groups, various commentaries and posts kept a mixture of ideas, aspirations, and concerns alive and accessible.

Thanks to some Russian websites I became aware of the fundamentally important *The Book of Tasty and Healthy Food*, and it is on the Internet that I was able to find the texts of some 18th, 19th, and 20th century cookbooks. The Internet provided electronic versions of books that enabled me to compare recipes from different editions. Fortunately, the Russian Internet world is not as fiercely Balkanized as the American one, into profit-making satrapies making serious research expensive and difficult. For example, one American site with a 5-page paper of interest demanded 40 dollars for access to it. There has been a boycott of Elsevier for what many scholars consider predatory pricing.

As a consequence of the more liberal and informal attitudes in Russia I was able to view and sometimes download significant old cookbooks and many articles. That is how I acquired a recipe for **Siberian Borsch** and the wonderful recipe for **Cossack Borsch**. Were it not for the Internet, I would never have discovered how my reprint of *Culinary*, while shorter overall in page count than the original, could claim to be "expanded." The Internet yielded the Dukhobor and Molokan borsch recipes found here, and it is the Internet that gave variant recipes for Mennonite borsch and helped me to understand the sheer volume of community cookbooks in the Russo-German and Jewish communities.

More importantly, in terms of the experience of people living as ethnics in the diaspora, discussion groups on the Internet provide a way to share experiences and to help self-define any particular participant in that discussion, and in that way assist in the process of ethnic identification. If the telephone replaced the village well as the means of sharing informal community information, then the Internet is replacing the strictly person-to-person landline phone. One can have private conversations and also participate in a "party line" through chat rooms, listserves, and websites. That ability to create a discussion group that becomes a kind of new community is illustrated by an edited number of group "conversations," recorded in 2008, that center on proper preparation of Polish *biały barszcz*:

> *"tatianalee623   Dec 20, 09, 18:39   Reply / Quote #38*
> *This is definitely a Christmas Eve dish, as up until Alzheimer's has afflicted my grandmother, we had it every year. Her recipe is much simpler, but slightly confusing as she wrote it for herself!!*
> *1 small container old fashion oatmeal*
> *1 small fresh yeast*
> *2 quarts of lukewarm water*
> *Dissolve yeast in 1/2 cup of lukewarm water. Mix oats with 2 quarts of water add yeast. Put in small bowl and place in warm place until it smells sour (2-3 days). Strain mixture, cook in double boiler until thick. Add more water if necessary. Add salt, white pepper and caraway seed if you like the flavor. We are making the recipe now, but did not have luck with the yeast we used!!*
> *PS- when this dish was eaten on Christmas Eve (in our Ukrainian-Russian Orthodox house) it was used as the base of the meal. First the soup was poured in the dish and then all the other non-dairy, non-meat items were placed in it. These items were served family style and guests chose from pierogi (potato or sauerkraut (or cabbage) and mushroom), sauteed mushrooms, peas, bulbulkie (spelling is probably wrong, but it was a buttered finger shaped noodle), butter beans, and potatoes. Side dish's included prunes with oranges and a Russian Christmas Bread. The bread was served first with the oldest male handing the portion- then salt and a clove of garlic was wrapped in the bread and eaten for good luck.*
>
> *Rakky ♂   Dec 20, 09, 23:42   Reply / Quote #39*
> *tatianalee623: our Ukrainian-Russian Orthodox house*
> *Are you sure you're Ukrainian? Is it possible that you are descended from Carpatho-Rusyns who identify themselves as "Ukrainian" because it's simpler than explaining what Rusyns are? I thought I was Ukrainian until I discovered the truth 6 years ago.*
> *Thanks for the recipe and the sharing of your memories around this soup. Sorry about your baba.*
>
> *SherryD   Dec 29, 09, 17:34   Reply / Quote #40*
> *I just happened to see all the posts on this soup. Our family is Polish and I have been eating our Christmas Eve Mushroom Soup for 50 years. Very simply, we break up a loaf of rye bread with caraway seeds, sprinkle about a cup or two of oatmeal (not instant), a tablespoon or two of salt in a non-reactive bowl, cover with water. Lay a piece of cheesecloth, or a dish towel over. Once water is absorbed, add a bit more to keep moist. Every few days, scrape off any bits of mold, and stir.*

Once the fermenting is done (about 10 days?) strain everything through a cheesecloth. We get good dried, Polish mushrooms and soak, soak, soak and rinse, rinse, rinse (lots of sand). Always keep the liquid and add to the soup. Once mushrooms are thoroughly cleaned, add as well. Then season to taste with salt, pepper, and ALWAYS served over diced, boiled potatoes.

Rakky ♂   Dec 30, 09, 16:32   Reply / Quote   #41
SherryD: Every few days, scrape off any bits of mold. That's just so great... I love these recipes. Thanks for contributing to this thread. Szczeslyoho nowoho roku!

cemeterywoman ♀   Jan 8, 10, 04:39   Reply / Quote   #42
Hi!
I am senor citizen, 2nd generation Russian, not Polish. was doing a search for Keselitza and ended up here. My mother used to make this, but we thought of it as a cereal not a soup. It is delicious!! I am copying this from my mother's hand written recipe card....she died at almost 90 in 1999almost 90.
Keselitza
2C old fashioned oatmeal
3 heaping T flour
1 pkg dry yeast
4C lukewarm water (whatever temp the yeast specifies)
4 slices rye bread
Put all ingredients together and let stand overnight in bowl with clean dishtowel over it. Next day put through a strainer or Foley mill. Add 2C warm water and boil VERY slowly over low heat 15 minutes, stirring continuously. It sticks very easily. Add 1 t salt and 1 clove crushed garlic. Remove from heat. Add 3 bays leaves. Reheat when ready to serve.
My notes make sure the bowl you use is ceramic or glass, NOT metal. I usually leave out the salt but then I am a low salt freak. And I love garlic so sometimes I add extra, justifying this since garlic cloves vary so widely in size.
Please let me know how this turns out and if you and your father like it. Also feel free to write if you have any questions.
andrea
cemeterywoman@gmail.com

Polonius3 ♂   Jan 8, 10, 06:05   Reply / Quote   #43
KISIELICA AND KISIAŁKA are eastern versions of ŻUR

susanneiles   Mar 1, 10, 19:03   Reply / Quote   #44
It's called flummery or 'kaerakile' or 'kaerakiisla', and I'm making some right now. Don't let the naysayers get you down. I found a wonderful step by step recipe for you at this girl's blog. The link is entitled "The Story of a Fermented Oat

*Flummery." Here is the link: nami-nami.blogspot.com/2008/05/story-of-fermented-oat-flummery.html
[link is good ed].
You can also find the traditional recipe if you google, "Llymru" because it is also a traditional Welsh dish.
Best to you!
Susanne*

krysia ♀   *Mar 1, 10, 19:24   Reply / Quote #45*
*The person who posted this almost 2 years ago died from eating moldy, fermented oatmeal soup.
Good luck to you.*

polishlady   Apr 5, 10, 21:39   Reply / Quote #46
*Fermented Oatmeal Soup is called Borscht. My grandmother was Polish and we had it all the time when I was a child. Fortunately for me, I have her recipe and make it on Holidays.
You take equal amounts of water and Oatmeal (Quaker Old Fashion) and put it in a bean pot. Put the heal of rye bread (stale) on top. Cover with cheese cloth. Let it stand for about 3 days. You'll notice the bread is starting to get mold on it. Remove the bread when it does. Add a little water if it gets a little dry. Let it stand for about 5 days.
It will start to smell pretty ripe. After the five days is up strain through either cheese cloth or strainer. This is your base for your soup. Next cook a kielbasa. Save the water. Take the kielbasa water and bring it to a boil. Start adding your base and keep stirring. It will thicken. Add more water if it's too thick. The kielbasa water gives it flavor.
Thats all there is to it. It's a simple recipe. Pour into a bowl and add some hard boiled eggs, pieces of rye bread and chunks of Kielbasa. You can also add mushrooms and beets. It's a hardy meal and sticks with you. Enjoy!*

polishlady   Apr 5, 10, 21:41   Reply / Quote #47
You should try it. Did you know that when you eat oatmeal it ferments inside you anyway. The fermentation process is a natural process. Your not eating mold. You boil it before you eat it anyway.

jonni ♂   *Edited by: jonni Apr 5, 10, 21:41   Reply / Quote #48*
polishlady: Fermented Oatmeal Soup is called Borscht. Barszcz. It's usually a beetroot soup, but there is a white barszcz (and a rarer green one). The recipe you gave (a good one) is for Żurek.

Madge   Apr 9, 10, 23:19 Reply / Quote #49

Hi ... I just finished eating the last of it for lunch! I'm Polish, naturally, and it's our traditional after Lent/Easter meal. Borscht. We always had it after church. You have to allow at least one week before you want it, depending on your climate. If in a humid climate, it could turn moldy, so check daily.

I put about 2 cups of regular (not instant) oatmeal, with water to cover, in a sort of crockery/china type bowl. Cover with a towel and let set in a corner of the kitchen counter.

I check it every couple of days to see if it needs a bit more water. It usually takes about 7 days to ferment. My Mom used to put a piece of rye bread on top .. as the yeast helps the process.

When ready, spray a pot with Pam, etc. and add about 2-3 cups of water to the pot. Put the pot on medium low heat. Next, take some of the mushy mixture and glop about a cup's full into a medium sized strainer with a handle.

Take a wooden spoon and start grinding and straining the fermented oats into the pot. You'll see the whitish thicker mixture dropping from the strainer into the pot of water.   As you push it through, pour some water into the mixture in the strainer to continue getting all the essence possible out.

As your oatmeal gets used and dried out and expended, plop that mixture into a plastic bag or old newspaper to toss away when you're all finished, and pour in another batch of the oatmeal and continue massaging it into the strainer.. getting the essence into the pot. Once you've got all the strained oatmeal in the pot you want, KEEP STIRRING THE POT, preferably with a wooden spoon. You'll see it thickening more and more, and will add more water so that your final result is a smooth substance, like thickened cream or a creamy soup.

Use just as much of the fermented oatmeal to make what you want to consume at that meal, as you can refrigerate the rest for another meal. It should have a tinge of fermented sourness, but if the fermenting process hasn't done enough, just add teaspoon or so of white vinegar to taste, depending on how big a pot you've made. On the side, I have my bowl filled with cooked kielbasa slices, a couple of cut up hard boiled eggs, cut up cooked ham and either bits of fried salt pork or you can cheat like I do with the real bacon bits from the store.

The feast is complete when you pour the hot borscht over the bowl of goodies described above, and add a healthy dollop of beet horseradish and stir in.

Your initial starter of a couple of cups of oatmeal will make A LOT of borscht, with the additional water you will have to add. It's definitely an acquired taste; but for me ...YUMM! That's when it all comes together and you get the point. You wouldn't want to consume the creamy mixture alone. The leftover fermented oatmeal keeps in the fridge in a container for quite awhile, which is why I was able to enjoy this last treat for Easter today. Hope this helps.

Iamlemko ♀   *Jul 27, 10, 16:40*   *Reply / Quote #50*
Hi Rakky,
I am Lemko myself (my fathers family was born in the region around Krynica South Poland before they were deported to Legnica in 1947) and I just came back from Ruthenia (we visited the Lemko Watra in Zdynia) and ate the original Lemko-Kyselica (thats the right spelling).
I still have family in South of Poland, where the Lemkos lived until 1947. As I am also researching for years about my roots (I live in Germany now) I would love to contact true Lemkos because of course there is still much to learn. My grand-aunt is still alive and knows a lot of original Lemko recipes. So do not hesitate to contact me for more questions.
By the way: "Rusyn" is the name the Polish people and the Austrians gave us. We ourself call us Lemko (pronounce: "Uemko")!!!!!!

Ewapgo   *Oct 23, 10, 21:13*   *Reply / Quote #51*
My grandparents were Lemko-Ukrainians from Galicia; keseitsa was always served as the first course of Christmas Eve dinner. As far as I remember, it was not served at any other time; this may be due to the fact that it was a staple for the poor in the "old country." The recipe below is from "Favorite Recipes" a cookbook compiled by the Ladies Aid of the Three Saints Church in Ansonia, Connecticut.
1/2 box old-fashion Quaker Oats (or any oat of that sort)
1+1/2 cakes of yeast (or equivalent of dry yeast)
1 quart lukewarm water
2 Tbsp. flour
salt (to taste)
garlic (to taste - my family used a good deal, tasting and adding very thin slices as the soup cooked)
1 tsp. caraway seeds (optional) - my family did not add caraway
Place oats in a large bowl - Add flour - Crumble in yeast - Add water - Stir well - Cover and place in a warm spot to ferment for 24 hours - Add, gradually, 3 quarts lukewarm water to bowl - Stir well - Strain though sieve into a large pot - Discard oats - Cook slowly, stirring frequently - Add sliced garlic as soup cooks - If too thin, add flour - If too thick, add water- Soup is done when it coats a spoon - Serve with boiled potatoes.
This soup is not difficult to make but it can be ruined by cooking at too high a heat because it will burn. This is pure starch and will stick to the bottom and burn if not stirred frequently.

partlyPolish   *Nov 30, 10, 04:37*   *Reply / Quote #52*
I've been looking for my Babcia's recipe for what she called barszcz but can't find it; should have paid more attention when she made it! I know she fermented

oatmeal with a slice of rye bread for a few days, then strained it and cooked till thick, maybe stirring in some browned salt pork -- we ate it for Easter dinner with hard-cooked eggs and kielbasa sliced into it.

Ashleys mind ♀   Nov 30, 10, 08:48   Reply / Quote #53
Wow! 2 pages dedicated to oatmeal soup. Quaint

Clearly, the transcription of the messages shows that an active community discussion about making white borsch stretched over months, with the topic being revisited at times when the dish becomes important in celebrating major holidays. I've recorded similar conversations in Russian and in those cases, just as in this one, the circle of discussants (and lurkers) was global. Interesting that for those who have observed these sorts of interactions in personal settings, the online discussion is similar, both in content and the ongoing nature of the communicative interaction. For a folklorist, ethnographer, anthropologist, or sociologist these types of discussions are redefining the concepts of fieldwork.

To round out this chapter on the relationship of the Internet to borsch I was planning to share one short online piece out of a number of fascinating ones I have collected over the years. In my collection are magazine and newspaper articles, odes to borsch, borsch joke collections, a description of cooking and borsch in the Russian submarine forces, an article entitled "100 Recipes for Hangover" that includes a humorous account of finding Chinese borsch in Harbin, China, a wonderful memoir piece by William Pokhlebkin recounting his experiences with an Army mess sergeant who was instrumental in inspiring him to study cookery, a beautiful article about the hogweed (*borschevik*) plant, and a host of others. Before I could decide on my final choice, however, life took one of its twists.

For the past sixteen years I have been friends with Sheldon "Shelley" Blitstein. We grew close after our misadventures in Yonkers, New York, and our relationship deepened after we discovered that we were both Buddhists. In a way, we formed a two-man sangha. The last three years of Shelley's life were marred by an illness that proved fatal. During that time we shared a weekly lunch, and when Shelley became too ill to travel I would bring lunch from his favorite restaurant. Less than two weeks before he died I went over for our appointed lunch and brought Chapter Six of this book to read to him (by this point he didn't have enough energy to be able to read on his own) and to solicit his views on the chapter. Shelley had been an early reader of the book and kept up his interest in its progress. His comments were clear and cogent and disturbing, essentially challenging me to rewrite the chapter. I responded to the challenge with a rewrite, and a few days after that he was dead.

After the funeral I was thinking about how I could mark Shelley's passing and his involvement with this work, and then I remembered that in my collection I had a wonderful piece about memorial borsch preparation. The piece was too lengthy as written, but with judicious condensing it could retain its flavor and serve as a memorial to a friend. I also wanted to include a recipe of Bessarabian borsch since Shelley's father emigrated from there. I went on the Internet to look for a likely candidate.

This is how **Green Borscht Mama Regine's Way: Bessarabian Stew with Lamb Ribs** became part of this book. The author of the recipe is a German lady who worked for many years in Berlin and other cities, spent some time working at a refugee camp for Cambodians in Thailand, and then retired to Thailand. The recipe was Doris' favorite dish that she asked her mother to make every time she came for a visit. The serendipity in this chain of events is improbable if we consider that Shelley's grandson is of Thai heritage.

"Memorial Borsch"
Original title "The High Poetry of Borsch" by Lady Di -Translated and condensed by N. Burlakoff

A formula for borsch is impossible. Borsch that is prepared on a Sunday for Monday—that is, an everyday borsch, smells and sounds completely different from a Christmas borsch. And, a Christmas borsch does not resemble the borsch cooked for the church—obviously; each village has a different church.

The causes for the continual difference in taste of this dish are unclear. They have not been determined to this day, in part because the investigators usually lean back sluggishly, burp quietly, think a bit, and silently reach out with their soup dish for seconds. After that, there is sex and sleep. Sex after a couple of bowls of borsch is particularly good. Sleep with a borsch aftertaste in the mouth is also sweet. It is because of this that investigators cannot finish researching the delights of the flavor varieties of borsch—the flavors are infinite. In the course of my life I have cooked borsch more than one thousand times, each one tasting different

But there is a special borsch: the memorial borsch. When I find myself being invited for a memorial dinner, I become immediately afraid. I know that there will be a memorial borsch which must be eaten to the last spoonful. Afterwards, I will feel ill and I will not be able to move away from the table on my own, and my kind neighbor, who with difficulty pressing-in his belly will move me away from it, so that I will be able to crawl away, and dragging my belly move on to dessert.

I took part in one such memorial borsch preparation. My auntie, Stanislava, died suddenly. A heart attack—and she was no more. Aunt Stacy was the kindest auntie; she was the sister of our great grandmother. She was the kindest, I repeat that, and will continue repeating that. She was 200 pounds of kindness of the highest manifestation.

She died, and the relatives who came together for the funeral dissipated. All of the elders sat in the yard under the apple tree and began to cry, and cry. The nephews also cried but ran around, digging the grave, finding a car for the casket, bringing the casket over. The nieces? I turned out to be the only niece present. The other nieces had not arrived yet at the old apple tree in the yard.

Mother nodded to me and I began working. I knew precisely that during funeral services everyone must be fed. I brought out the 16 gallon pot which is used by the clan at such occasions, and which was kept by Aunt Stacy, poured water into the pot, placed the pot on the heat and began to peel the potatoes uncomprehendingly.

With dismay I heard the hum of voices under the apple tree—the clan was arriving, and was hungry. I looked with fear at the meat which was lying on the next table. The pork, beef, veal, goose, and two ducks were lying before me in a red-pink-beige mound and were differentiated from the chickens by the fact that the chickens still needed to be caught, killed, and de-feathered.

To catch, kill and de-feather—was not my concern. There were experts for that; my task was to use my finger to point out the candidates, so to say—future participants in the potential borsch.

I needed to choose one kind of meat from a variety of meats. Not an easy task when I know that Mother has diabetes, Nikolai Petrovich suffers from obesity, auntie Asya has hypertension, and aunt Vita has pancreatitis. I understood that with my choice I will definitely doom someone.

I made a Solomon's choice and pointed my finger at two chickens. When the experts caught, slayed and finished de-feathering the candidates, my older sister Olya entered the hot kitchen. Olya flowed into the hot kitchen where I stood mechanically removing the peel from the potatoes and looking blankly at the meat.

Olya flowed to the table covered with meat and examined it, critically, the red-pink-beige mound. "And why aren't you cooking the meat yet?" she furrowed her brows sternly.

"I am; the chickens are already in the broth."

"Oh," Olya nodded. "And what kind of chickens do we have here? Oh, yellow. Aunt Stacy did not spare the grain." She nodded contentedly.

My heart felt relieved although I had hardly any connection to Aunt Stacy's chickens.

"And you decided on two chickens for the whole borsch?"

"Yeah" I shyly nodded, "Two will be good. There's 16 gallons of borsch. One would not be enough."

Olya laughed, shook her head, and for some reason said: "God, you're so skinny."

And we started making the borsch!

I looked on in horror, afraid to utter a word of resistance as three pounds of pork tenderloin, six pounds of beef, and three pounds of veal, set forth into the huge pot.

"And give me about forty potatoes. They will cook and make the borsch a bit thicker" I handed them over to her.

"Oh, and that bowl of onions. Let it also cook."

"How about the garnishing?"

"For the garnish you'll peel some more. Right? Only a bit more, this time."

Resigned, I nodded. The tub, similar in its diameter to those we use at home to wash our feet, was upended over the pot and the onion, rinsed with my tears in the process of peeling and slicing, went to its holy purpose of making the borsch more substantial.

While I continued to do the manual labor—peeling and scraping the vegetables, Olya thought a bit, chuckled, and added a duck to the pot. My late aunt did not spare grain for the ducks either, and in their fat content and size they were equal to three chickens. I shuddered. But this was only the beginning.

I didn't understand, or see, how and when, a pot, smaller than the one with borsch, appeared on the table. Boiled potatoes were steaming in the pot. Olya took a few cans of potted meat, opened the cans, and scraped out the contents into the potatoes.

"Great!" I said happily, and grabbed the pot to take it into the yard to feed the hungry clan.

"Where are you going? It'ssss not ready!" hissed Olya at me. She pulled out the duck from the broth and tore it into shreds, threw it into a frying pan, poured half a can of lard into it, and began calmly but quickly mincing onions into the fry pan.

I was beginning to feel ill.

The potatoes, swimming in golden oil, enriched with potted meat and shreds of duck meat, fried to an orange hue and the crispness of skin, was swept up instantaneously by the clan; who hiccupped, and began to cry again. We continued to work

Another duck was conveyed to the pot which was already inhabited by a dozen pounds of meat.

"For flavor," responded Olya to my questioning look.

"Oh. And the chickens?" I asked, and in fear of the anticipated response I pulled my head into my shoulders.

"The chickens are put in last, what's with you?"

I sighed. Under the ribs on my left side I began to feel pain. "I should have brought my pancreatin," I thought out loud.

"I have some. Take two," said Olya as she handed me the pills, looked me over, and repeated: "God, you're so skinny."

A bucket of potatoes and two chickens went into the borsch.

"A rooster would be good … what kind of borsch is it without a rooster?" Olya frowned.

"We can do without. Rich food is unhealthy," said our aunt Asya (300 pounds) appearing in the door of the kitchen—Aunt Asya didn't see well but she always, consistently, went towards the smells.

"Yes, unhealthy," Olya sighed.

I was silent. I rushed around the kitchen, cutting vegetables.

Olya was smoking, sitting by the open door in clouds of steam that escaped from the kitchen to the street with help from the draft …

In the hunger-pang evoking odor and the smoke stream of her unfiltered cigarette, Olya reminded me of a shaman. A woman shaman. The woman shaman was working her magic. I began to relax. Diabetes, pancreatitis … they long ago became immaterial.

Olya was talking, I was listening. She was reminiscing about the departed, Aunt Stacy, who was lying on the other side of the kitchen wall.

"Don't cut the cabbage! I'll do it myself, you don't know how," Olya would say at times, and picking up the knife she would shred the cabbage for the borsch into thin-thin slices—transparent and weightless. "Mix it; mix the borsch, that won't hurt it."

"It's no help when a child is involved in business," she grinned under her breath

There was a fifteen-year difference in our ages.

"Now, the main thing!" The river flowed upstream and Olya arose smoothly. She placed the roaster on the heat. Two pounds of margarine, a quart sized jar of pork lard, a pound of butter, a quart of sunflower oil, and a minced slab of fatback went into to the roaster, cast into it by Olya's accurate, smooth, plump hand.

The substance was crackling in the roaster and began gaining a golden color. Having come to the color of 24-carat gold the substance accepted into itself carrots, onions, beets, parsley root, and a few other kinds of roots; afterwards the tomato was poured in—homemade, with tomato pulp, and thick.

In the meanwhile I was directed to prepare the bell peppers in the quantity of a tub for the washing of feet, and a couple of dozen eggs. Need it be said that all that was consequently minced and thrown into the giant pot?

"A baffling borsch" said Olya, tasting it. "Something is missing. It seems it needs a rooster! What kind of borsch is it without a rooster?" Olya flowed to the refrigerator, carefully examined the contents, pulled out a pound of fatback and seemed satisfied. "Ah! That's what it needs!"

I didn't have time to grunt when the fatback departed into the red, insanely aromatic, boiling contents of the pot.

"Half hour cooking and it's enough." And she commanded me to prepare a bowl of greenery. And to get the small pail of sour cream from the refrigerator, so that everyone who returned from the funeral to Aunt Stacy's house could get a bowl of borsch (besides other dishes) after putting a dollop of sour cream and greenery and attempt to surrender to the god of Borsch, which for a time would dull the pain from the death of the loved one.

"The borsch is delicious! And it is so thick, a spoon stand -up in it!" said the neighbor lady as she fell away from the memorial table at which all those who came sat, in turns, in three shifts. Olya sat at the table.

I, and the younger sisters, who finally arrived, ran around the table serving guests.

"What kind of borsch would it be if the ladle in it did not stand upright? Aunt Stacy, God rest her soul, made delicious borsch," Olya said humbly.

"And she poured it into a bowl always to a mound," Uncle said. And started to cry.

12. COOKING WITH MATZA

"It was hard when we came here. The Korean War was going on. People thought we were Japanese, Chinese, Korean. It was hard."
Matza Andreyev Interview, 2013

The two most dangerous moments in any flight are the takeoff and landing. These are the moments in which pilots feel the greatest stress, and which account for somewhere between 50 and 80 percent of all accidents. For writers, the beginning and ending of a work have the same challenges. The phenomenon of "blank-page paralysis" is well known, and the Internet is replete with tips on how to overcome this difficulty. Less examined, but perhaps even more challenging, is deciding how and when to end a work. The father of modern American academic folklore studies, Richard Dorson, once asked me, "What's the biggest problem in writing a dissertation?" I answered that I did not know. He chuckled and said, "Knowing when to end."

And so it is with every book or any story. With a magic tale there is no issue: the ending coda, decreed by tradition—"And they lived happily ever after"—says it all; the trial is over, normalcy is restored. With a classic meal there also is seldom a problem—dessert marks the ending. In all other situations, however, endings are more problematic. As I was driving on the New Jersey Turnpike to Howell, New Jersey, for my scheduled interview with Matza Andreyev, little did I suspect that this interview was fated to become the final chapter of this book.

I wanted to get a Kalmyk borsch recipe from Matza, whose cooking I had previously enjoyed and admired. Earlier, I was particularly taken by her stuffed cabbage, which was indistinguishable from Mother's. As a nomadic people, Kalmyks (Mongolian people who have lived in Russia since the 17th century) traditionally did not have soups as part of their cooking. Their soup equivalent was Kalmyk tea—a potent brew of green brick tea, salt, mutton fat, milk, and nutmeg. Therefore, this would be an unusual addition to my book—a traditional soup recipe collected from a member of an ethnicity that does not have a soup tradition.

There was also a more personal reason for my wanting to interview Matza. We share an unusual characteristic of having been born into an ethnic immigrant community and also being immigrants ourselves. Many people do not understand that there is a difference between immigrant experience and ethnic experience. Ethic groups are part of a host culture, but they also have distinct features that differentiate them from the dominant culture. Immigrant groups are simply complete outsiders who try to survive in a new culture. Both Matza and I share some common elements in our heritage. My biological father came out of the Don Cossack group, while Matza's people were of the Buzava clan, which is the clan of Kalmyk Cossacks. The Buzava and Don Cossacks were neighbors, and the Buzava were part of the Don Cossack Host. Lastly, both Matza's and my parents came from the Yugoslav emigration, and so there were many similarities in the experiences of both sets of parents.

How close the experiential connection is was demonstrated one cold morning after Tsagan Sar (Kalmyk Arrival of Spring) services at the Buzava Buddhist temple in Howell. A group of parishioners and I were breaking fast after the service with Kalmyk tea and *bortsek* (Kalmyk ritual fry-bread) and Sara Andreyev suggested that I talk to one of the community elders, a woman who came to the U.S. as an adult. The woman, Sania Dzevzinow, a beautiful woman near her 90s, and I began to talk in Russian and I discovered in our conversation that she went to the same secondary school as my mother. I asked Sania if she were acquainted with mother. She asked me for Mother's name, and I gave it to her. Sania smiled broadly and said, "Oh, Sveta [the affectionate diminutive of Mother's given name, Svetlana]; is she still living?" "No," I responded, "She died some years back."

It is hard to describe the feeling that came over me at that moment. I almost felt as if Mother were there with us. It was a beautiful sunny morning, that Tsagan Sar holiday. Matza was there with us, as well as Matza's daughter Sara.

As I was heading to Matza's I had a feeling of going to talk to a cousin whom I did not know very well, and was not going to interview a complete stranger. The fact that I was about to learn a borsch recipe from a person and not from a book added a sense of reviving the initial motivation for this book, and that felt good. Fortunately, over the years, I had gathered a number of recipes from people and I did not have to feel that my original intent was forgotten.

Overall, my focus on studying cookbooks resulted in a more historic approach than I had originally envisioned. From a book planned to be about people, it evolved into an exploration of the history of borsch, then into a historical review of cookbooks, and then into borsch as a cultural expression and symbol. Throughout, and despite the changes in focus, I kept the introductory reminiscence about borsch in Shamokin and fretted about how to ensure that the story of the people involved in borsch would come through. In part, this was accomplished by examining the authors or personalities responsible for some important cookbooks, but the periodic injection of personal experiences with practicing cooks became a "leavening" device, reminding readers that cooking is really about people and experiences and not marks on a page.

It was a sunny February day as I was driving to "Little Kalmykia," as I call Howell, and the book was not really on my mind. I was more concerned with the traffic bottleneck I encountered around Woodbridge, which would make me late for our appointment. I was looking forward to this interview and the Jersey traffic was irritating.

Howell is an interesting township in Southern New Jersey; it was settled by Europeans in the 18th century and officially incorporated in 1801. Together with its neighbors, Jackson and Lakewood, it has a vibrant concentration of Eastern European immigrants and their descendants. First attracting Jews from the Pale of Settlement who were escaping pogroms and came to America after 1882, and who by the 1920s began establishing chicken farms in the area, these townships also appealed to Christian Russians, Estonians, Latvians, Lithuanians, Cossacks, Byelorussians, Ukrainians, and people of other ethnicities found in the Russian Empire. The later immigrants were particularly attracted to the area after 1934, when the United Russian Mutual Aid Society (original acronym ROOVA) established a 1,400-acre farm in Jackson, New Jersey, that provided work and homes for new immigrants and later became a cultural magnet.

When the Kalmyks originally arrived in 1951-52, they landed in Windsor, Maryland. Part of the group went on, with the help of Quakers, to Philadelphia, Pennsylvania; the bulk of the immigrants, however, through the intercession of Russian Cossack Nicholas Korolkov, wound up in Howell. Some went on to New Brunswick and Patterson, New Jersey.

Korolkov began to work assiduously to bring Kalmyks to Howell, finding for them jobs and places to live. As a mark of the close connection between the Cossacks and Kalmyks (and Korolkov's real estate interests), the first Kalmyk Buddhist temple, founded in 1952, was located only a few blocks from the Cossack St. George Church.

By the time I got to Howell on that February day, I was quite late and flustered. I entered Matza's comfortable, spotlessly clean ranch house and was engulfed by the bright welcome I remembered from my previous visit. Matza was, as usual, impeccably dressed in a dark skirt, a conservative and high-quality beige top, a spotless apron, and her hair "just so." She graciously accepted my apology and we proceeded to the kitchen.

Matza did not waste the time while I was driving and fuming. She had prepped all the vegetables for the pot and was only waiting for my arrival to begin cooking. All the ingredients came from the local supermarket. She had three packages of meat: two **beef shanks**, **cut-up boneless chuck**, and a package of cut-up **baby back ribs**, in all, about three to three and a half pounds of meat total. On the table was half a head of **white cabbage**, quartered and sliced into noodle-width ribbons; one **diced onion**, three stalks of **sliced celery**, two finely minced **garlic cloves** on top of which were piled two tablespoons of finely minced **parsley** and **dill**. On the back counter was a bowl filled with vegetables and water. In that mix there were two **sliced carrots**, half a **parsnip root**, diced, one **diced turnip** and three small **diced potatoes**. On the other side of the counter stood a jar of **Ragu Garden Combination Pasta Sauce**, a package of **Lipton's Onion and Mushroom Soup Mix**, and a box of **Idaho instant mashed potatoes**. Matza pointed to the mashed potato and said, "It helps thicken the soup."

Matza pointed out the manufactured ingredients somewhat sheepishly, but given that health problems made it difficult for her to use her hands, these substitutions for raw ingredients made a great deal of sense. In general, I have noticed over the years that ethnic cooks in America gravitate toward using certain manufactured ingredients in traditional dishes, ingredients that somewhat reduce the labor involved in cooking, but more importantly give a consistency to their dishes that cannot otherwise be achieved because of the constantly shifting sources of raw produce found in supermarkets. My godmother, for example, always used the bouillon cube from a package of Lipton's Chicken Noodle Soup whenever she was braising meat, and my mother always insisted on using only Libby's tomato juice whenever she made her "Greek Sauce."

A large stainless steel cook pot stood ready on the stove. Matza opened the packages of meat and placed all of the meat in the pot. I helped, by filling the pot with water and returning it to the large electric heating element on the stove. Matza put the range on high, and we sat down to chat. Soon the water began to boil and Matza got up to begin skimming the foam from the surface with a stainless steel skimmer. Matza's daughter, Sara, came in, and we talked for a while before Sara left with her daughter.

After Matza had skimmed off all the foam and scraped off most of the film that formed on the sides of the pot at the water's edge, we sat down again to continue talking. After about 40 minutes she added the potatoes and then, after another ten minutes, the cabbage, and then the carrots, parsnip, turnips, leeks, and onions. We kept talking, and throughout the conversation Matza would periodically get up, perform some necessary task, then sit down again and continue our conversation. There were no recipes, no timers, no glancing at watches—in short, I was observing and participating in a cooking process so internalized and habitual that the internal clock, supplemented by the sense of smell, (a good cook can smell when a dish is done) were sufficient guides.

Our conversation started about displaced person (DP) camps. Matza told me about arriving in the U.S. on Christmas and spending a whole day aboard the ship, waiting to disembark because all staff had the day off, and about the relocation to Howell. Matza was very concerned that Nicholas Korolkov be recognized for help-ing the Kalmyks. We talked how I might possibly find his son, who lives around Howell, to establish a history of events in those days.

A bit of a comic interlude interrupted our conversation. I noticed that the track shoes I was wearing had begun to shed mud on Matza's impeccably clean kitchen floor. I was mortified and asked Matza if it were customary to shed one's shoes in the house, and she nodded. I did that, and began to clean up the floor with a couple of paper towels. Soon, cleanliness restored, we continued our talk.

We talked about making borsch and how Matza, whose full name is Edmaska in Kalmyk, learned to cook it from her grandmother. When I mentioned to Matza that her recipe was close to Mennonite borsch she was not quite sure about my reference, until I explained to her that I was talking about the "Volga Germans." "Ah, yes," she exclaimed, "they lived next to our *stanitsa* (Cossack village)."

Matza's husband passed away some years back. When we started talking about married life I mentioned that I had been divorced, and that in my subsequent marriage things have worked out well and that, in my view, the first two decades of a marriage are more challenging but that after that life becomes easier. Matza smiled at that, and shared with me some of her thoughts when she was newly married at nineteen. The atmosphere shifted. We began to talk of children and grandchildren, and suddenly it dawned on me that we were no longer a cook and a fellow collecting borsch recipes, but two elderly people sharing the events of their lives, experiences, and lessons learned.

We commiserated a bit about changes we observed that are not to the best, in our view, and Matza expressed great pride in the Kalmyks' maintenance of their Buddhist heritage. She reminisced about how the men would each donate a pallet of cinder blocks and then spend their weekends building the Tashi Lhunpo Temple. She expressed great satisfaction in being related to Tsem Tulku Rinpoche, whom she visited in 2010 in Malaysia. She also was quite happy that the little band of Kalmyks in the U.S. produced two leaders of Buddhism, including Telo Tulku Rinpoche, the head of the Buddhists in Kalmykia, Russia.

By this time the borsch was ready. Again, without a watch or timer, Matza got up and began serving us. As guest, I received a choice piece of shank meat in my bowl. We sat at the kitchen table, quietly ate, and continued to talk. The borsch was delicious, with just a hint of garlic. I shared my admiration with Matza and remarked how subtle the garlic taste was. "I cut it really fine," Matza replied, and smiled.

Among other things, we talked about the various personalities in the community, and it was remarkable how similar our views often were. Matza was very generous in giving me ideas about those folks who might be particularly good for me to get to know in my quest to know the community better. But mostly we talked about the difficulty of maintaining a culture in a different land, the problem of having so few Kalmyks, and the difficulty of finding Kalmyk marriage partners. Only one of her married children married a Kalmyk. She also shared stories of her grandson, who is studying Russian in high school and, on vacations, chided her for telling him that certain words are Kalmyk when, in fact, they are Russian. Matza said, "How would I know? I was taught that those were Kalmyk words." We both smiled.

And then the borsch was eaten. We talked a bit more, and then it was time for me to leave. I thanked Matza again and went off in a happy mood. As I was driving toward Route 9 I recalled how similar Matza's borsch was to what I remembered of my godmother's. And then it dawned on me—this interview is the ending of the book—we have come full circle. What began some 30 years ago, as a sharing of life after a day's hard work, over a bowl of delicious borsch, ended fortuitously with a sharing of life after many years of hard work, over another bowl of delicious borsch. And interestingly enough, in both cases the dish was cooked by Cossack women; the first from the Kuban and the other a Kalmyk, originating from the Don.

APPENDIX: BORSCH RECIPES & COOKING TIPS

"... This is like a recipe for Ukrainian borsch. If you take three liters of water, half-head of cabbage, meat and cook it for forty minutes, you already have sixty percent borsch. If you add beans, pepper, ten potatoes, and beets then you have ninety percent borsch; agrarian policies also consist of sharply delineated components."

Viktor Yushchenko, former President, Ukraine.

COOKING EQUIPMENT

Pots

The most important piece of equipment for cooking good borsch is a good pot of proportions sufficient for your style of cooking (borsch prefers to be cooked in large quantities). The pot does not have to be expensive. I have never had a decent borsch that was cooked in an All Clad, but I have had some superb versions of the dish from cheap, thin, enameled soup pots. I cook borsch in the same old 8-quart covered Farberware stainless steel pot I bought some three decades ago when I was cooking Cioppino regularly. I use the pot for making broth and for cooking the soup itself. For most people a 4- or 5-quart pot is perfect.

My wife, who is an excellent baker and cook, has a penchant for periodically creating a particular minestrone and also a lentil soup, and she always uses her grandmother's venerable cast iron Waring Round Roaster for those. The point? Get the pot you can afford and are comfortable with, and don't think that a $300 soup pot will add anything to a peasant dish that was originally cooked in clay pots.

For those cooks who want to imitate the traditional Russian stove without the bother of getting a kit for it, which would entail a load of bricks imported from Russia and instructions written in Russian, a slow cooker is a great alternative. Or you can purchase a multi-cooker (a countertop device that can sear, sauté, roast, slow-cook and steam—all in one pot) and join many modern Russian home cooks.

Frying Pan

Some kinds of borsch require the braising and sautéing of certain vegetables. While this can be accomplished in one pot, if the different steps are broken down sequentially it is simpler and a more efficient use of time to use a separate frying pan, or a different pot with a heavy bottom.

Knives

I love tools. A good tool has that combination of form and function that makes my heart sing. Therefore, I am a bit of a knife nut. I own a handful of knives that range from the internationally recognized Henkel utility knife to a no-name folding Greek fisherman's knife with an aluminum blade and a crudely made plastic handle. I prefer my carbon steel Chinese chef's knife and the American-made utility kitchen knife for most tasks.

A first-class paring knife and a very good utility knife are quite sufficient for anyone who is not a professional chef or a knife lover. My wife seldom uses my knives; she feels that they are too sharp for her and she is quite happy with a no-name stainless steel paring knife and dull utility knife. She manages, however, to cut her ingredients as well as I cut mine.

Chicago Cutlery makes excellent knives, ranging in price from $8 to $20. Whatever you do, don't buy a whole knife set; most of them you will not use. Few things are sillier than a $200 knife that is never used.

Heat Source

Unless one has access to a traditional Russian stove, one normally uses a range or stove for borsch making. Preferences vary, but I like gas ranges, particularly small restaurant-type ones. A ready substitute for a Russian stove is a slow oven or a slow cooker.

Other Equipment

Other equipment used in borsch cooking includes the following: a good vegetable peeler, a cutting board, and a good sturdy spoon for stirring the ingredients. (I like wooden spoons.) You'll also need a skimmer, to remove the foam that rises as a result of cooking meat for broth; bowls to rinse vegetables and store processed/prepared ingredients; cheesecloth for bouquet garni; and a ladle to transfer the soup to a tureen or eating dishes.

All these items can be purchased in almost any sizeable department store or supermarket. If you want something that will last your whole lifetime for a reasonable price, go to a restaurant supply store and buy what you need, used.

INGREDIENTS

In American supermarket culture, anything that is not canned or frozen is called "fresh." When a vegetable takes a week or more to get from grower to buyer, it can hardly be called "fresh." "Raw," yes, but not "fresh." Anyone who has been able to pick their own produce knows the vast difference between that vegetable and what is available in supermarkets. I urge borsch makers to patronize a local farmers' market whenever possible.

Meats

Borsch can be made with any kinds of domesticated meat, most fatty fishes, and with vegetable broth. And I have known of borsch made with seal meat. If you use vegetable broth, mushrooms (either fresh, dried, or in bouillon cubes) will give you a much richer-tasting broth. Always wash meat before cooking; this lessens surface foam. Begin cooking meat in cold water.

The best American cuts of meat for borsch are brisket, shank, and ribs; chuck is also quite good. Marrow bones are a favorite with aficionados. Ukrainian borsch usually calls for a combination of pork and beef. Some recipes call for smoked meats. I have used smoked hocks successfully. Poultry is used in some traditional borsch recipes. Turkey, which is ubiquitous in America, makes a very nice broth, particularly when used in a slow cooker. I suggest skinning the turkey meat before cooking to reduce the fat content.

Avoid using frozen or thawed meats; they will usually give you a cloudy broth. Using frozen or thawed meats in a slow cooker, however, seems to avoid that problem.

Vegetables

The rule of thumb is that fresh, ripe vegetables picked in season are best. More mature vegetables are more flavorful, and are really great in soups. Supermarket tomatoes ought to be avoided. Diced, canned tomatoes, particularly fire-roasted ones, are much better than fresh supermarket tomatoes. I have also used dried tomatoes successfully.

The one non-meat ingredient that, under normal conditions, is best to use dried rather than fresh, is mushrooms. The traditional mushroom used in borsch cooking is the *boletus edulis,* commonly know as porcino or porcini. In Russian it is called "white mushroom." Fresh porcini mushrooms are expensive and hard to find in markets and, besides, dehydrated foods usually give a much stronger flavor if they are properly stored. Dry porcini are quite expensive; mushroom bouillon cubes are acceptable substitutes.

Another reasonable substitute for porcini are regular supermarket mushrooms that have been sliced and oven dried. I was taught that trick by my Carpatho-Rusyn friends while doing folklore fieldwork in Cleveland, Ohio. Especially good are large mushrooms that are being sold at a discount because they begin to turn brown. These fungi will give the strongest flavor. Quickly rinse and slice them, and place them on a cookie sheet in a low oven till completely dried. They keep "forever" in a tightly closed glass jar.

Spices: Balancing the Flavors

Russian cooking has sometimes been described by outsiders as bland. That characterization I cannot understand, either from personal experience, or based on ingredient lists found in recipes. The list of traditional spices used in Russian cooking includes: salt, black pepper, garlic, onion, horseradish, celery, dill, parsley, ginger, hot peppers, mustard, allspice, saffron, bay leaf, and lemon. Dill is almost a national icon, and bay leaf is used in virtually every soup. The Russian armed forces even specify a ration of two bay leaves per serving of soup in their instruction to cooks. Different spices enjoy popularity at different times. Any borsch recipe that calls for allspice, in my experience, is a 19th century recipe. The spice lost its popularity in the Soviet period and its antique name, "English pepper," is unrecognizable to anyone but students of culinary traditions. Today, allspice is called "fragrant pepper" in most books I have encountered. In Brighton Beach stores, "allspice" worked quite well when I tried my experiment in modern spice-recognition competence.

Hiawatha Cromer, an extraordinarily good cook who taught me the Living Food Cuisine, continually repeated when she was instructing me: "Cooking is about balancing the five flavors—sweet, sour, bitter, salty, and spicy." If you remember and practice that injunction, you will become known as a good cook. Traditional borsch is a complex dish, with some versions requiring 20 or more ingredients but, in the end, if the five flavors are in balance people will enjoy the dish.

Spices are meant to help achieve the sought-after balance and should never dominate. While the ideal borsch has a light sweet-sour taste that allows the flavors of the various ingredients to be tasted, historically a more sour taste has been the preference (probably to offset the fattiness of traditional borsch). Again ideally, while a spoonful of borsch should reflect a flavorful harmony in the balance of flavors, that spoonful needs to be so delicate that each ingredient can be tasted without infringing on the flavors of the others.

I learned about respecting the flavors of individual ingredients during a visit to Vietnam, where dishes of lightly cooked and seasoned pond greens not only had individual flavors that reflected the place where the dish was served and eaten, but even led me to imagine that I could taste the flavor of the water in which the plants had grown. All too often, in America, we are unable to taste the individual flavor that a particular soil has imparted to an ingredient because of the heavy use of chemical fertilizers.

Oversalting and overspicing are a common problem in modern American cooking, where ingredients often have inherently weak flavors due to agricultural, transportation, and storage techniques. Local produce eaten in season or properly stored to be used out of season can go a long way to restoring appreciation for the inherent flavor in all things. Spices should enhance, not mask, flavor (although sometimes they help to correct errors made by the cook).

COOKING BORSCH

For some people borsch is an acquired taste. These people are won over to the dish, not as a result of an initial tasting that makes them want to immediately repeat the experience but as a consequence of exposure to it in specific situations over a period of time. Often, enjoyment of borsch is as much dependent on a desire to re-create a certain social reality as it is on the flavor of the dish.

Borsch is a food of ritual. Literally, this is demonstrated in the Polish *Wigilia* borsch on Christmas Eve, or the Easter *żurek,* where the borsch is part of the holiday fare, if not the star. More generally, the ritual nature of the soup is reflected by the occasions at which the soup is served or eaten (such as on a visit by a beloved child). Even when eaten daily it is often done within a ritual context. One co-worker shared with me a reminiscence of his father, a German concentration camp survivor, daily eating borsch together with white bread as a celebration of survival and a sign of well-being achieved in America. The reminiscence offered in Kyra Petrovskaya's cookbook clearly shows the ritual manner with which the soup is approached.

The best way to learn how to cook borsch is to find the version you really enjoy and learn to make it from the cook who creates it. If that is not possible, the following advice will help ensure a consistent result.

Slicing Cabbage

One of the trickiest techniques to learn in making a traditional cabbage borsch is the proper slicing of the cabbage. While Maritime, and a few individual borsch recipes, call for square or diamond-shaped cuts of cabbage, the most common manner of cabbage preparation is a julienne. Excellent and quick results can be achieved by using the slicing disk of a food processor, such as a Cusinart, or a mandolin (no, not the musical instrument). A mandolin has definite cost advantages over a food processor; a good one can be purchased for as little as $10, and they are easier to clean.

Traditionally, cooks have used utility or even paring knifes and achieved excellent results. The trick is to cut the cabbage into quarters, and then "shave" or shred the vegetable into match-sized slices from the inside. This way you will soon learn to produce thin spoon-sized bits of cabbage that will make your cooking reputation.

Eight Steps to Better Borsch

The necessary steps and proper sequence to create a "classic" (Ukrainian/Russian) meat borsch are laid out nicely by William Pokhlebkin in *The National Cuisines of Our Peoples* (*Nacional'nye kukhni nashikh narodov*) and served as the foundation in developing the following steps. I put in bold the key concepts made by Pokhlebkin and followed with more detailed elaborations:

1. **The key to a good borsch is the broth.** There are many varieties of it. One can have bone, meat-and-bone, and just meat stock. Borsch can also be based on goose, chicken, or duck broth (Poltava, Odessa, and some Polish varieties). In those cases only poultry is used as meat. Borsch can also be prepared with fish stock. Of course there is also purely vegetarian borsch, particularly important in Lenten fare, but a classic Ukrainian and Russian borsch is based on meat stock. Bone stock is cooked slowly (4-6 hours), while one made of meat seldom takes more than two hours. By consensus of many writers and cooks, the bones and meat for the most flavorful borsch come from the rib primal cut (located between the chuck and short loin on a carcass). The most flavorful meat broth is cooked on a high flame. The most velvety broth is done in a slow cooker. Once the broth is done the meat is removed and set aside until about 10-15 minutes before the borsch is done, at which point it is combined with the rest of the soup.

2. **The vegetables for borsch are prepared separately from the broth.** The traditional vegetables (besides beets) in a classic borsch are cabbage, carrots, potatoes, parsley root (if parsley root is unavailable, parsnips and extra leaf parsley make an acceptable substitute), onions, and tomatoes. Optional vegetables include beans, apples (tart Granny Smith are best), squash, green and dried beans, and turnips. Vegetables are normally julienned, except for potatoes and squash, which are cubed. Dry beans are cooked separately from the other vegetables and added about 15 minutes before the dish is done. Turnips (and other root vegetables) are sautéed with carrots. Apples and squash are not sautéed; they are added raw after all the other vegetables, approximately 15 minutes before the soup is done.

The main vegetable, beets, are prepared separately. Julienned beets are first sprinkled with vinegar or lemon juice (to retain the red color during cooking) and are stewed in a bit of broth. Sometimes the beets are baked or boiled to semi-doneness before they are julienned and placed in the broth.

Finely cut onion, julienned carrots, parsley root or parsnips, and/or turnip are sautéed (traditionally in fatback/lard or butter); there needs to be enough fat to visibly coat the vegetables. Before the sautéing is finished, tomato paste or small-dice tomatoes are added, and the mixture is cooked until the fat turns orange.

3. **It is important that the vegetables are placed into the broth in a specific order.** The order is determined by the cooking time for each vegetable.

- Potatoes, 30 minutes before end of cooking
- Cabbage, 20 minutes
- Braised beets, 15 minutes
- Sautéed vegetables (onion, carrots, parsley root) and the meat from making the broth, also 15 minutes
- Aromatic herbs, 5 to 8 minutes
- Garlic (added separately), 2 minutes

4. **To give the borsch its most traditional sweet-sour taste, it is prepared with the addition of fermented beet juice (beet *kvas*).** When the meat has been cooked and removed from the broth, this juice is added to the broth. Be sure not to boil it for a long time or the flavor will dissipate.

5. **When the borsch is ready, place it on a very low heat so as not to allow it to cool too much, and let it rest for about 20 minutes before serving.** It takes anywhere from three to seven hours to prepare a traditional borsch.

6. **The rule of thumb is that in order to get 1½ to 2 quarts of broth one begins with 4 quarts of liquid.** Some types of borsch require the addition of flour or roux to thicken the broth further. In general, borsch needs to be a very thick soup; according to folk belief: "In a good borsch, a spoon can stand upright."

7. **Sour cream in traditional borsch is obligatory.** Russian sour cream is more fluid than American. (A good substitute is Mexican *crema*.) Garnishes, which can vary widely, most often include dill weed, minced hot pepper, sliced scallion, additional garlic, and salt and pepper.

8. **No soup in Russia or the Ukraine is eaten by itself.** At a minimum, a nice slice of bread accompanies any soup. Borsch has its own traditional accompaniments, from the ubiquitous *pampushki* to a whole range of delicious tidbits.

Eating Borsch

Making borsch is the opposite of cooking fast food. Depending on the recipe, borsch can take from an hour to days to make. It is gratifying that even in today's "hyperdrive" world there are people who will take a week to re-create a recipe passed on from grandma. That, in itself, is an indicator that this food is viewed as more than simple nutrition or a way to generate energy; a spiritual value is associated with it.

The eating of borsch should, therefore, also be accorded a certain degree of respect and involve a bit of ceremony. In a simple setting, such as feeding a multitude of diners in an outdoor venue, disposable soup bowls and utensils make sense; at home a bit more care is nice. A nice bowl or dish makes a difference. For guests, serving from a soup tureen makes a bit of a fuss and adds a touch of ceremony. A soup plate with a wide rim is a nice touch at any table.

I favor eating borsch with a Russian painted wooden spoon. The colored traditional pattern from Khokhloma gives a bit of color and cheer on a dreary cold day when borsch is particularly welcome.

The wooden spoon also never gets hot, so you cannot burn your lips with it.

Recipes

Kvas, Rejuvelac, Borş, Żurek

Beet Kvas

4 lbs. beets	Salt
14-21 oz. sugar	1 piece of rye bread
Lemon salt	3-4 qt. water
1½ oz. yeast	

Take well-washed beets and grate them on fine grate. Cover with cooled boiled water. Add sugar and lemon salt to taste, yeast, and mix well; add bread. When signs of fermentation begin to appear, filter the liquid through a few layers of cheesecloth and pour into bottles. Cap tightly and after 12 to 24 hours take the bottles to a cool place. The kvas is ready to use the next day.

Bread and Beet Kvas

1 qt. hot water	1 rye bread crust
1 lb. beets, pared and sliced	

Pour hot water over beets in an enamel, stainless steel, or ceramic pot. Add bread. Cover with cloth. Let stand 3 to 4 days.

Drain off clear juice and use for soup.

Rejuvelac
Makes 2 quarts

1 c. wheat grains
2 qt. filtered water

2-qt. wide-mouthed glass jar

Rinse wheat in water. Add the wheat to the glass jar. Fill with filtered water and cover with gauze held securely in place with an elastic band. (It is important to prevent the entry of insects.) Soak for 12 hours.

Pour off the soak water and refill. Leave the jar on a kitchen bench out of direct sunlight. Give the jar a gentle twirl, but not a shake, every 12 hours. Once a light foam develops it should be ready for use. It may take anywhere from 2-5 days to ferment the Rejuvelac, depending on the ambient temperature. In hot weather, where it may ferment too quickly (around 24 hours) it is possible for the Rejuvelac to go putrid. Rejuvelac should have a pleasant yeasty smell with a lemon-like flavor.

Once the Rejuvelac is ready, then carefully decant the liquid into a clean container and refrigerate. The sediment can be used to make a second culture. Refill the jar with filtered water and ferment for another 24-36 hours. Decant the Rejuvelac and refrigerate. Discard the wheat grains and the sediment.

Notes and Cautions:

It is possible for Rejuvelac to go bad (as it is for sprouts and probably any fermented culture). You can generally tell if the Rejuvelac is okay by the smell and taste. It is good practice to observe, smell, and taste the Rejuvelac periodically to become accustomed to the changes that occur (as it is for any fermented culture). Rejuvelac should keep in the fridge for a week or more, and will gradually sweeten with time.

Romanian Borş Recipe
Makes 4 pints

8 oz. wheat bran
1 tsp. instant yeast
2 Tbs. cornmeal
4 pt. water

Combine 2 tablespoons of the wheat bran with a cupful of warm water and add the yeast. Leave to froth for a couple of hours, then drain and reserve the bran, discarding the liquid.

Put the remaining dry bran and cornmeal in a clean bowl. Boil the water and pour it into the bowl. Mix and leave to cool until tepid, then stir in the yeasty bran.

Cover with a clean cloth and set aside for three to four days in a cool place, stirring regularly, until delicately soured. Strain into a clean glass jar, store in the refrigerator, and use as required.

To start another batch without yeast, reserve a cupful of the strained-out bran and proceed as above, adding the yeasted bran to the new batch at the stage when the bran-and-water mixture has cooled to tepid.

Simple Beet Infusion

Beets
Water (in proportions of 1:2 beets to water)

Take peeled and grated beets and pour boiled water over them. Let stand in a warm place for 3 to 4 days.

Sourdough Kvas

For every 2 quarts of **water** *use one pound of* **rye flour** *and ½ oz. of* **yeast.**

Dissolve 1-2 tablespoons of flour and yeast in a cup of warm water, and allow it to ferment (starter). Cover the remaining flour with hot water and mix the dough to a sour cream or yogurt consistency, and place it in a warm spot. Add the starter to the dough and dilute it with warm water to the consistency of kvas (liquid).

As you use the kvas, add water in the ratio of ½ quart water to each quart of kvas used.

Zurek-Simple Rye Kvas

¾ c. rye flour
Crust from one slice of rye bread
2 c. of warm pre-boiled water

In a scalded crock or glass jar whisk the rye flour and water until lump free. Add rye bread crust. Cover mouth of container with cheesecloth and fasten with string or rubber band. Put in warm 75°-80° F place for two to five days or until the liquid is pleasantly tart. Taste every day. When it's to your preference of tartness, go to the next step.

A comment about tasting: There will be froth on top; skim it, then taste. When it's ready, strain through cheesecloth and pour the liquid into scalded jars or bottles. Cover and refrigerate. You aren't trying to achieve a clear liquid–cloudy is good.

Borsch

1. Anna Alexandrovna's Borsch (Chapter 1)
Anna Alexandrovna Osetrova

4 qt. cold water
4 lbs. beef brisket (2 beef shank slices and 2 to 2½ lbs. of boneless chuck are a good substitute if you are not making pirozhki out of the meat)
½ small cabbage (about 1-1½ lbs.)
2-3 medium potatoes
2 medium carrots
2 stalks celery
1 onion
1 parsley root
2 medium beets
4 ripe or 1 can of fire-roasted diced tomatoes
1 red or green bell pepper
3 cloves garlic
1 small hot pepper or dried red-pepper flakes (optional)
Salt
Black pepper
White, cider, or wine vinegar
2-3 bay leaves
Fresh parsley
Fresh dill
Scallions
Sugar
Sour cream

Pour four quarts of cold water into large (8 quart) pot. Rinse meat under cold running water (that will result in less foam when you start boiling the meat). Cut meat into 2 to 4 pieces. Put water and meat on high flame to boil. When water boils up, adjust flame to maintain a low boil. Skim foam from pot. Cover; cook for approximately 90 minutes, or until meat is quite tender. If you cook the meat longer you will have a richer broth but a less flavorful piece of meat (an important consideration, if you are making *pirozhki* from part of the meat).

After skimming the foam, and while the meat is cooking, prepare the vegetables. Slice cabbage into noodle-like strips. Peel root vegetables. Cube potatoes; chop onion; slice in half (lengthwise) the remaining root vegetables, then slice into half-moon slices, then quarter those slices. Dice fresh tomatoes or use canned. Chop bell pepper. If you like some spiciness to your soup you can use a Poblano chile instead of a bell pepper. Mince fine garlic and about 2 tablespoons of fresh parsley and dill. I rinse all vegetables under cold running water after prepping them, and hold them in bowls to add to the soup.

When the broth is ready, remove the meat from the pot and set aside. Wipe any foam remnants from the side of the pot with a paper towel or clean wet cloth. Make sure you have 2 to 2½ quarts of liquid. If not, add hot water to the broth. The cooking of the vegetables should take about 30 minutes.

Add cabbage, potatoes, and onion first. After about five minutes, add celery, carrots, parsley root, and tomatoes; after another five minutes add beets and a good dose of vinegar to help preserve the beet color. After 20-25 minutes the vegetables should be close to done. Add chopped bell pepper, minced garlic, parsley, dill, and bay leaf. Correct seasoning (salt, pepper, sugar) as needed. Cook for an additional 5-7 minutes. Correct seasoning again. Let the borsch "rest" on very low flame for at least 20 minutes. (The idea is not to allow it to completely cool.) This borsch should have a bright red color.

If you want your borsch with meat, dice meat and add to bowls before adding soup. Anna would grind the meat and use it in making *pirozhki* that accompanied the soup.

Serve borsch with sour cream. Anna used only Breakstone sour cream, which in those days came in a glass tumbler with colorful polka dots or a flower design. All the glasses in her house were acquired that way. Also have freshly minced dill, parsley, garlic, scallions cut into ringlets, and hot pepper on hand for diners to add at will.

To make Lenten or vegetarian versions of this borsch one can either make a vegetable broth or use low-sodium canned vegetable broth. When using vegetable broth I also like to use dried tomatoes instead of fresh or canned. If using dried tomatoes, chop them and add them to the first batch of vegetables being cooked. Adding reconstituted dried mushrooms or a mushroom bouillon cube to the broth will make it much richer and "meaty" tasting. A trick I learned from Matza Andreyev is to add Lipton's Mushroom-Onion soup mix. Works well.

2. Cow Parsnip Borsch (Borschevik) (Chapter 2)
Modern Version (Ingredients per serving)

½ lb. young cow parsnip or young nettles	1 egg
½ lb. beets	1 Tbs. sour cream
¼ lb. potato	¼ tsp. sugar
1 Tbs. green onion (scallion)	Salt, vinegar, dill to taste,

Boil potato, cool, and peel. Dice into medium-sized cubes. Mince green onion.

Fill pot with water, salt it, bring to boil and blanch the cow parsnip. Remove the greens from the pot and dry them on paper towels. Cut finely.

Dice beets, place in a large pot, add vinegar, and fry. Add water, salt, sugar, blanched cow parsnip or nettle and bring to boil. Allow the borsch to cool, add potato, and the minced green onion.

Sprinkle the borsch with minced dill and serve with sour cream. Instead of using water for the borsch you can use beet, vegetable, or meat broth.

[The egg may be added to the soup, raw, to thicken it, or used hard-boiled and chopped as a garnish—cook's choice. If you use raw egg it is best to temper it. To temper the egg add a bit of broth to the egg and mix well. The pour the mixture slowly into the soup while stirring.]

3. WHITE BORSCH (BARSZCZ BIAŁY) OR ŻUREK (CHAPTER 2)

Serves 6

6 c. sausage cooking water, fat removed
1 clove minced garlic
2 c. sour cream
¼ c. all-purpose flour
1 link white Polish kielbasa sausage, casing removed, sliced ¼" thick
1 link smoked Polish kielbasa sausage, casing removed, sliced ¼" thick
6 medium potatoes, peeled, cut into chunks and boiled
6 c. żurek
6 hard-cooked sliced eggs
6 slices light or dark rye bread
Salt and pepper to taste

In a large pot or Dutch oven, add sausage water and garlic. Bring to a boil, reduce heat and simmer, partially covered, for 5 minutes. Add *żurek*.

Blend the flour and sour cream. Temper the sour cream with a little hot sausage water, return to pot, stirring until thickened. Add sausages, potatoes and eggs to pot and heat until warmed through. Season to taste. At this point, some people add a pinch of sugar or a tablespoon of vinegar. The soup should have a pleasantly sour taste.

To serve, tear rye bread into bite-sized pieces, place in heated bowls. Ladle hot soup over bread.

4. CIORBĂ DE PERIȘOARE (ROMANIAN SOURED MEATBALL SOUP) (CHAPTER 2)
Elisabeth Luard, *Zester*

Serves 4

A *ciorba*, or sour soup, can also be soured with vinegar, lemon juice, pickle brine, or sauerkraut juice.

¾ lbs. ground beef	2 pt. strong beef bone or chicken broth
2 heaping Tbs. rice	1 c. shredded lovage or celery leaves
1 small onion, grated	1 pt. borș (soured bran) or plain water
1 medium egg, forked to blend	plus 2 tablespoons wine vinegar
1 c. chopped dill or fennel tops	Sour cream
1 c. chopped parsley	Fresh red chilies

Work the ground meat with the rice, onion, egg, half the dill and half the parsley until well-blended and smooth. Roll into balls about the size of a walnut.

Bring the broth to a boil and gently slip in the meatballs. Return the pot to the boil, turn down the heat and leave to simmer without bubbling for 30 to 40 minutes, until the meatballs are tender and cooked through.

Strain the soured bran into the broth (or add the extra water and vinegar), reheat and bubble up for no more than 2 minutes.

Finish with the shredded lovage and the rest of the parsley and dill. Ladle into bowls and add a dollop of sour cream. Serve the fresh red chilies separately, one for each person.

5. NICK'S GREEN SORREL BORSCH (CHAPTER 2)
Nikolai Burlakoff

1 qt. beef or vegetable broth	3 scallions
1 large Idaho potato	2 hard-boiled eggs
1 bunch of sorrel (about 20 plant leaves, the size of a palm)	Fresh dill, salt, pepper to taste

Nick's Green Sorrel Borsch (Continued)

Pour broth into 2-quart pan, bring to boil, add a medium-cubed large potato. While potato is cooking slice the sorrel leaves into ribbons; mince dill; cut scallion into ringlets; chop eggs.

When the potato is done, increase the heat to high and add the prepared greenery and eggs. Bring to boil and when the soup boils up, shut off the heat and serve immediately. The soup should turn dark or olive green.

[Sorrel can vary in tartness. If it is too tart for your taste, you may mix in spinach in proportions that suit your taste. If it is not tart enough, add lemon. Summer spinach, Swiss chard, nettle may be substituted for sorrel; the taste will differ but it will still be good.]

6. ANNA'S ŠALTIBARŠČIAI (LITHUANIAN COLD BEET SOUP) (CHAPTER 2)
Anna Hylton

4 hard-boiled eggs (chopped)
1 can beets (grated) save liquid
2 cucumbers (medium)
¼ c. green onion (chopped fine)
3 blossoms fresh dill or ½ tsp. dill salt
2 Tbs. sour cream
2 qt. buttermilk

Mix sour cream with eggs, beets, cucumbers, onion, and dill. Add buttermilk and beet juice.

7. "LAZY" SLOW COOKER BORSCH-RUSSIAN (CHAPTER 2)
Svetik21-Internet

I layered the bottom of the slow cooker with sliced **cabbage** and cut **potatoes** (the potatoes I put to the sides of the pot since my cooker heats from the sides).

Then add a layer of cut **beets** and **carrots** and **meat** directly from the freezer. Then **onion,** frozen **broth** (I freeze broth I make, for later use—no chemicals) and **tomato paste**.

Cover everything with **water**; add a handful of washed **dry beans**; also **salt, pepper, bay leaf**.

Set on low for 9 hours.

Serve borsch with **sour cream** and **minced dill**.
[Svetik21 has cleverly solved the problem of the different cooking times for meat and vegetables by placing frozen meat in the slow cooker. This eliminates the need to separately braise the vegetables.]

8. CROCK POT RUSSIAN BEEF BORSCHT-AMERICAN (CHAPTER 2)
Lorac, Internet

Servings: 8-10

4 c. thinly sliced green cabbage
1½ lbs. fresh beets, shredded
5 small carrots, peeled and sliced
1 parsnip, peeled and sliced
1 c. chopped onion
4 garlic cloves, minced
1 lb. beef, cut into ½ inch cubes
1 (14½ oz.) can diced tomatoes, undrained
3 (14½ oz.) cans beef broth
¼ c. lemon juice
1 Tbs. sugar
1 tsp. black pepper
Sour cream
Fresh parsley, minced

In a slow cooker, layer ingredients (except sour cream and parsley) in the order listed.

Cover and cook on Low 7-9 hours or until veggies are just tender. Add more pepper, lemon or sugar to balance taste. Serve with sour cream and parsley.

9. NICK'S VEGETARIAN LUO SONG TANG (RUSSIAN SOUP) (CHAPTER 3)
Nikolai Burlakoff

1 medium can tomato puree*
1 lb. tomatoes, ½ in. cubes
1-2 large carrots, ½ in. cubes
4 sticks celery, ½ in. lengths
2 large potatoes, ½ in. cubes
1 medium beet (optional), ½ in. cubes
1 large onion, ½ in. cubes
2 large bay leaves
¼ tsp. freshly ground black pepper
Salt to taste

*If you don't want to add tomato puree, increase the fresh tomatoes to 2 lbs.

Boil about 8 cups of water, add the onion and tomatoes, and simmer 45 minutes.

Add the celery and beet [optional] to the soup and let simmer for about an hour. Then add the carrots, potatoes, and tomato puree and the seasonings and boil until potatoes are slightly soft. Last five minutes add the bay leaf. If the water level is too low, add 1 or 2 cups of water, let soup come to a boil again, and switch off the heat and leave the vegetables to rest.

Just before serving, heat soup.

10. Nick's Living Foods Raw Borsch (Chapter 3)
Nikolai Burlakoff

1 Serving

1 small beet, scrubbed, quartered
½ parsnip root, scrubbed
Piece of celery root the size of the parsnip piece, scrubbed, or stalk of celery, rinsed and quartered
1 very small onion, peeled, quartered
White cabbage, about ½ c.
1 kale leaf
Small slice ginger
1 or 2 sprigs of parsley
¼ tsp. raw apple cider
¼ lemon with peel
½ tsp. agar or raw honey
Cup of beet kvas or buckwheat Rejuvelac
Salt and pepper to taste

Place ingredients in blender, add kvas or Rejuvelac. Blend. Correct seasonings. Possible additions:

Walnut/sunflower seed "meatballs": ½ c. walnut meats, ¼ c. sunflower seeds. Blend, season to taste, form into small "meatballs."

Avocado "sour cream": ¼ avocado, lemon juice to taste. Blend avocado until it is the consistency of sour cream, season with lemon.

Add sprinkling of minced dill weed, garlic mashed with salt and olive oil, few dashes of cayenne or hot pepper chiffonade.

11. Zaporozhian Borsch [Brezhnev's Favorite] (Chapter 3)
Culinary, Voskresenie

For this preparation one needs a good piece of meat—the best is **brisket**. Wash 1 pound of meat; cut into pieces; cover with 3 quarts of **bone stock** and put on the fire. Wash, peel, and cut 1 medium **beet**, ½ **celery root**, 2 **carrots** and sauté them in a tablespoon of butter and 3-4 tablespoons of stock. In the process of stewing add the stock. After 30 minutes add ½ head of chopped **cabbage** and stew it together with the other vegetables until they are soft; then transfer all to a pot with boiling stock. After this, fry a finely diced **onion** until golden together with small diced **corned beef** (optionally, **fatback**), with a pinch of **red pepper**; to that, add 2-3 tablespoons of hot stock and put all the sauté into the borsch. To this, add 7-8 **whole peppercorns**, 1-2 **bay leaves** and 2 **teaspoons of vinegar**.

After 10 minutes one can remove the borsch from the heat and serve it. But it tastes even better if it rests for at least a few hours.

12. Prune Borsch (Chapter 3)
Victoria Petrovna Brezhneva (Wife of Leonid Brezhnev)

4 Servings

¾ lb. fresh white cabbage	1 parsley root
½ lb. prunes	1 carrot
⅓ to ½ oz. of dried porcini (boletus) mushrooms	½ Tbs. flour
4 beets	2 Tbs. tomato paste
4 potatoes	3 Tbs. vegetable oil
1 onion	1 Tbs. parsley greens
	1 Tbs. sugar
	Salt and pepper, to taste

Soak mushrooms in 2 quarts of water for 2 hours. Then bring to boil and cook for 1 to 1½ hours. Take out the mushrooms and slice. Save the broth. Wash the prunes and cover with 2 cups of water, add sugar and cook until soft—10 minutes; then remove from heat. Peel the beets, then julienne. Heat half the oil in fry pan, add the beets, a tablespoon of tomato paste, and some mushroom broth; stew on low, stirring periodically, for 10 to 15 minutes.

Peel and slice the onion, carrot, and parsley root, and sauté with the remaining oil, tomato paste and flour for 5 to 7 minutes.

Finely slice the cabbage; peel the potato and slice it. Add the cabbage to the boiling mushroom stock. After it boils again, add the potato and cook for 10 to 15 minutes.

Then add to the pot the beets and braised vegetables; add the sliced mushrooms, cooked prunes, and the prune broth. Salt and pepper and continue cooking for 7 to 10 minutes. Before serving, sprinkle the borsch with minced parsley.

13. *Carême's Borsch for Tsars (Chapter 3)*
Internet

Place in a pot a spit-**roasted chicken**, a piece of **veal**, marrow **bone**, one pound of **bacon**, two **carrots**, stalk of **celery**, two **onions** (one stuck with six **cloves**), bunch of **parsley**, a little **thyme, basil,** and an ounce of **white peppercorns**.

Cover all this with a **beet decoction** and cook for one hour. Then add a **duck**, a corn-fed **chicken** that has been slightly fried, and **six large sausages**. As the ingredients become done take them out and retain them for further use. Continue to cook the broth. Take a **beet** from those that were used to make the beet decoction and cut into matchsticks. Cut a **celery root** and onion in a similar manner. Lightly fry the vegetables in **clarified butter**, add a small amount of broth, and braise until the broth is cooked away.

In the meantime, mince 4 ounces of **beef filet** and 4 ounces of **beef fat**. Add a little **salt, pepper**, ground **nutmeg**, and two **egg yolks**. Make out of half this stuffing 30 small round cakes, fold them in half in the form of a half moon, and cook them in a small amount of broth for 10 minutes.

Make remaining half of the stuffing into quenelles the size of hazelnuts, bread them in **flour**, and brown them in clarified butter immediately before serving the borsch.

Hard boil two **eggs**, cut each in half lengthwise, remove the yolks, mix them with one **raw egg yolk**, salt, pepper, and ground nutmeg. Add a little ground **horseradish** and finely sliced **parsley**. Stuff the egg whites with the resulting stuffing, moisten with some **liaison** (cream and egg-yolk thickener), bread with **bread crumbs**. Brown in clarified butter immediately before serving the borsch.

Cook the broth for five hours, strain, clarify. Place in the soup tureen the meat taken from previously cooked **ox-tail**; also place in it the cooked and sliced bacon, chicken, and duck breast, and sausages, each of which has been quartered.

On top of the meat assortment place the prepared quenelles, the half-moon stuffing, and the browned egg halves. Then add the braised beets, onion, and celery. Place the soup tureen in a warm place. In the meantime grate **one peeled beet**, squeeze the juice out of it, bring it up to boil and pour it into the boiling clarified broth so as to give it the color of Bordeaux.

Pour the resulting broth into the tureen. Serve the **marrow bone** separately on a very hot serving plate surrounded by heart-shaped **croutons** browned in butter.

14. LOUIS P. DE GOUY'S BORTSCH POLONAISE (CHAPTER 3)
Hot or Cold
Louis P. De Gouy, *The Soup Book*

Roast a whole cleaned **domestic duck** of about 6 pounds in a hot oven (450° F.) until well browned (seared). Drain, put it in a soup kettle with 1 pound of **beef bone** and ¼ pound of **bacon** in one piece. Add 3 quarts of cold salted **water**; the pulp of 12 medium-sized fresh **beets**; the pulp of 2 small **carrots**; 5 small **leeks**, carefully washed and passed through a food chopper; 1 **bouquet garni**, composed of 1 large **bay leaf**, 12 sprigs of **fresh parsley**, and 1 large sprig of **thyme**, tied together with a kitchen thread; 2 stalks of **celery**, scraped and chopped; 2 medium-sized **onions**, quartered, 2 quarters being stuck with 2 cloves each; 1 large clove of **garlic**; 12 **whole peppercorns**, gently bruised; and a grated **nutmeg**.

Bring slowly to a boil, skimming off all scum carefully. When boiling, lower the flame, let simmer gently, covered, over a very low flame for about 4 hours without disturbing.

When done and tender, strain the bouillon through a fine-meshed sieve or fine cheesecloth into another soup kettle. Add 3 **egg whites** and their crushed shells, and gradually gently but thoroughly mix them into the bouillon.

When the boiling point is reached, let simmer very gently for 12 to 15 minutes, but do not stir or beat any more. Strain through a fine cheesecloth over a sieve, taste for seasoning, and serve either very hot or very cold, but always with plenty of rich **sour cream** on the side. When served cold, sour cream whipped with a few grains of salt may be forced through a pastry bag with a small fancy tube to decorate the top of each cup.

Note: You may, if desired, cut the duck meat into small cubes, and serve in the soup. Polish peasant women usually use goose or chicken fat instead of the diced duck meat, and add barley and caraway.

15. Jellied Bortsch I (Chapter 3)
Louis P. De Gouy, *The Soup Book*

Pour into a saucepan 1½ quarts of **Beef Consommé** (recipe follows). Add 2 cups of peeled, cored chopped **beets**, ½ cup of chopped **onion**, and 1 cup of green **cabbage**. Cook until the vegetables are tender, adding more beef bouillon as necessary. Remove from the fire, and stir in 2 teaspoons of granulated **gelatin**, softened in 2 tablespoons of cold water. Stir until the gelatin is dissolved. Taste for seasoning, and cool to lukewarm, stirring occasionally so as to mix the vegetables. Fill six chilled cups with the mixture, and chill in the refrigerator for at least 3 hours. When ready to serve, gently break the jellied mixture with a fork, and cover the entire surface of each cup with plain **whipped cream, slightly salted**, and forced through a pastry bag with a small fancy tube. Serve a side dish of finger lengths of **brown bread and butter sandwiches**.

Jellied Beef Consommé or Bouillon

Master recipe—called Pot-au-Feu when the soup is served hot with the vegetables.

To obtain a really good consommé or *pot-au-feu*, both time and patience are required. Hours of slow and steady simmering will alone extract all the substance from the meat, bones, and vegetables. The French peasant deliberately refrains from skimming the soup, in the belief that it is more nourishing, and all good French cooks, be they men, women, or chefs, recognize the importance of this, but carefully skim the scum from the top of the boiling liquid before adding the vegetables, which give the indefinable flavor to the bouillon. The meat should never be cut up but left whole and secured with kitchen string.

For a very good French consommé, place in a special earthenware dip [clay] pot, with a cover, the following ingredients:

For each quart of cold—remember, cold—**water**, take 1 pound of **beef** from the shin and ½ pound of **beef bone**, cracked, and add **salt** to taste.

Place the pot on the fire, add the meat and bones, well washed and sponged, then pour in the water. Very, very gently bring to a boil. Let it "smile" until the scum rises to the surface, which should be skimmed carefully with the perforated ladle if a clear consommé is desired.

When the scum has all disappeared, then and only then add: 2 large **carrots**, scraped and cut into quarters, lengthwise, then into inch pieces; 1 white **turnip**, peeled quartered; 1 large **onion**, peeled, left whole, and stuck with 2 or 3 cloves, heads removed; 1 small clove of **garlic** (optional), left whole after being peeled; 1 small **parsnip**, peeled, quartered, core removed; 1 **bouquet garni** (composed of 1 large or 2 small **bay leaves**; 2 small **leeks**, cleaned, quartered lengthwise, carefully washed in several changes of cold water; 2 small

parsley roots, scraped or 8 sprigs of **fresh parsley**; 1 sprig of **thyme**, all tied up with kitchen thread; 10 **whole peppercorns**, gently bruised).

If the meat is to be served at table, as it is in most French households, it is usually removed after 3 hours of simmering; only the bones and vegetables are left in. If its sole purpose is the actual making of a rich consommé which will congeal by itself, the meat is left in to the end of the simmering. Besides the shin of the beef, the *menagéres* also use the thin flank and brisket, if the meat is to be served at table as *boeuf bouilli*, or boiled beef.

Caution. Never use game, mutton, pork, lamb, or ham for making real *pot-au-feu*, or consommé. Only beef will do, to the exclusion of any other kind of meat, including poultry or poultry trimmings, as when these are added, it is called *Petite Marmite*, with, of course, the marrow bones of the beef.

The vegetables and seasonings being added, gradually bring to the boiling point. Cover, and allow to simmer, to "smile" imperceptibly for 3½ to 4 hours, and without disturbing. The longer it smiles, the better the consommé or bouillon will be.

When done, strain the stock through a cloth wrung out in cold water. Keep the stock (until now, it is called stock and not consommé) in a cold place, and the next day remove carefully any fat that has set on the surface.

Following these simple directions, you will have a real consommé in natural jelly without the addition of any gelatin.

If the stock is not sufficiently strong enough to jell well, you may add a little unflavored granulated gelatin softened in a little cold water. But it is preferable to omit the gelatin, as the fine delicate flavor of a jellied or hot consommé is a little impaired, unless red, white, sherry, Madeira, or port wine is added.

Important: In these jellied consommés or soups, it is recommended that the jellied soup be not too stiff, and before serving, it should be beaten with a fork.

16. Russian Borshch (Potage Bortsch à la Russe) (Chapter 3)

Mary Henderson, *Paris Embassy Cookbook*

4 pt. stock	3 Tbs. of tomato purée or ¼ lb. fresh tomatoes
3 to 4 beets	2 Tbs. vinegar
½ lb. fresh cabbage	1 Tbs. sugar
2 carrots	1 to 2 bay leaves
1 parsnip	Sprig of dill
2 stalks celery	Sprig of parsley
¼ lb. boiled ham (optional)	1½ tsp. salt,
6 frankfurter sausages (optional)	½ tsp. pepper
1 large onion	¼ pt. sour cream

Prepare stock. Clean and shred beets, carrots, parsnip, celery, and the onion. Cut the root vegetables into slices first, then into little "matchsticks." The decorative appearance of the vegetables in borshch is very important.

Put vegetables into a saucepan, add tomatoes or tomato purée, sugar and enough stock, with a little fat (if the stock has no fat, add 1 to 2 tablespoons butter) to cover the vegetables. Simmer for 15 to 20 minutes, stirring from time to time and adding stock or water to prevent sticking. Add shredded cabbage, mix well, and simmer another 15 to 20 minutes. Pour in all the stock, add salt and pepper to taste, bay leaf, 1 tablespoon vinegar, and simmer until the vegetables are done. Potatoes may be put in the borshch—whole if they are small, cut into chips if large. When the borshch is ready and just before serving, a few slices of boiled ham or sausage (frankfurter) can be added to it.

To give it its characteristic, attractive color, keep one beet for last minute use. Rub it through a fine grater, cover with a cupful of stock, bring to the boil, simmer for 2 to 3 minutes with a teaspoon of vinegar and strain the liquid into the borshch. Sprinkle with finely chopped parsley and dill. Add the sour cream and serve. Mushroom patties or buckwheat croutons may accompany the borshch.

17. British Royal Navy Bean Borsch
(Chapter 3)
Master Chef, Internet

1 c. dry navy beans
2½ lbs. lean beef
½ lb. slab bacon
10 c. cold water
1 bay leaf
½ c. sour cream
8 whole peppercorns
2 cloves garlic
2 Tbs. dried parsley
1 carrot
1 celery stalk
1 large red onion
1 tsp. salt (optional)

8 beets for soup
2 small beets
2 c. shredded green cabbage
2 large sliced leeks
3 medium potatoes, cut into eighths
1 can (1 lb. 13 oz.) tomatoes
1 Tbs. tomato paste
3 Tbs. red wine vinegar
4 Tbs. sugar
1 lb. kielbasa (optional)
2 Tbs. flour
1 Tbs. butter

Cover beans with water and allow to soak overnight. Cook until tender; drain; set aside. Place beef, bacon, and water in large soup pot; bring to a boil. Skim fat from surface. Add bay leaf, peppercorns, garlic, parsley, carrot, celery, onion, and salt. Cover and simmer over low heat for about 1½ hours. Scrub beets for soup and cook in boiling water until tender, about 45 minutes; drain and discard water; cool. Peel and cut each beet into eighths. Scrub small beets; grate; cover with water to soak. Remove meat from soup; set aside.

Strain soup into another pot and add cooked beets, cabbage, leeks, potatoes, tomatoes, tomato paste, vinegar, sugar, beef, and bacon. Bring to a boil and simmer 45 minutes.

Cut kielbasa into chunks and add with navy beans to soup. Simmer 20 minutes more. Mix flour and butter together to form a paste. Stir into soup to thicken slightly.

Strain raw beets, saving liquid and discarding beets. Add beet liquid to soup. Additional sugar or vinegar may be added for a sweeter or more sour flavor.

Slice meat and arrange in individual soup bowls. Pour hot soup with vegetables over meat. Garnish each serving with a dollop of sour cream, if desired.

18. Nina Nicolaief's Maritime Borsch (Flotski Borsch) (Chapter 3)

8 Servings

1½-2 lbs. bacon or ham bones; enough water to cover bones and make a broth	4 Tbs. butter or ¼ c. oil for frying
1 onion	1 c. tomato puree
1 small cabbage	Pepper
3 medium-sized carrots	Salt to taste
1 small parsnip	2 bay leaves
3 medium-sized raw beetroots	1-1½ lbs. frankfurter sausages
3 medium-sized potatoes	½ c. sour cream

Make a broth by putting ham bones or bacon into saucepan, cover with cold water, bring to the boil, turn down the heat and simmer for 45 minutes.

Prepare vegetables. Peel and chop onion, cut cabbage into 2-inch chunks, peel carrots, parsnip, beetroots and potato and cut into slices, not strips.

Fry the vegetables in butter or oil and add to the broth when it is ready and has been strained. Add tomato puree and simmer for 30 minutes; 10 minutes before finishing add bay leaves.

Just before serving cut the frankfurters into 1-inch pieces, fry lightly, add to soup, and boil up for 3 minutes. Serve with or without sour cream.

Taste this soup carefully before adding salt since broth from the bacon or ham bones will already be salty.

19. Lake Smelt Borsch—Pskov Style (Chapter 3)
Internet

1-2 beets
11 oz. sauerkraut
6 oz. dried smelt
1 carrot
2 onions
1-2 Tbs. tomato paste

2-3 Tbs. butter
1 Tbs. sugar
1½ Tbs. vinegar
4 tsp. sour cream
Greenery, to taste

Cook the dried smelt and strain the broth. Prepare a borsch with sauerkraut in that broth. When serving, add the smelts, sour cream, and sprinkle with minced greenery.

20. Galina's Ukrainian Borsch (Chapter 3)
Galina Chernykh
Time: 47-56 minutes

Serves 4

1 qt. good beef or chicken stock
10 oz. boiled beef or chicken cut in bite-size pieces
1 medium beet, diced
1 onion, diced
2 new potatoes, peeled and cubed
1 c. cabbage, chopped
3 carrots, peeled and diced
1 Tbs. sunflower, peanut, or other vegetable oil
2 Tbs. tomato paste

2 bay leaves
2 tsp. vinegar
1 tsp. sugar
2 garlic cloves, minced
1 small piece (size of a quarter) fatback/salt pork, minced
2 Tbs. sour cream
To taste: salt, ground pepper, fresh minced or dried dill
Garlic rolls (Pampushki)

Sauté beets in part of oil with sugar and vinegar. Add onion and carrots and rest of oil. Cook till onion is translucent and carrots begin to soften. Add tomato paste. Mix. Take off heat.

Bring stock to boil. Add cooked meat and potatoes to stock. Cook until potatoes are almost done (12-20 minutes). Add chopped cabbage and simmer for another 5 to 7 minutes. Add the sautéed ingredients and simmer for another 10 minutes.

While soup is simmering blend minced garlic, salt, and minced fatback (if using salt pork, omit additional salt) in a mortar with a pestle until you get a paste.

Bring soup to boil. Add dill, bay leaf, and pepper. Add garlic-fatback paste. Cover pot. Take off heat and let stand for 20 minutes.

Serve with sour cream and *pampushki* (garlic rolls) on the side.

21. CHRISTMAS EVE BORSCH (WIGILIA BARSZCZ) (CHAPTER 4)

International Institute of Youngstown

1 celeriac root
1 parsley root
2 carrots
2 leeks
1 onion
4 red beets, peeled and sliced thinly
10 grains of whole black pepper
2 grains of allspice
Small piece of bay leaf

2-3 oz. of dried boletus mushroom
Soured beet juice
Clove garlic, crushed
Salt, to taste
Sugar, to taste
Water
Dry red wine or lemon juice (optional)

Combine the first nine ingredients and prepare a concentrated vegetable stock. In a separate pot cook the dried mushrooms in two cups of water until soft. Pour vegetable stock through a sieve into another pot. Pour mushroom stock through a sieve into the pot with the vegetable stock. **Save the mushrooms.** Add soured beet juice to pot. Heat until boiling and then remove from heat.

If the soup is not a bright red color, correct the color with the juice of a fresh beet grated to a pulp. To balance the taste use salt and sugar. To sharpen the taste, add a wineglass of dry red wine or lemon juice. Do not use vinegar. Fifteen minutes before serving, add a crushed garlic clove to the soup.

The traditional Christmas Eve borsch is served with *uszkas* [stuffed ravioli shaped like "pigs ears"]. The cooked *uszkas* are placed in the soup tureen and then covered with the hot borsch; 6-8 *uszkas* are served per person. *Pierozki* that are filled with mushroom filling can also be served with the borsch. The Christmas Eve borsch becomes a traditional Easter borsch with the addition of meat to the vegetable stock.

22. SEA CABBAGE (KELP) BORSCH (CHAPTER 4)

Holy Presentation of Mary Female Monastery

7 oz. marinated kelp*	*2 tsp. sugar*
4 beets	*1 tsp. salt*
2 potatoes	*3-4 whole cloves*
1 carrot	*1 bay leaf*
1 parsley root	*Vinegar, to taste*
2 onions	*1½ qt. water, plus water for marinade*
1½ oz. tomato puree	*To taste dill, chives, or parsley*

Thaw or rehydrate kelp. Rinse thoroughly. Place kelp in cooking water. Boil up water, lower the heat and simmer for 20 to 30 minutes. Drain kelp but reserve the liquid. Let kelp cool. Slice noodle-width.

For marinade: Combine sugar, salt, cloves, bay leaf and water. Boil it up for 2 to 3 minutes, then let cool. Place sliced kelp in water and marinate from 8 to 10 hours. Pour off marinade.

Braise julienned beet, carrot, parsley root and onion with the addition of tomato puree. After 20 to 30 minutes add marinated kelp and continue braising.

Boil up the reserved kelp water and add potato. Ten to 15 minutes before potato is done add the braised vegetables and correct the seasoning. When serving, add minced greenery.

*[If there is no fresh seaweed readily available, Japanese dried *kombu* can be bought at any Asian market, or better supermarket.]

23. BEET BORSCH WITH BARLEY (CHAPTER 4)
(Lenten Memorial Borsch)
Holy Presentation of Mary Female Monastery

1½ qt. water	1 onion
3 potatoes	2 Tbs. green peas
¼ head cabbage	3 Tbs. tomato sauce
⅓ c. barley	3 bay leaves
1 carrot	Dried potherbs*, dill, parsley, pepper and salt to taste
1 large beet	2 cloves garlic, ground to a paste

*Potherbs can include celery, kale, Swiss chard, spinach, etc.

Lower into boiling water diced potatoes, shredded cabbage, and barley. Cook for 25 minutes. In the meantime cut beet and carrot into matchstick-sized pieces and sauté in oil; add finely diced onion and tomato sauce. Braise, stirring frequently. Add to the borsch bay leaves, potherbs, dill, parsley, salt and pepper. Lower the braised ingredients into the borsch and cook for another 15 minutes, having added the green peas. When the borsch is ready add garlic, cover with a lid, and immediately remove from heat. Let it stand for 30 minutes. Serve the borsch with garlic rolls (*pampushki*).

24. COLD BORSCH WITH FARMER'S CHEESE (CHAPTER 4)
L.I. Nichiporovich, *Orthodox Culinary*

¾ lb. beets	1½ qt. water
½ lb. cabbage	2 Tbs. parsley, minced
½ lb. squash or pumpkin	Salt to taste
6 oz. farmer's cheese	

Julienne the squash, beets and cabbage, add the **beet vinegar** and water and braise for 5 to 6 minutes. Put the farmer's cheese through a food mill and dilute it with boiled cold water. Add the vegetables, salt, sour cream and sprinkle with minced parsley.

25. BORSCH WITH RADISH (CHAPTER 4)
L.I. Nichiporovich, *Orthodox Culinary*

¾ lb. beets	¾ c. sweet cream
½ lb. cabbage	2 qt. water
½ lb. radish with leaves	1 tsp. minced dill
2 Tbs. minced onion	Salt to taste

Julienne the beets, cabbage, radish, add minced onion and a small amount of boiling water and braise 6 to 8 minutes. Cool, add salt, add the remaining boiled cold water, and cream. When serving, sprinkle with minced radish leaves and dill.

26. SMOLENSK BORSCH (CHAPTER 4)
Spasso-Avramiev Monastery (Smolensk)

14 to 28 oz. beef	1 Tbs. lemon juice
14 oz. pork	1 wine glass of Madeira or Port
2 onions	Dried bay leaf, allspice, salt
3 beets	To taste: fresh parsley, dill

Make a broth with the beef and pork, adding onion, bay leaf, allspice, and salt. Bake the beets, peel them, slice them like noodles, place in soup tureen, add lemon juice, Madeira or Port, add meat that has been cut to bite-size pieces; if desired, add minced parsley and dill, add the broth, and serve.

27. BORSCH WITH TURNIP (CHAPTER 4)
Orthodox Cuisine

1 turnip with greens	4 tablespoons sour cream
1 beet with greens	1½-2 qt. water
3 tomatoes	

Separate the turnip and beet from the leaves. Peel them and grate on the large grating slots. Wash the leaves and chop. Slice the tomatoes into wedges. Mix the beet with the tomatoes. Add the turnip and beet leaves into boiling water and return to a boil, add the beet with tomatoes. Bring to boil, cool, and add the grated turnip and sour cream.

28. TURKISH BORSCH (CHAPTER 4)
Martha Rose Shuleman, *Gourmet Vegetarian Feasts*
6 Servings

1 Tbs. safflower oil
2 onions, chopped
3 cloves garlic, chopped
1 lb. beets, chopped
2 c. shredded cabbage
2 stalks celery, sliced
2 medium potatoes, diced
1 medium green or red pepper, chopped

2 qt. water or vegetable stock
½ lb. tomatoes, chopped
Salt and pepper, to taste
½ tsp. dill seeds, crushed
Juice of one lemon
3 Tbs. chopped fresh dill
1 c. plain yogurt

Heat oil in a large heavy-bottomed soup pot and add onion and garlic. Sauté for a couple of minutes and then add the other vegetables, dill seeds, salt and pepper. Cook, stirring, for another minute; then add water or stock. Bring to a boil, cover, reduce heat and cook for 1 hour.

Remove 2 cups from pot and puree in a blender or put through a food mill. Return to soup pot. Correct seasonings. Serve, topping each bowl with a spoonful of yogurt.

29. COSSACK HAPPINESS LENTEN BORSCH (CHAPTER 4)
Elizabeth Vereya Old Ritualist Community
3-5 Servings

1 large or 2 medium beets
⅓ small head cabbage
1 carrot
1 onion
3½ oz. tomato paste
1 Tbs. catsup

3-4 prunes
3-4 slices lemon
3-4 cloves garlic
1 Tbs. sugar
2 Tbs. sunflower oil
Salt, pepper

Cossack Happiness Lenten Borsch (Continued)

Fill pot with water and bring to boil. Wash the beet(s) and peel. Place beet(s) in the pot whole, adding a tablespoon of vinegar; and cook on medium for 30 minutes. In the meantime peel the carrot and onion. Cut the carrot into long thin "straws" (cut the carrot in half, then cut each half lengthwise into 3-5 slices, then julienne each slice) and slice the onion fine. Add sunflower oil to a heated frying pan and add the carrots and onion. Brown slightly and salt generously (because the water was not salted in the beginning); add a few tablespoons of "broth" from the pot, cover, and stew until the vegetables reach a medium softness (7-9 minutes).

Take the beet(s) from the pot (the water should have acquired a red color). Slice the cabbage into "straws" and place it in the pot, adding to that the carrots and onion. Add pepper; if necessary, add salt. Cook on low, approximately 35-45 minutes (until the cabbage is almost done).

Cut beet(s) into "straws" (like the carrots). Add sunflower oil to a heated frying pan, add beet(s); adding 1 tablespoon of vinegar, brown lightly until the beets acquire a "caramelized" look, add tomato paste, catsup and sugar, cook the mix on medium heat until it begins to gurgle. Place the resulting product into the pot and cook it for another 30 minutes. Five minutes before finishing cooking, add prunes that have been cut in half and round slices of lemon. Serve the borsch with garlic and bread.

30. Molokan Borscht (Chapter 4)
From the Internet

1½ c. thinly sliced potatoes
1 c. thinly sliced beets
4 c. vegetable stock or water
2 Tbs. butter
1½ c. chopped onions
1 tsp. caraway seed (optional)
2 tsp. salt
1 celery stalk, chopped
1 large carrot, sliced

3 c. coarsely chopped red cabbage
Black pepper to taste
¼ tsp. fresh dill weed
1 Tbs. cider vinegar
1 Tbs. honey
1 c. tomato puree
Sour cream, for topping
Chopped tomatoes, for garnish

Place sliced potatoes and beets in a medium saucepan over high heat; cover with stock, and boil until vegetables are tender. Remove potatoes and beets with a slotted spoon, and reserve stock.

Melt butter in a large skillet over medium heat. Stir in onions, caraway seeds, and salt; cook until onions become soft and translucent. Then stir in celery, carrots, and cabbage. Mix in reserved stock; cook, covered, until all vegetables are tender, about 10 minutes.

Add potatoes and beets to the skillet. Season with black pepper and dill weed. Stir in cider vinegar, honey, and tomato puree. Cover, reduce heat to medium low, simmer at least 30 minutes.

Serve topped with sour cream, extra dill weed, and chopped fresh tomatoes.

31. Lil's Doukhobor Borsch (Chapter 4)
From Lil Potapoff via her daughter Michelle Barabonoff

4 qt. water
1 medium beet, peeled and quartered
6 medium red potatoes, peeled (3 quartered, 3 diced)
3 carrots (1 grated, 2 diced)
3 onions (2 diced, 1 for processing)
2 green peppers (1 diced, 1 for processing)
1 small head of cabbage, finely shredded

1-1¼ qt. stewed tomatoes or whole canned tomatoes
2 c. 10% cream (often called "half and half" cream)
¾ c. butter
6 Tbs. fresh dill
3+ Tbs. salt
To taste, black pepper

Prepare veggies. Peel and quarter the beet and 3 of the potatoes. Dice the 3 remaining potatoes, 2 carrots, 1 onion, and 1 green pepper. Grate or finely shred the cabbage. Set the vegetables aside.

Place the quartered beet and the quartered potatoes in a large soup pot with 4 quarts of water. Bring to boil, reduce heat slightly and let cook until vegetables are tender. Once the potatoes are tender, remove from the water and mash in a large bowl. Add ¼ cup of butter, 4 tablespoons dill, 1 tablespoon salt, and black pepper to taste. Warm the cream, and stir into the potatoes. (Make sure to warm the cream first, otherwise it may curdle when added to the potatoes.) Set this mixture aside.

When the beet is tender, remove from the water and set aside to cool. Grate the beet once it has cooled. Leave the water in the pot; this is the base for the borscht.

In a separate pot, pour in the stewed tomatoes. Add 1 grated carrot and the grated beet.

Place 1 onion and 1 green pepper in a food processor until coarsely processed. (Alternatively, you can chop them finely by hand.) Add this onion and green pepper to the tomatoes, along with ¼ cup of butter, 1 tablespoon salt, and pepper to taste. Cook over medium-high heat until vegetables are tender. Stir this tomato mixture into the bowl with the mashed potatoes and cream, then set aside.

Add the diced potatoes and carrots to the soup pot with the water which had the beets and potatoes in it. Cook over medium-high until vegetables are tender. Once tender, put the temperature to low until all of the other ingredients have been added.

Place the shredded cabbage in a separate pot with water. Boil the cabbage until tender. (Boiling the cabbage first gets rid of the gas-producing components in the cabbage; you can skip this step, but you may regret it later.) Strain the cabbage and place in a pan with 2 tablespoon of butter; fry lightly. Add to the soup pot.

Melt 2 tablespoon of butter in a frying pan and sauté the diced onion and green pepper over medium-high heat. Once tender, add to the soup pot.

Slowly add the potato, cream, and tomato mixture to the soup pot. You can use a cup or a large ladle to transfer it without making splashes.

Add 2 tablespoon of dill, and salt and pepper to taste.

Now all the ingredients should be in the soup pot. Bring to a boil and then remove from the heat. You're finished! Leave the borscht uncovered in the pot.

Borscht can be served immediately, or be left for a while to allow flavors to go through.

Extra borscht should be placed in glass jars while it is still hot. To seal the jars, make sure the mouth of the jar is clean; boil sealable lids in water, then place the lids on the jars. Once the jars have sealed the borscht will keep in the fridge for up to 3 months. Storing borscht in this way is a much better alternative to freezing, as freezing will alter the consistency.

Serve borscht with fluffy fresh bread (generously buttered, of course) and slices of cheddar cheese on the side. You can let the cheese slices melt in the borscht for added tastiness! This may not be the traditional way of eating it, but it's how it was served in my childhood, so I can't have it any other way.

Read more at: http://flowingfree.org/how-to-make-borscht-doukhobor-style/#ixzz2I6lsqiyl

32. KOMMST BORSCHT (CABBAGE SOUP) (CHAPTER 4)
Bob Strong Menno Recipe Project
http://www.mts.net/~bobstron/recipes.html

2 lb. soup bones
2 qt. water (cold)
2 carrots, cut
1 medium head cabbage, chopped fine
2 medium potatoes, diced
1 medium onion, chopped

1 tsp. salt
1-2 hot chili or cayenne peppers, or ground cayenne to taste (optional)
1/2 tsp. star aniseed (optional)
10 allspice (whole)
1 small bay leaf

Small bunch dill - fresh or frozen
1½ Tbs. parsley chopped (add more if using dried parsley)
1½ c. tomatoes

2 Tbs. tomato paste (optional)
1 can tomato soup (optional)
½ c. heavy cream (optional)
Dash of pepper

Boil the soup bones for at least 1½ hours. (They can be oven-roasted first for a richer flavor.) Add enough water to yield 2 quarts stock. Add all vegetables except tomatoes and add seasonings. Cook until vegetables are done. Add tomatoes and bring just to a boil.

Options: Just before serving, add cream, or let each person add cream to taste. White vinegar can be added to individual taste. Instead of using a soup bone, use ham or farmer sausage to make the broth. Chop up the ham or sausage and leave it in the borscht if you like. More veggies can also be added.

Like most soups, this tastes better the day after it was made because all the flavors blend more. This soup also freezes well - just microwave for a quick meal.

33. ZHURE KOMMSTBORSCHT (SAUERKRAUT SOUP) (CHAPTER 4)

Bob Strong Menno Recipe Project

1 lb. smoked farmer sausage (or kielbasa), casing left on
6 Tbs. chopped onion
¼ c. flour
½ tsp. dried thyme, rounded
½ tsp. pepper

3 c. milk
1 c. half and half
8 oz. can sauerkraut, with juice
1½ Tbs. lemon juice
2 Tbs. finely chopped fresh parsley

Chop the sausage coarsely by hand or in a food processor. Transfer the chopped sausage and onion to a deep pan and sauté over medium heat until the sausage is lightly browned, about 8 minutes. On a small plate or wax paper, combine the flour, thyme, and pepper. Add to the sausage and brown all together until the mixture bubbles up, about 5 minutes. Add the milk and half and half all at once, and cook, stirring until the mixture again bubbles up, about 5 minutes. Add the sauerkraut and its juice and bring to a boil;

the mixture will continue to thicken. Taste for tartness, and add lemon juice if desired. Add parsley, and serve at once.

34. CELERY BORSCH (CHAPTER 5)
Ekaterina Pavlovna Avdeeva, *Handbook of the Experienced Russian Mistress*

Make a broth out of three pounds of **beef** with **root vegetables** (if you want, you can add a pound of **ham**), strain. Take a pound of **celery**, separate the leaves, add the stalks to boiling **water**, cook till they are soft; drain and chop finely. Take **shortening** and ⅔ cup **flour**, fry lightly, then add the celery, then dilute with **sour cream**, and then the broth; boil up while stirring. Add two minced celery leaves and **dill**.

35. BAKED BEET BORSCH WITH WINE (CHAPTER 5)
Elena Molokhovets, *A Gift to Young Housewives*

1-2 lbs. beets	5-10 allspice seeds
2 onions	½ lemon
1-2 bay leaves	1-1½ glass French white
1-2 lbs. beef	wine or Sauterne
1 lb. pork	Parsley greens and dill

Cook a clear broth as usual, out of 1-2 pounds of beef and 1 pound of fresh young pork loin with two onions and aromatics. Remove meat. Strain. Cut pork fine and reserve.

Bake a good-quality red beet; slice finely and place it in a soup cup; squeeze out lemon juice; pour in French white wine or Sauterne, place finely cut cooked pork in soup cup, and dill. Dilute with hot strained broth, having previously placed into the soup dish ½ glass of juice from a grated beet that has been strained and boiled-up once.

36. BORSCH WITH FRIED HERRING (LENTEN DISH) (CHAPTER 5)
Elena Molokhovets, *A Gift to Young Housewives*

Make a broth from **potherbs**, a bundle of **greens**, and 2 oz. of **dried boletus**; strain. Bake a pound of **beets**, peel them, slice them, place them in a pot and cover with the strained broth. Add separately boiled-up **beet pickle liquid**, add **salt, pepper, parsley, dill**, and finely diced mushrooms. Heat it to the utmost level and add 2 to 3 **Scottish herring** [any fresh herring will be an adequate substitute], which were previously soaked, cleaned, flattened, cut into pieces, dredged in **flour**, and fried in **oil**. Add them to the borsch, allowing it to come to boil once.

37. "LITTLE RUSSIAN" BORSCH AS IT IS PREPARED IN PETERSBURG
(MALOROSSIISKI BORSCH, KAK EGO PRINYATO PRIGOTOVLYAT V PETERBURGE) (CHAPTER 5)
Pelagia Pavlovna Aleksandra-Ignateva, *A Guide to the Fundamentals of Culinary Arts*

For five servings:
2 lbs. meat
½ lb. root vegetables (turnips, carrots, celery, parsley root, etc.)
1 lb. beets
½ lb. fresh cabbage [blanched and shredded]
2 Tbs. flour
3.5 oz. butter

Bouquet garni
Salt, pepper, bay leaf- according to taste
2½-3 qt. water
5 to 10 tomatoes or 3.5 oz. tomato puree
½ lb. ham bone with meat
3.5 oz. pork fatback
5 Tbs. sour cream

[Following the cooking directions there is an extensive description of ingredients and techniques.]

Cooking Directions. Having chopped the plate meat [rib plate meat will give the best flavor but brisket or even chuck are good substitutes] into serving pieces, being sure that each piece has some bone, begin preparing the broth. After removing the foam, add salt and *bouquet garni*, peel the beets and root vegetables.

Then, in a separate deep cooking utensil, sauté the finely sliced onion in browned butter, add to it beets that have been sliced into thin, small ribbons; if there is not enough butter for sautéing the onion then add another piece. Permitting the beets to sauté a bit (do not cover the utensil), add the root vegetables (turnip, carrot, and celery) sliced in the same manner as the beets, and add two soup spoons of broth. When the vegetables are cooked through and completely done, add the blanched and finely shredded fresh cabbage, and when the latter has sautéed a bit, mix in some wheat flour (as substitute for a separately prepared roux), and following that, fry a bit more.

One to one-and-half hours before serving, when all the added ingredients become ready, strain the broth into them, rinse the stock meat in hot water and lower it also into the soup and, without covering, continue cooking the borsch on a low flame. At this time one ought to add the blanched ham bone, a few allspice berries, and the bay leaf. One half-hour before dinner, place into the pot tomatoes that have been cut into wedges. Ten minutes before serving, one can add separately cooked beans, and after removing the extra fat, add to the borsch the minced fatback with sour cream.

Right before serving add to the borsch the coloring, which is prepared as follows: grate a peeled beet on a grater, cover it with broth, let stand for 15-20 minutes, then place the pot with the coloring on the stove and, without covering it, bring to boil a few times, then strain it through a strainer and put the resulting decoction into the borsch.

One half-hour before serving one can also add to the borsch duck meat, roasted and cut into serving pieces, which will add a very pleasant taste to the borsch. One can also add pieces of peeled tart apples and separately cooked potato, cut into wedges. The potato is added immediately before serving because if it is added earlier it can overcook and lose its shape.

Explanations and notes:

Meat: For borsch one needs to buy beef plate, the type of meat that most fully meets the requirements of a good borsch. Borsch must be 1) full flavored, 2) fat, and 3) contain a decent amount of meat. Plate meat contains short bones with a large amount of red marrow, which yields a good broth. As with any kind of meat that is selected for soup-making, plate needs to be chopped into small pieces; in addition, one needs to take care that this rule is observed so that the bones are cut and their juices go to the broth.

Beets: For "Little Russian" borsch the beets need to be braised in the fat skimmed from the broth or in other fat, but not cooked in water because, in the latter case, they lose color and part of the flavor to the water; braised, they preserve color and flavor. To maintain color the beet needs to be braised in an open pan.

Ham: The bone of the smoked ham, which is to be added to the borsch, needs to be blanched, so that it would be easier to remove the accumulated soot. [Obviously, this instruction is not needed in modern mostly chemical curing processes.] The ham can be cut into servings pieces before cooking, but that also can be done right before serving the borsch.

Tomatoes: Tomatoes are an essential ingredient in "Little Russian" borsch. Tomato seeds need to be removed before cooking because they can make the borsch bitter. Tomatoes need to be placed in the borsch at least ½ hour before table service; otherwise, they won't have enough time to cook to softness and to give up their flavor to the borsch. If there are no fresh tomatoes one can add canned tomato puree. If one places many tomatoes in the borsch then there is no need to add vinegar because the tomatoes add a pleasant tartness to the borsch.

Pork fatback: With a knife one should finely chop the pork fatback on a board and then mix it in a cup with a good-quality sour cream; thin it a bit with some borsch liquid. Having added it to the borsch it needs to be boiled up. Pork fatback, as well as fresh tomatoes, are necessary ingredients in "Little Russian" borsch, no matter if it is prepared in the "Great" or "Little" Russian manner.

One uses fresh or salted fatback, but not smoked. After adding fatback the borsch should not be boiled long; otherwise, it will develop a smell of lard.

Coloring: Since the beets are cooked in the borsch for a long time (otherwise they will not transmit their flavor) and because of that lose their color, it is necessary to color the borsch before serving.

The coloring should be cooked in an enameled or other nonreactive pot; reactive cooking pots will give the broth a bluish tint and also change its flavor. The coloring needs to be strained so that the grated beets do not get into the borsch. Many people color their borsch with raw grated beets, but one should not do that because the raw beets will give the borsch a raw flavor.

Vinegar. Normally, one does not add vinegar to a "Little Russian" (Ukrainian) borsch, especially if the borsch is made from rye **kvas**, and a sufficient quantity of tomatoes are added.

38. *Ukrainian Borsch (Chapter 6)*
The Book of Tasty and Healthy Food

Serves 5

For 18 oz. of meat:	*1 parsley root*
14 oz. cabbage	*1 carrot*
14 oz. potato	*1 celeriac*
9 oz. beets	*1 onion*
½ c. tomato puree	*¾ oz. fatback*
½ c. sour cream	*1 Tbs. butter*

Cook and strain **meat broth***. Take peeled root vegetables and beets and julienne into straw-like pieces. Braise the beets in fat, tomato puree, vinegar and some broth (you can also add bread or beet kvas). Lightly fry the julienned roots and onion in butter, mix with fried flour (roux), add broth and bring to boil.

Place potatoes, cut into large cubes, chopped cabbage, braised beets, and **salt** into the prepared broth and cook for 10 to 15 minutes. Then add the fried roots with flour roux, **bay leaf, allspice, pepper** and continue cooking until done.

Add to the borsch fatback ground together with **garlic**, **tomatoes** cut into wedges, and bring to boil. After that let the borsch rest for 15 to 20 minutes.

When serving borsch add sour cream to each dish and sprinkle with minced **parsley greens**.

***Meat Stock or Broth**: You can use any homemade or canned meat stock for this borsch recipe. If using canned broth be very careful about using additional salt.

39. BORSCH WITH PICKLED BEETS (CHAPTER 6)
(To counteract obesity)
The Book of Tasty and Healthy Food

Make a broth out of **meat** and **water**. Peel the **beets** and slice into noodle shape, cover with 1 to 2 quarts cold water, adding **vinegar** and letting it steep for 2 hours, changing the water twice during this time.

Julienne the peeled **onion, parsley root,** and **celery root** and fry it in **butter**, together with **tomatoes**. Add the **pickled beets**, ½ cup broth and braise covered for 20 minutes; add shredded cabbage and the braised beets to the strained broth and cook till done. Serve with a piece of meat, sour cream and minced parsley or dill.

40. LENTEN BORSCH WITH FISH (CHAPTER 6)
Cookery–(1999 Reprint) recipe from Ekaterina Pavlovna Avdeeva's
Handbook of the Experienced Russian Mistress

Cook a few pieces of **salted** and **fresh sturgeon** [Acipencer] and **white sturgeon** [Huso huso] or any fat fish. Chop **fermented beets** with the addition of fresh **beet greens**, dredge in **flour** and fry. Cut into a number of strips a head of **cabbage**; fry in **shortening** and add all that to the cooking fish. If it is not sour enough, add some **kvas**. Add to this brew fried **crucian carps**, or other fish; pieces of **carrots**; **onion**; **salt** and **pepper** to taste.

41. UKRAINIAN BORSCH (CHAPTER 6)
Cookery, Ukrainian Section

Per serving:

2 oz. meat	.1 oz. wheat flour
2.2 oz. beets	.18 oz. bacon
2.8 oz. fresh cabbage	.36 oz. lard
3.5 oz. potato	.18 oz. sugar
.71 ounce carrots	.18 oz. vinegar (3 percent acidity)
.3 oz. parsley root	.36 oz. bell pepper
.53 oz. onion	.53 oz. sour cream
.05 oz. garlic	To taste, pepper, bay leaf, parsley and
.71 oz. tomato puree	dill greenery

Braise beets that have been cut into straw-like pieces with salt, vinegar, lard, tomato puree and sugar. Julienne carrots and parsley root into straw-like pieces, cut onions into wedges, and sauté everything together.

Place potato and cabbage into boiling broth* and cook for 10 to 15 minutes, adding the sautéed root vegetables, flour, bell pepper, and spices. Before serving add garlic that has been ground together with parsley and dill greens and bacon and then let it rest; add to the borsch sour cream and minced greens.

*Meat Stock or Broth: You can use any homemade or canned meat stock for these borsch recipes. If using canned broth use additional salt very sparingly.

42. KIEV (KYIV) BORSCH WITH CHICKEN (CHAPTER 6)
Z. Klinovetska, *Dishes and Drinks in the Ukraine*

Dilute three cups of **beet kvas** and one cup of **rye kvas** with **water**, and add **salt**. Add two pounds of **beef**, one **chicken**, and cook. When the chicken is done remove it, add three large sliced **beets**, diced **carrots, parsley roots, celeriac**, and fresh young **beans**. When the beets are done add a pound of **lamb or mutton**. At that time add a **cabbage** cut into six or more pieces, and some potatoes. Finish off with **fatback** ground with **onion, parsley**

greens, and **dill**. When everything is done add strained **tomato** which was braised with fat or oil (or pickled tomato in winter), and whiten the soup with **sour cream**. Cut up the meat and chicken and place them in bowls. The borsch is served with Easter eggs (hard boiled eggs), *pirozhki*, or kasha.

Note: The lamb or mutton should be taken from the rib area. One can add one large or two small cucumber pickles when the broth begins to boil. This will add a nice flavor, but then you should reduce the amount of beet and rye kvas.

43. Byelorussian Borshch with String Beans and Apples (Chapter 6)
Byelorussian Cuisine

Make stock* with **beef** and **ham bones** and separately boil the **string beans**. Shred the **carrots, parsley** and **onion**, sauté, add **tomato paste** and keep over a low fire for another 10 minutes. Drop cubed **potatoes** into the ready stock. After bringing to a boil add shredded boiled **beet** roots sautéed with tomato paste with some stock mixed in. Five minutes before the borshch is done add **apples** cut into quarters and with their skins and core removed, boiled string beans, **salt, sugar** and **vinegar**. Serve together with **meat, sausages** and **sour cream**.

*****Bone Stock**. Chop up the **bones** and wash in cold water. Veal and pork bones are better browned in the oven. Place in a saucepan, pour cold **water** over the bones, cover the saucepan with a lid and rapidly bring to a boil. Remove the scum with a skimmer and let simmer for 2 to 3 hours. Partially skim the fat on the surface, leaving intact a very thin layer which helps retain the savory matter in the stock. Forty to 60 minutes before the stock is done, add the **salt**, browned **carrots** and **onion**s, **parsley** and **celery**. Strain the stock.

44. ONION BORSCH (LENTEN) (CHAPTER 6)
1000 Antique Recipes

20 onions
3½ oz. oil
4 carrots
¼ head of soured cabbage (sauerkraut) [1-2 lbs.]
1 Tbs. flour

Spices to taste
Sugar to taste
Vinegar or kvas to taste
Greens (dill, parsley, celery leaves)

Chop onion and fry in oil. Add sufficient amount of water; add pieces of carrot and ¼ head of soured cabbage and spices and cook everything well, adding water as it evaporates. Thicken with flour; add sugar and vinegar to taste. Sprinkle with minced greens.

Serve separately croutons made from sweet-sour dark bread or some kind of thick porridge.

45. "AUTUMN-WINTER" TURKEY BORSCH WITH FETTUCCINI (CHAPTER 6)
William Pokhlebkin, Internet

1-2 turkey legs (remove half of the turkey meat for another use)
1-2 beets
1 small carrot
2 fettuccini "nests"
2 onions
2 tomatoes
½ small cabbage
1 potato
½ small parsley root

½ bunch of green parsley
½ inch slice fresh, or small piece of dried, ginger
Small piece of raw celery root
1-2 tsp. apple vinegar
1-2 bay leaves
6 black peppercorns
½ head of garlic
½ bunch of dill greens
Knife tip of red pepper (cayenne)

Introductory note: 1) Remove skin, tendons, and knee joints from the turkey legs. Leave meat on that is harder to remove. Chop the bones in half, across. 2) The fettuccine noodle is wound into a ball or "nest." There are two kinds of fettuccine: plain noodle and spinach. This borsch is particularly good if both kinds are used. Substituting other kinds of noodle products is not recommended.

In a deep pot containing 1½ quarts of boiling water place turkey bones from two turkey legs. After five minutes of cooking, covered, and after removing the foam from the top, add the ginger, parsley and celery roots. Make sure that the ginger is thoroughly peeled and that only the insides of the root go into the soup. Before adding the vegetables one can cook with the lid covering the pot, but afterwards leave the pot uncovered.

Prepare (slice) the vegetables and place them in the soup in the following order: beets, cabbage, potato, onion, and tomato (as you ready each) and continue cooking, uncovered, over medium heat.

After removing any additional cooking foam add the bay leaves, and the black and red pepper. After the vegetables have cooked, correct the salt and add the vinegar, particularly if there has been a loss of the bright-red color of the borsch. (Practically speaking, if the cooking was done properly—uncovered—there should not be any color change; in that case, add the vinegar at the end of the cooking time).

Raise the heat, and when rapid boiling resumes, add the fettuccine; after 3-5 minutes of boiling, lower the heat to medium.

After 10 minutes, check the fettuccine for doneness, add the vinegar, add the greenery (minced parsley, dill, garlic). Take off flame and allow it to rest for 3-4 minutes, covered. Serve immediately.

46. Borsht *(Chapter 7)*
Florence Kreisler Greenbaum, *The International Jewish Cookbook*

Take some **red beetroots**, wash thoroughly and peel, and then boil in a moderate quantity of **water** from two to three hours over a slow fire, by which time a strong red liquor should have been obtained. Strain off the liquor, adding **lemon juice**, **sugar**, and **salt** to taste, and when it has cooled a little, stir in sufficient **yolks of eggs** to slightly thicken it. May be used either cold or hot. In the latter case a little homemade beef stock may be added to the beet soup.

If after straining off the soup the remaining beetroot is not too much boiled away, it may be chopped fine with a little **onion**,

vinegar, and **drippings**, flavored with **pepper** and **salt**, and used as a vegetable.

47. CABBAGE BORSCH (CHAPTER 7)
Jennie Grossinger, *The Art of Jewish Cooking*

Serves 6-8

2 lbs. brisket	2 tsp. salt
Beef bones	½ tsp. pepper
2 qt. water	¼ c. lemon juice
2 onions, diced	2 Tbs. sugar
3 c. canned tomatoes	3 Tbs. seedless raisins
3 lbs. cabbage, coarsely shredded	

Combine the brisket, bones and water in a deep saucepan. Bring to boil and skim. Add the onions and tomatoes. Cover and cook over low heat one hour. Add the cabbage, salt and pepper. Cook one hour. Stir in the lemon juice, sugar and raisins. Cook 20 minutes. Taste and season if necessary. Serve with meat as garnish.

48. BORSCH WITH FRESH CABBAGE (CHAPTER 7)
Ukrainian-English Cookbook

Prepare normal **kvas** [beet kvas is assumed, but not mandatory]. Steam **cabbage**, shred it, and cook it with the kvas. You can add **garlic** ground together with **fatback** and **parsley** greens or **sour cream**.

49. LENTEN BORSCH II (CHAPTER 8)
Sophia Nabokova, *The Complete Russian Cookbook*

Serves 8-10

Water	2 parsnips, thinly sliced
3-4 oz. dried mushrooms (boletus), or 1½ lb. domestic fresh mushrooms, thinly sliced	2 leeks, chopped
	2 stalks celery, chopped
	7 medium beets, peeled and sliced
2 carrots, thinly sliced	¼ lb. Greek or Italian black salted

olives, or ¼ lb. canned domestic black olives, pitted and halved
1 lb. shredded cabbage
5 medium potatoes, cut in bite-sized pieces
5 tomatoes
2 Tbs. tomato paste

2 medium onions, chopped
Vegetable oil
2 Tbs. lemon juice
1 clove minced garlic
2 Tbs. minced dill
Salt and pepper

If dried mushrooms are used, wash them and soak in two cups water for 2 hours; then bring to a boil and simmer 15 minutes. Remove mushrooms, reserve their liquid; slice them and sauté in 2 tablespoons oil for five minutes. Put mushrooms, their cooking liquid, and 8 cups water in a soup pot. If using fresh mushrooms, sauté them in 2 tablespoons oil and then add to soup pot with ten cups water. Add carrots, parsnips, leeks, and celery. Bring to a boil and simmer ½ hour, partially covered. Sauté beets in 2 tablespoons oil, stirring constantly until shiny. Add to soup and simmer along with olives, cabbage, potatoes, tomatoes and tomato paste for 45 minutes. Sauté onions in 1 tablespoon oil until golden brown and add to soup. Simmer for 5 minutes. Add lemon juice, garlic, dill, and salt and pepper to taste

50. PASSOVER RUSSELL BORSCHT (FERMENTED BEETS) (CHAPTER 8)
The Molly Goldberg Jewish Cookbook

8 c. russell*
2 c. water
3 beets, peeled and grated
2 onions, finely chopped
3 lbs. beef (brisket or plate flank)

Beef bones
2 tsp. salt
2 Tbs. lemon juice
3 eggs

Combine the *russell*, water, beets, onion, beef, and beef bones in a saucepan. Bring to a boil. Skim the top. Cover and cook over medium heat for 2 hours. Add salt, sugar, and lemon juice. Cook for

30 minutes. Correct seasoning, adding a little more sugar or lemon juice. Remove the bones and slice the meat.

Beat the eggs in a bowl. Gradually add 3 cups of the soup, beating constantly to prevent curdling [temper].

Serve with pieces of meat in the soup, or serve the meat as a separate dish.

*Note: *Russell*, fermented beet juice, is prepared by the following method. About 12 very large **beets** should be peeled and cut into quarters. Place them in a large pot or stone jug and fill with 5 quarts of water. Use a container that will permit the 5 quarts of **water** to come within an inch of the top. Put the top on the container at a very slight angle and cover with thin cloth to keep out the dust. After 10 days, remove the cover and skim the surface carefully; stir well and re-cover. The *russell* should be ready for use 2 to 3 weeks later. The liquid should be completely clear, bright red, and have a winelike aroma. If preferred, *russell* may be purchased in bottles.

51. Moscow Borsch (Chapter 8)
(Moskovskiy borsch)
Nina Nicolaieff, *Cooking with Nina*

8-10 Servings

A few beef bones
A 5 lbs. piece of fresh beef brisket
1 clove garlic
2 bay leaves
1 Tbs. salt
Pepper
Enough water to cover meat and bones
1 onion
1 small cabbage
3 medium-sized carrots
1 small parsnip
3 medium-sized raw beets
3 medium-sized potatoes
1 c. tomato puree
1 lb. bacon, in one piece
1 Tbs. oil or bacon fat
1 extra raw beet
½ c. sour cream

Wash the meat and bones; put them into a big saucepan with garlic, bay leaves, salt and pepper. Cover with water, bring to boil and simmer for 1 hour.

Meanwhile prepare vegetables. Peel and chop the onion, cut the cabbage into 2-inch chunks, peel and cut carrots, parsnip, and the 3 medium-sized beets into thin strips, 2 inches long. Peel and cut potatoes into ½-inch dice.

When the meat and bones have simmered for 1 hour take them from the pan and strain the liquid through a fine sieve. Put the meat back into the saucepan, add the strained broth and the cabbage.

Cut the bacon into ¼-inch dice and fry in oil or bacon fat for a few minutes. Add the cut-up vegetables, all except potato, and fry for 10 minutes with the bacon. Add to the broth, bring to the boil, then simmer for 45-55 minutes. Add tomato puree and diced potatoes and simmer another 20-25 minutes.

Taste carefully for salt, since bacon is salty.

To give the extra deep red color, the additional beet is shredded and fried quickly for 5 minutes, then added to the borsch just before serving. One teaspoonful of sour cream is put into each plate. [Moscow borsch is traditionally served with Vatrushki.]

52. THE RED SOUP (CHAPTER 8)
Betty Grant's Russian Cookbook

1½ lbs. soup meat	Fresh dill
1 large onion	9½ c. water
2 carrots	Salt

Rinse meat. Put 2 tablespoons water in saucepan so as not to have it dry. Add vegetables and cook on slow fire, turning meat constantly and stirring vegetables so that they do not burn, but turn a little brown. Add tablespoon water as needed in cooking. When the meat forms a very thin blanket over it and the bones have sheen, add 9½ cups water. Turn on high flame and boil 3 times, each time pushing aside and removing the skin.

Add salt to taste and cook on a slow fire. Remove excessive fat. Half hour before serving, remove meat and put soup through a sieve. Cook again for another half hour. When ready, serve with blinchikee [blinchiki].

53. PRINCESS ALEXANDRA'S QUICK BORSCH (CHAPTER 8)
Princess Alexandra Kropotkin-*The Best of Russian Cooking*

2 cans consommé
1 can bouillon
1 c. water
½ tsp. vinegar
½ tsp. Worcestershire sauce
½ c. juice from canned beets
½ c. sour cream

Mix the consommé with bouillon and water. Bring to a boil. Add the vinegar, Worcestershire sauce, and beet juice. Put in a pinch of sugar if the beet juice doesn't give the soup a slightly sweet taste. But be very careful not to over-sweeten! Stir the sour cream smooth with 1 tablespoon of water, and then add the consommé, a little at a time. Reheat but do not boil.

When you serve this borsch cold, do not add the sour cream before chilling. Instead, put the sour cream in just before serving. This borsch should always be sprinkled with finely chopped parsley when you serve it either hot or cold.

54. RUSSIAN BORSCH (CHAPTER 8)
Kyra Petrovskaya *Russian Cookbook*

9-10 c. boiling water
2½ lbs. soup meat (with a marrow bone if possible. You may also use a left-over bone from a baked ham instead of the meat.)
2 large carrots, sliced
2 stalks of celery with leaves, sliced
2 onions, sliced
2 bay leaves
8-10 medium-sized beets
½ head of medium-sized cabbage, sliced not too fine
8 peppercorns (or freshly ground pepper)
1 Tbs. vinegar
2 c. raw, cut tomatoes (skinned), or drained canned tomatoes

6 Tbs. butter *Salt according to taste*
1 Tbs. flour
Sour cream to heap in plates when soup is served

Put the washed meat in a large pot with nine cups of boiling water. (Later on you may add the tenth cup of boiling water if the borsch looks too thick. My grandmother always kept a kettle of boiling water on the stove when she was cooking, just in case she needed to add a little water to something, or to melt something over it quickly. Or simply to have a cup of tea while she was cooking!)

Add bay leaves, cabbage, peppercorns and start simmering.

Brown slightly, in 2 tablespoons of butter, cut onions, carrots and celery and add them to the simmering soup.

Peel beets, cut in strips, and simmer them in another pot with vinegar, the rest of the butter, and just enough water to cover the beets.

When the beets are tender, add flour, mix well, and combine with the meat stock, which should be ready whenever the meat becomes tender (it takes less time, of course, if you have used a left-over ham bone). Add cut tomatoes to the meat stock and boil quickly for 8-10 minutes. Take the meat out, cut into serving pieces and return them to the soup.

Or save the meat for the next day's main dish of cold boiled meat with horseradish. Serve borsch very hot in large soup plates or bowls with one tablespoon or more of sour cream for each serving.

55. BORSCH (NO MEAT) (CHAPTER 9)
Mrs. Helen Kozyreff, *Just a Pinch of Russian*

Make several days in advance for *Sviata Vecheria* (Christmas Eve).

½ c. butter
1 Tbs. flour
Parsley (chopped)
Celery (chopped)
1 carrot (diced)
1 turnip (diced)
Salt and pepper
1 tsp. paprika

1 large potato (cut up)
½ head medium cabbage (cut up)
1 (12 oz.) can vegetable juice
1 (8½ oz.) can cut beets
½ can tomato paste (small)
3 to 4 qt. water

    Boil water in pot. Meantime, put butter in large pot (3-4 quart). When butter melts, add flour and fry a little. Add parsley, celery, carrot, and turnip. Let stand on low flame a few minutes. Add paprika. Add just enough hot water to cover the mixture. Add cut potatoes, cabbage, and more hot water till pot is ¾ full. Simmer 20-25 minutes. Add vegetable juice, tomato paste, and beets. Add more water if needed. Add salt and pepper to taste. Simmer 10 minutes. Refrigerate for a day or two before serving. Plan on approximately one hour to prepare.

56. POSNEE [LENTEN] BORSCH (VEGETARIAN)
Mary J. Bogdanov, *Recipes of San Francisco Russian Molokans*

    This meatless soup can be made the day before you plan to serve it, and is enough for a fairly large crowd.
    Start with a soup kettle large enough to hold two gallons of **water**. Bring water to a boil and add **salt** to taste, ½ cup each of baby **lima beans** and **green split peas**. Cook for ½ hour. After this add 4 small peeled **potatoes** (whole). Take out and mash after borsch is done. Meanwhile grate or chop: 1 **onion**, 2 **leeks**, 1 small **cabbage**, some fresh **spinach**, 3 **carrots**, 1 **bell pepper**, 1 **zucchini**, ½ bunch **parsley**, chopped fresh **mushrooms** (about ½ lb.) and 1 quart whole **tomatoes** (mashed). Add to soup and continue to cook another hour

or until done. Remove from heat and add ½ cube **butter** and ½ pint ½ 'n ½ (**half and half**). DO NOT BOIL ANYMORE. For garnish add 3 hardboiled **eggs**, mashed with a fork.

57. BORSCH FOR A LARGE CHURCH DINNER (300-350)
Mrs. Anna A. Seminoff, *Recipes of San Francisco Russian Molokans*

250 lbs. meat	*3 large bottles ketchup*
10 to 15 lbs. soup bones	*10 lbs. carrots*
Salt	*4 bunches beets*
2 lbs. large limas, dried	*9 lbs. zucchini*
3 lbs. lentils (split peas)	*6 lbs. string beans*
30 lbs. potatoes	*6 bunches parsley*
8 lbs. onions	*6 lbs. spinach*
9 large cans tomatoes	*15 heads cabbage*
8 cans tomato paste	*8 large bunches celery*
24 cans tomato sauce	

Prepare the fresh vegetables 1 or 2 days in advance. Wash and chop fine: carrots, beets, zucchini, string beans, parsley, spinach, cabbage and celery. Cabbage may be chopped in little larger pieces. Mix and put into large enamel or stainless kettles, sprinkling lightly with salt. Cover and set in a cool place until needed.

On the night before the dinner: wash the bones thoroughly and soak in salted water overnight.

On the day of the dinner, start at 4:30 AM, turning on all stoves. Wash meat in salted warm water thoroughly, repeating 3 times. Trim off all dark spots, prints, and blood clots. Rinse and wash the bones.

Divide meat and bones evenly into 4 large commercial kettles. Add enough hot water to cover meat to about ¾ full of kettle.

Bring to a boil and when it has boiled 15 minutes, add 5 to 6 wooden spoons salt to each kettle (about ¼ cup). Cover partially and let boil 2 to 2½ hours.

While meat is boiling:
1. Pour boiling water over limas and boil for 20 minutes. Strain and remove skins.

2. Peel and boil potatoes in salted water until done. Strain, mash and keep hot. Reserve some potato water.
3. Wash lentils; add to the skinned limas. Add reserved potato water to cover and cook over low heat until done.
4. Bring all tomatoes, tomato sauce, tomato paste and ketchup to a slow boil; set aside. Keep hot until needed.
5. Chop the onions finely and set aside.

Time now about 7:45 AM. Take out meat; trim away all bones and large pieces of fat. Lay aside; do not throw away. Cut meat into about 2" pieces.

Put meat in layers into commercial size roasting pans. Sprinkle each layer with salt. Do not fill more than ⅔ full. Cover the meat with the bones that were trimmed off. Some of the fat may be added, but not too much. Pour about 2 cups broth over meat to each kettle. Put in oven at 300° and bake for 2 hours.

Strain the broth through clean cloth. Repeat 2 times, wash the kettles after each time. The cloth must be rinsed in hot water. DO NOT USE SOAP.

Divide broth into four kettles for the borsch, making each kettle about ¾ full. Bring to a boil. To each kettle: equally divide the prepared vegetables. When it has boiled about 15 minutes, add equally the mashed potatoes, lentils, tomatoes and onions. Bring to a boil, and let boil for 15 minutes longer or until vegetables are done. Shut off heat and cover.

This will serve 300-350 people, about 5 rows of tables.

58. OLD COUNTRY BORSCH (CHAPTER 9)
Mrs. Josephine Racine *Just a Pinch of Russian*

6 c. water
1 lb. beef brisket (cut into 6 pieces)
2 medium onions (sliced)
2 stalks celery (cut into 1-inch lengths)
4 medium beets (pared and sliced) or
  1 can of beets
6 chicken or beef bouillon cubes
  (optional)
4 carrots (pared and thinly sliced)
1 small head of cabbage (cut into
  pieces)
1 bay leaf
Salt (use sparingly if using bouillon)

2 beets (coarsely grated) or
  1 can of beets
1 (6 oz.) can tomato paste
2 Tbs. vinegar

1 Tbs. sugar
½ pint sour cream

    Place water, brisket, onions, celery, beets, carrots, cabbage, bay leaf, bouillon cubes, and salt in a large kettle. Cover and simmer 1 or 2 hours or until beef is fork tender.

    Add beets, tomato paste, vinegar, sugar, and more salt, if needed. Cover and simmer for 15 to 20 minutes. Serve topped with sour cream.

59. SARA'S BORSCH (CHAPTER 9)
Sara Kharitonoff, *Joys of Ethnic Cooking*

2 lbs. shank meat, with bone
5 medium potatoes, peeled and cut into
  fourths
2 medium onions, diced
1 can tomatoes
¼ can tomato paste

3 medium beets, peeled and cut into
  strips
4 carrots, peeled and diced
5 pieces of celery, diced
½ to ¾ medium head of cabbage,
  shredded

    Use a large pot filled ¾ full of water. Boil the meat until tender. Add the potatoes and cook until well done. Remove and mash potatoes and return to the pot. Remove the meat, take the meat from the bones and cut into small pieces. (I use scissors to cut this meat.) Add tomatoes, tomato paste and onions to pot and cook about 30 minutes. Next, add the beets and cook for about 10 minutes. Add carrots; cook for another 5 minutes. Add celery, cook slightly. Return meat to the pot and perhaps a little beef bouillon will give more flavor. Lastly, add the cabbage and turn off the heat. Since my husband likes sauerkraut in his borsch, I cut up a cup or so, depending on how sour you may like it, and add at the same time as the cabbage. Also, I add chopped parsley and dill (if I can obtain it!). Serve with sour cream.

60. MATUSHKA GIZETTI'S BORSHT (CHAPTER 9)
Matushka M. Gizetti, *Joys of Ethnic Cooking*
[Matushka—literally "Little Mother," is an honorific title given to priests' wives]

1 qt. Manischewitz Borsht	Chopped green onions
¾ qt. buttermilk	Chopped dill
2 hardboiled eggs, chopped	Ice cubes
1 large cucumber sliced	

Combine the first 4 ingredients and chill well. To serve, dish up in chilled bowls, garnish with chopped onions and dill. Add an ice cube to each bowl.

61. VEGETARIAN BORSCH (CHAPTER 9)
Ukrainian-American Cultural Society, *Indy Cooks International*

Dried mushrooms, 1 oz. [boletus are assumed]	4 Tbs. vegetable oil
2 onions, chopped	1 carrot, sliced or chopped
1-2 stalks celery, sliced	3 medium beets, julienned
1 potato, diced	½ c. cooked beans (white, lima, butter, green)
2 c. shredded cabbage	1 clove garlic, minced
¾ c. tomatoes or juice	1 bay leaf
9-12 c. water	Fresh or dried dill weed
Salt and pepper to taste	

Boil mushrooms in 3 cups water until tender, remove and chop into pieces. Save liquid. Sauté onions, carrots, garlic and celery in oil until tender. Add beets (and chopped beet tops, if available), potato, beans, cabbage, tomatoes or juice, mushrooms and mushroom stock. Simmer 40 minutes until vegetables are tender; add salt and pepper. (Lemon juice or vinegar may also be added for tartness.) Add dill near end of cooking time.

62. BORSHCH (CHAPTER 9)
Mrs. Harold Eisenberg, *The War-Time Edition Russian Cook Book for American Homes*

Serves 4 - 6

1 lb. soup meat	½ Tbs. vinegar
5 c. water	2 Tbs. butter or table fat
Soup greens	½ Tbs. flour
1 onion, sliced	1 c. strained canned or chopped
Salt and pepper	fresh tomatoes
5 beets	Sour cream

Wash meat; place in large pot with 5 cups boiling water, soup greens, sliced onion, salt and pepper to taste. Simmer until meat is tender. Peel and cube beets, put in separate pot, add vinegar and butter or fat, cover with water and cook until tender. Add flour to beets, mix well, then add to strained meat stock. Add tomatoes and boil for 10 minutes. Serve 1 tablespoon sour cream with each portion.

63. MEATLESS BORSHCH (CHAPTER 9)
Concord Committee, Russian War Relief
The War-Time Edition Russian Cook Book for American Homes

Serves 8-12

2 large carrots	*1 small cabbage*
2 large beets	*2 medium potatoes*
2 large onions	*½ lb. mushrooms*
Table oil	*6 tomatoes*
12 c. water	*1 small can ripe olives*
Salt	*Sour cream (optional)*

Slice or cut into strips the carrots, beets, and onions. Brown lightly in enough table oil to keep from burning but not enough to make vegetables greasy. Add water and 1 tablespoon of salt; bring to boil. Simmer 1 hour. Cut cabbage in 8 pieces, cube potatoes, and slice mushrooms; brown in table oil. Add to soup with quartered tomatoes. If desired, add pitted olives. Simmer another hour, or longer if beets have not lost their color. Add more salt to taste, skim off fat. Serve with spoonful of sour cream in each plate, if desired.

64. BORSHCH UKRAINSKY (UKRAINIAN STYLE BEET SOUP) (CHAPTER 10)

Time-Life

Serves 6 to 8

- 4 medium tomatoes
- 4 Tbs. butter
- 1 c. finely chopped onions
- 2 cloves garlic, peeled and finely chopped
- 1 lb. beets, trimmed of leaves and coarsely grated
- ½ celery root, peeled and coarsely grated
- 1 parsley root, peeled and coarsely grated
- 1 parsnip, peeled and coarsely grated
- ½ tsp. sugar
- ¼ c. red wine vinegar
- 1 Tbs. salt
- 2 qt. beef stock, fresh or canned
- 1 lb. boiling potatoes, peeled and cut into 1½-inch chunks
- 1 lb. cabbage, cored and coarsely shredded
- 1 lb. boiled brisket or 1 lb. boiled ham, cut into 1-inch chunks
- 3 Tbs. finely chopped parsley
- ½ pint sour cream

Drop the tomatoes into boiling water for 15 seconds. Run them under cold water and peel them. Cut out the stem and then slice them crosswise. Squeeze the halves gently to remove the juices and seeds and then chop them coarsely and set aside. In a heavy 10- to 12-inch skillet or casserole, melt the butter over moderate heat. Add the onions and garlic and, stirring frequently, cook 6 to 8 minutes, or until they are soft and lightly colored. Stir in the beets, celery root, parsley root, parsnip, half the tomatoes, the sugar, vinegar, salt, and 1½ cups of stock. Bring to boil over high heat, then partially cover the pot and lower the heat. Simmer for 40 minutes.

Meanwhile, pour the remaining stock into a 6- to 8-quart casserole and add the potatoes and cabbage. Bring to boil, then simmer, partially covered, for 20 minutes, or until the potatoes are tender but not falling apart. When the vegetable mixture has cooked its allotted time, add it to the casserole with the remaining tomatoes and the meat. Simmer, partially covered, for 10 to 15 minutes, until the borshch is heated. Taste for seasoning. Pour into a tureen, sprinkle with parsley and serve accompanied by sour cream.

Beef Stock

1 lb. fresh lean brisket of beef
5 lbs. beef marrow bones, cracked
1 large onion, peeled and quartered
1 large carrot, scraped

2 celery tops, 6 sprigs of parsley and 2 bay leaves tied together
1 Tbs. salt

In a heavy 6- to 8-quart pot, bring the pound of beef, beef bones and 4 quarts of water to boil over high heat, skimming off any foam and scum that rises to the surface. Add the onion, carrot, tied greens and salt, partially cover the pot and reduce the heat to low. Simmer 1-1½ hours, or until the meat is tender but not falling apart. Remove the meat from the pot with a slotted spoon, cut it into small dice and set the dice aside. Strain soup through a fine sieve set over a large bowl, discarding the bones and greens. Continue to simmer the stock and, with a large spoon, skim off and discard as much of the surface fat as you can.

65. POTAGE BORTSCH (BORSCHT SOUP) (CHAPTER 10)
The Escoffier Cookbook and Guide to the Fine Art of Cookery

Cut in julienne fashion the heads of **two leeks, one carrot, half a root of parsley,** the white part of a **stalk of celery** and **four ounces of beets**; cook gently in **butter**. Moisten with one quart of white **consommé** and two or three tablespoons of the **juice of grated beets**; and a small bunch of **fennel** and sweet **marjoram**, two pounds of moderately fat **brisket of beef**, and half of a **partly roasted duck**; set to cook gently for four hours.

When about to serve, cut the beef into large dice, and cut the duck into smaller slices; finish the soup with one quarter pint of **beet juice**, extracted from grated beets pressed through linen, and a little blanched and chopped fennel and **parsley**. Put the beef dice and sliced duck into the soup, with twelve grilled **chipolatas** (Italian or Polish sausage).

Serve separately a sauceboat of **sour cream**.

NB: The chipolatas may be replaced by very small patties made with duck forcemeat, which should be served separately.

66. BLENDER BORSCH II
Irma S. Rombauer, *Joy of Cooking*

Combine in a blender:

2 c. tomato juice	3 Tbs. finely grated onion
2 c. canned beets	1 drop hot pepper sauce
3 dill pickles	1 clove minced garlic

Chill the soup and serve garnished with four thinly sliced hard-boiled eggs, cultured sour cream: fresh chopped dill or fennel

67. RUSSIAN CABBAGE BORSCHT
Molly Katzen, *The New Moosewood Cookbook*

1½ c. thinly sliced potatoes	3 c. coarsely chopped red cabbage
1 c. thinly sliced beets	Black pepper to taste
4 c. vegetable stock or water	¼ tsp. fresh dill weed
2 Tbs. butter	1 Tbs. cider vinegar
1½ c. chopped onions	1 Tbs. honey
1 tsp. caraway seed (optional)	1 c. tomato puree
2 tsp. salt	Sour cream, for topping
1 celery stalk, chopped	Chopped tomatoes, for garnish
1 large carrot, sliced	

Place sliced potatoes and beets in a medium saucepan over high heat; cover with stock, and boil until vegetables are tender. Remove potatoes and beets with a slotted spoon, and reserve stock.

Melt butter in a large skillet over medium heat. Stir in onions, caraway seeds, and salt; cook until onions become soft and translucent. Then stir in celery, carrots, and cabbage. Mix in stock; cook, covered, until all vegetables are tender, about 10 minutes.

Add potatoes and beets to the skillet. Season with black pepper and dill weed. Stir in cider vinegar, honey, and tomato puree. Cover, reduce heat to medium low, and simmer at least 30 minutes.

Serve topped with sour cream, extra dill weed, and chopped fresh tomatoes.

68. BARSZCZ-POLAND (CHAPTER 10)
Could I Have Your Recipe? An International Cookbook

Chicken or beef broth	*Sugar*
2 bunches of beets	*1 or 2 lemons*
Salt	*"Pig's ears"*

This is a soup which all Polish people love and it is a special favorite after a hunt.

The foundation is a broth made from chicken or beef. Take two bunches of beets, clean them well but do not remove skin. Put the beets in hot water until they can be pierced with a fork. Empty water, peel cooked beets and cut up into small pieces. To the beets add salt and sugar to taste and the juice of 1 or 2 lemons. Let stand for five minutes, then pour boiling broth over beets and cook for another 5 minutes. Pass vegetable through a sieve and a beautiful red soup is made. Serve soup hot with "pig's ears."

69. CHLODNIK (SOUPE FROIDE AUX BETTERAVES)-FRANCE KHOLODNIK (COLD SOUP MADE FROM BEETS)-FRANCE (CHAPTER 10)
Madame G. Frumkin, *Could I Have Your Recipe? An International Cookbook*

2-3 betteraves, en fin tranches (avec tiges si assez jeunes)	*Quelques petits radis*
	1 concombre
Sel	*Ciboulette*
Sucre	*L'aneth, haché*
Vinaigre, filet	*2 oeufs durs, coupés en morceaux*

2 deciliters de créme aigre

Peler et couper 2-3 betteraves en fines tranches, avec les tiges (si assez jeunes), et les cuire dans assez d'eau, à laquelle on ajoute un peu de sel, de sucre, et un filet de vinaigre. Mettre au frais.

Disposer au fond de la soupière: 1 concombre coupé en fines tranches, quelques petis radis coupés en fin tranches, de la ciboulette et de l'aneth (dill) haché, 2 oeufs durs coupés en morceaux. Verser là-dessus un peu de betteraves cuites et autant de leur jus qu'il faut pour qu'il y ait assez de soupe et y mélanger environs 2 déciliters de crème aigre. Servir bien froid.

70. BORSCH (CHAPTER 10)
Cook Book/Libro de cocina Recipes Collected by The American Women's Literary Club, Lima, Perú.

Beef stock
5 large uncooked beets, finely shredded
Butter
Salt and pepper to taste
Sour cream

Melt butter in saucepan and when hot add the beets and cook for 20 minutes. Stir in a little hot stock and when this is absorbed, stir in more stock. Repeat the process until the beets are tender. Pour the contents of the pan into another saucepan containing hot stock and simmer gently for ½ hour. Strain. To serve, sprinkle with finely chopped uncooked beets and sour cream.

71. BORSCHT (CHAPTER 10)
101 Recipes of Old Russia

1 small head cabbage
1 medium onion
1 16 oz. can stewed tomatoes
1 16 oz. can sliced beets
Beef or vegetable broth
Salt and pepper
Oil

Core and slice the cabbage thinly. Dice the onion. Sauté onion and cabbage in oil until they become a little soft. Chop the tomatoes and add to cabbage and onions. Cut beets into thin strips (julienne). Add beets and beet juice to above mixture. Add enough beef broth (or vegetable broth) to bring to the consistency of soup. Salt to taste. Simmer for about an hour.

Sliced cooked carrots and diced cooked potatoes may also be included in the borscht. For borscht that contains meat, add shredded cooked beef or chicken.

Serve with sour cream

72. BORSCHT WITH SOUR CREAM (CHAPTER 10)
Mrs. Chris Cummins, Indianapolis Collects & Cooks

Serves 8

1 c. canned beets with juice	1 tsp. monosodium glutamate
1 medium onion, chopped	1 tsp. liquid Maggi
3 kosher dill pickles, chopped	1 drop Tabasco
½ c. dill pickle juice	1 can tomato juice:(46 oz.)
1 Tbs. dill weed	1 c. julienne beets
Ground black pepper	6 hard-cooked eggs, sliced
1 tsp. garlic salt	Yogurt or sour cream

Place first ten ingredients in blender or food processor bowl. Blend on medium speed until finely pureed. Place in serving bowl, and add the tomato juice, julienne beets, and sliced eggs. Stir and chill several hours. Serve with scoops of plain yogurt or sour cream.

Sprinkle with chopped parsley or dill, and serve with a thin rye crisp. May be strained and served over ice with vodka as a Bloody Russian. Keeps beautifully in the refrigerator.

73. BORSCH (CHAPTER 10)
Patricia Morgan Swenson, *Dining with the Daughters*

This is for a one-dish meal, to be served hot in large soup bowls.

2 lbs. beef (2-inch cubes)	*1 can sliced beets, including juice*
2 qt. water	*1 lb. fresh cabbage, shredded*
1 large onion, cut up	*Salt and pepper (a pinch and a sprinkling)*
1 large can of tomatoes	*1 large container cultured sour cream*
2 lemons, juiced	
1 c. sugar	

In large stew pot put beef, water, onion, and salt and pepper. Bring to boil, stir, reduce heat, and simmer for ½ hour. Add canned tomatoes, lemon juice, sugar and cabbage, stir well, and simmer for at least 2 more hours. Add canned beets in their juice, stir again, and cook for another ½ hour. (Beets may be added earlier, but they are apt to become very pale in color after long cooking). A container of sour cream may be put on the table for each to serve himself. An attractive accompaniment is dark rye bread.

74. ALAN GINSBERG'S COLD SUMMER BORSCHT (CHAPTER 11)
Alan Ginsberg, Internet

12 beets with stems and leaves, cleaned and chopped	*Garnishes:*
Water to make gallon of beet juice	*Sour cream*
Lemon to taste	*Hot boiled potato (one per serving)*
Sugar to taste	*Salad greens: sliced scallions, tomatoes, lettuce, cucumbers, and radishes*
Salt to taste	

Boil beets and beet greenery in slightly salted water for an hour or more until beets are soft and you have a bright red soup. Add sugar and lemon to make soup sweet-sour like lemonade. Chill. Put hot boiled potato in dish; add chilled soup. Have garnishes and sour cream available at table.

75. SIBERIAN BORSCH (CHAPTER 11)
Internet

2 large beets	1 onion
5-7½ oz. fresh cabbage or a bit less sauerkraut	1 Tbs. tomato paste
	1 Tbs. rendered pork lard
1 potato	3-4 cloves garlic
3 Tbs. green beans	1 Tbs. sugar
1 carrot	1.5 qt. stock or water

For meatballs:
8-10 oz. beef	1 egg
½ onion	2 Tbs. water or milk
1 Tbs. butter	

Rinse the green beans, cover with cold water and cook on low heat in a covered pot until the beans soften.

Add to boiling stock or water the cubed potato and cook for 10-15 minutes. Add the braised beet and vegetables.

Take meat for the meatballs and run it twice through the meat grinder together with the onion that was softened in fat.

Add to the meat a raw egg, salt and pepper, cold water and mix everything well. Roll small meatballs from mix. Add the meatballs to the borsch 10 to 15 minutes before end of cooking.

Five to 10 minutes before the end of cooking add the cooked beans, sugar, spices, garlic ground with salt.

76. COSSACK BORSCH RECIPE (CHAPTER 11)
For an 80-gallon kettle to feed 600 monastic brethren
or 100 Cossacks

58 gals. water	*55 lbs. tomatoes*
14 lbs. carrots	*4 lbs. garlic*
16½ lbs. onions	*7 lbs. red pepper*
6½ lbs. parsley root	*4 lbs. salt fatback*
11 lbs. beets	*110 lbs. pork meat with bone*
40 lbs. cabbage	*6½ lbs. parsley and dill greens*
40 lbs. potatoes	*1 oz. bay leaf; to taste salt, pepper*

Place on a trivet a kettle of respectable size; pour in 22 buckets of clean spring water. Place wood under the kettle, light it with a candle, and cook the water until it boils. While the water is cooking cut up a small boar or pig. As a last resort, take about 100 pounds of cooled pork meat with bone, cut the meat into decent pieces, and lower it into the boiling water.

Cut a pound of fatback into small dice and render it in a separate small kettle. This will create a kettleful of boiling fat.

Thoroughly wash half a bucket of fresh garden beets and, after washing and peeling them, julienne them and place them in the boiling fat. Add a bit of water to the beets, let them cook, and when they are ready, add them to the large kettle. Cook the beets until they lose their color.

Wash and peel two buckets of potatoes; cut them into large pieces and pour them into the kettle. Let them cook till half-done.

In the meantime, take three one-pound pieces of fatback, dice them small, and render them in the small kettle. Cut up one bucket of peeled onions, two buckets of tomatoes, and place into the boiling fat, together with small diced parsley root. Shred a sufficient quantity of white cabbage and place it in the large kettle. Add the contents of the small kettle to it also. Peel, mince, and pound together with fatback, four large handfuls of garlic. Cut the red pepper into rings and chop the parsley and dill. Add all that, along with some bay leaves, to the large kettle right before it begins to boil. Salt and pepper to taste (the cook's and brethren's taste). Wait till it boils up and then remove the wood. Ladle the finished borsch into bowls, with an obligatory spoonful of cool sour cream.

77. Green Borscht Mama Regine's Way-Bessarabian Stew with Lamb Ribs (Chapter 11)

Dorrie-*Spaces and Spices*
http://spacesandspices-dorrie.blogspot.com/2011/09/grunborscht-nach-mama-regine.html

Serves 4-6

2 lbs. lamb ribs, roughly cut into pieces	1 bunch dill, chopped, save some to garnish the soup
2 qt. water	
Salt	1 bunch sorrel, chopped
1 onion, chopped	1 bunch of scallions, chopped
1 tsp. black peppercorns	1 bunch of beet leaves, chopped
Some allspice berries	1 bunch of parsley, chopped
Some juniper berries	1 Tbs. butter
4 bay leaves	2 tsp. hot paprika powder
1 clove garlic, minced	1 tsp. ground chilies
1 carrot, diced or grated	Some sugar
More salt, black pepper, freshly ground	Some vinegar
4¼ oz. rice	1 egg yolk
6 potatoes, peeled and coarsely diced	8 oz sou.r cream
	Some oil for frying

Put ribs in a pot and add water, bring to a boil. Add onion and spices (peppercorns, allspice, juniper berries, bay leaves, garlic, carrot): and cook on low heat for about 90 minutes.

Remove ribs and let them drain. Remove bay leaves. Blend soup using a blender.

Add rice and potatoes and simmer for 20 more minutes. Now, heat butter in a big pot and fry chopped dill, sorrel, chopped, scallions, chopped, beet leaves, and parsley for about 2 minutes. Add to the soup and allow it to simmer for some minutes.

Add salt, black pepper, hot paprika powder and ground chili and season to taste. Balance with enough vinegar and sugar to "round" the taste.

Whisk egg yolk and sour cream. Take the soup from the heat, add the egg yolk mix and stir well. Garnish with parsley and dill.

Pat meat dry and fry in some oil until crispy brown. Season with salt and pepper and serve with the soup.

The soup can also be cooked using beef or pork instead of lamb. [Chicken, particularly free range chicken, is also good.]

Garnishes and Borsch Accompaniments

Shkvarki

1 lb. goose, duck, chicken, or pork Skin with underlying fat.

½ lb. onion; halved and sliced into half-rings (optional)
Salt and pepper to taste

Shkvarki are cracklings—rendered and crisped skin or fatback. Shkvarki made from pork or goose skin are considered a delicacy in Ukraine. Shkvarki made from chicken skin were popular among Eastern European Jews. Shkvarki can be eaten out-of-hand as a snack with beer. Usually, however, they are toppings for kasha, other grains, or soups—particularly, Ukrainian borsch. The recipe given is for cracklings destined to be eaten as a snack. As a topping, the onion can safely be made optional.

Slice skin into small pieces and place it into a pan, salt to taste, and heat on low flame. When fat begins to render, add sliced onion and sauté together until caramelizing begins to occur. Pour off fat, remove the onion and slightly crisp the cracklings in the open pan on low heat until they crunch. Turn out on paper towels and pepper to taste. The rendered fat, if not over spiced is excellent for home fried potatoes.

Galushki

3½-4 oz. buckwheat flour
(Optionally, one can use wheat flour, but then use 5 Tbs. of butter or margarine instead of egg)
Water 2-3 Tbs.
Egg 1 small

Galushki are dumplings, usually made from buckwheat, but can also be made from all-purpose flour.

Add to 4-5 tablespoons boiling water 3½-4 ounces buckwheat flour, and mix well. Let cool. Add remaining flour and egg; make loose dough. Spoon bits of dough with tablespoon and immerse into salted boiling water. Cook till done (they will float to the top when done).

Buckwheat Croutons

1 lb. buckwheat groats (kasha)
8 c. water
1 egg
All-purpose flour
3-4 Tbs. butter
Salt to taste

Sift one pound of buckwheat groats. Heat 8 cups water, add 2 tablespoons butter and salt to taste. When water starts boiling, pour in buckwheat and cook; soon it will thicken. Add another tablespoon butter and cook to a well thickened mass. Empty the pot and spread out the porridge to about the thickness of a finger. Let cool. Slice layer of buckwheat into squares, dip in beaten raw egg and roll in flour. Heat frying pan, add butter and fry until golden.

Pig's Ears

Use one cup of **flour**, two **eggs** and a pinch or two of **salt** to make a dough. Roll dough out and cut into thin rounds with a glass. Use a mixture of **sauerkraut**, to which have been added some chopped **mushrooms**. Spread this mixture on the rounds of thin dough, fold over to make half-moons and make them into the shape of pig's ears. Boil in hot water and when done add to the Barszcz.

Uzhki

8 oz. dried boletus (porcini)
  mushrooms *
1 onion, chopped fine

1 egg
2 c. all-purpose flour
Olive oil or butter

Uzhki are a ravioli made in the shape of pig's ears. They are a traditional ingredient in Christmas borsch, which is strictly Lenten.

Filling:

Cover dried mushrooms with hot water. Soak until they become soft. Pour off the mushroom liquid into the borsch. Fry mushrooms with minced onion in olive oil or butter. Blend and season to taste

Note: A metal sieve, mincer, hand blender are best to use. If using a blender or processor, pulse the machine and stop before the mixture becomes totally homogeneous.

Pasta:

Place the flour into a bowl and break the egg into the flour. Mix together with sufficient cold water to obtain flexible dough. Roll dough out till thin on a floured board. Cut into circles using a 2-inch cutter or use a knife and cut into squares, approximately 2x2 inches.

Place a small quantity of mushroom mix on each piece of dough. Fold squares diagonally or fold circles in half. Pinch the edges together to seal. Fold over the two points of the semicircle or the two base points of the triangle so that they overlap, and squeeze together.

Cook in boiling, salted water for 5 minutes. When the uzhki float in water they are done.

*An acceptable homemade substitute for porcini mushrooms are thinly sliced raw supermarket mushrooms that are dried in a slow oven.

BLINCHIKI (SMALL PANCAKES)

Pancake:

2 eggs
½ tsp. sugar
½ tsp. salt
½ Tbsp. soft butter
3 c. milk

Filling:

½ onion
Meat from soup
½ Tbsp. shortening
Salt and pepper
1 hard-boiled egg.

Mix two eggs with sugar and salt. Add soft butter and milk. Grease small frying pan, put just enough batter to cover the bottom as thin as a wine glass (non-stick pan is best). Turn carefully. Fry both sides but brown only one. Put filling on browned side.

Filling:

Put boiled soup meat through grinder. Chop onion fine and fry in shortening until soft but not browned. Add meat, salt and pepper, and fry together. Remove from saucepan; cool. Chop fine the hard-boiled egg and add to meat mixture. Put two teaspoons mixture on each *blinchik*. Roll, fold the ends in, and fry until brown on all sides. Serve with Red Soup.

BAKED PIROZHKI

Dough:

8 oz. of all-purpose flour
5 oz. butter
1 small egg or 2 egg yolks

1 Tbs. sour cream
½ tsp. salt

Filling:
Same ingredients and preparation as Uszki filling.

To Prepare Dough: Mix above ingredients, cutting them with a knife. Knead quickly into dough and let rest for 30 minutes in a cool place. Roll dough out thin. Take glass and cut circles in the dough. Keep repeating until all dough is used up.

Place filling on each circle and fold in half. Crimp edges of the semicircle and place *pirozhki* on a baking sheet seam side down.

Bake in 350° oven till golden brown. Serve immediately or reheat in oven before serving.

SYRNIKI (CHEESE FRITTERS)

1 lb. farmer's cheese	1-2 Tbs. sugar
½ c. all-purpose flour	Salt to taste
1 egg	Butter to fry

Thoroughly mix the farmer's cheese with the flour, egg, sugar and salt until you get a smooth mass. Roll the mass into a 2-2½ inch roll. Refrigerate until the roll firms. Slice the cheese roll into ½ inch slices. Dust with additional flour. Fry in hot butter till each slice is golden brown. Serve with borsch and additional sour cream.

PAMPUSHKI (GARLIC ROLLS)

13 oz. flour	¾ oz. yeast
½ c. water	1 oz. sunflower oil
⅔ oz. sugar	1 oz. garlic
Pinch sugar	⅓ c. water for garlic baste

Dissolve yeast in warm water with sugar, salt, and mix with half the flour. Allow the dough to rise. Add the rest of the flour, sunflower oil, and mix well; allow to rise again. Make little balls out of the dough of about ¾ ounce weight and place them in a baking pan, and let then rise once more for about 20 minutes. Cover the pan so that the dough does not dry out. Once they have risen bake at 400° for about 20-25 minutes. To test for doneness pierce a roll with a wooden toothpick; if it comes out "clean" the rolls are done.

Garlic baste:

Grind together garlic and salt, add some vegetable oil and boiling water (kvas, optionally). Mix thoroughly. When the pampushki are done, immediately pour the baste over the rolls and shake them a few times. Serve immediately.

VATRUSHKA 1909 (CHEESE TARTS)
Pelagia Pavlovna Aleksandra-Ignateva, *A Guide to the Fundamentals of Culinary Arts*

Dough:
7 oz. flour	2 egg yolks
3½ oz. butter	1 tsp. salt
1 oz. sour cream	1 tsp. sugar

Make flour mound on a table and form a depression in the middle. Mix egg yolks and sour cream on the table with a knife. Put sour cream and egg yolk mix in the mound, add salt to taste. It is important to mix the sour cream and egg yolks first, and then com-bine with some of the flour, also using a knife. When the yolks and sour cream have been mixed well with the flour and you have dough the consistency of a loose porridge, then put in a piece of cold butter and mix it with the dough; then mix the dough with the rest of the flour. Knead the dough till it is smooth and does not stick to the knife when cut and has no lumps. Refrigerate the dough for 15 minutes.

Explanations and Comments

Where to prepare dough: This dough should always be made on a tabletop, or on a board, because it is much easier to combine flour and yolks, sour cream, and butter on a flat surface, and not in a bowl. When mixed with a knife all these ingredients will distribute themselves evenly, which will result in a smooth dough without lumps. If you mix the ingredients in a bowl it becomes more difficult to achieve the desired end.

Combining egg yolks with sour cream: To avoid having bits of egg yolk in the dough, they should always be first mixed with the sour cream and only after that with the flour.

Butter: Butter is added after the egg yolks and sour cream are already combined with a part of the flour. This method helps to mix faster the butter with the flour and that is necessary because the quicker the dough is made the softer and flakier the dough is. The longer the dough is worked the tougher it gets. Butter is always added cold and in one piece and never melted because melted butter makes the dough fatty and brittle

Baking sheet: A baking sheet for this dough is always powdered with flour and is not buttered.

Corrections

Correcting for fatty dough: If there is too much butter in the dough, or if it has been processed too long and in a warm place, and if because of that it acquires an unattractive color, becomes fatty and brittle, it can be improved by adding a bit of water or cold milk. The dough will cease to be brittle.

Correcting tough dough: If the dough becomes tough because there is insufficient butter or sour cream then it can be improved by adding one tablespoon of sour cream and be lightly kneaded.

Filling:

14 oz. farmer's cheese [Ricotta or cottage cheese can be substituted]	*1½ oz. butter*
	1 tsp. flour
3 egg yolks	*Salt and sugar to taste*

Preparing the filling: Place cheese in a muslin bag, or wrap in cheesecloth, and press out the liquid. When the liquid drains, process the cheese through a foodmill and afterwards add in the egg yolks and mash this together with butter. Stir and add salt to taste and a pinch of sugar. Add a bit of flour so that the cheese does not balloon when baking.

Directions for assembly and baking: Roll out the dough relatively thin and cut out dough circles with a glass or metal dough cutter. Place filling in the middle and level it off. Pinch the edges as illustrated below:

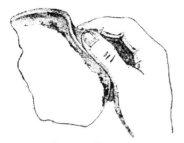 

Leave the center open, brush with egg, and place it on a flour-covered baking sheet, and put it in the oven. [350° F. for 40-45 minutes.] When the Vatrushka begins to color and moves easily from the baking sheet it is done.

The cheese needs to be dry, otherwise the filling will be liquid. If you want a more tart taste add sour cream. [Farmer cheese is dryer than ricotta or cottage cheese and therefore easier to use in this recipe.] You only put egg yolks in the filling because if you add egg whites the filling will become tough.

BIBLIOGRAPHY

Print

The American Women's Literary Club. nd. *Cook Book Libro De Cocina*, Tercera Ed. Lima, Peru: The American Women's Literary Club

Bardukharov, Stepan G., et al., eds. 1975-2008. *Slovar' russkogo yazyka XI-XVIII*. [The Dictionary of the Russian Language of the 11th to the 17th Centuries]. Vols. 1-28. Moscow-Leningrad: Nauka.

Bolotnikova, V. A. et. al. 1979. *Byelorussian Cuisine*. Minsk, U.S.S.R.: Uradzhai.

Christ the Saviour Orthodox Church. 1982. *101 Recipes of Old Russia*. Indianapolis, Ind.: Christ the Saviour Orthodox Church.

Cookbook Committee. 1976. *Joys of Ethnic Cooking*. Los Angeles: Los Angeles Orthodox Club Chapter Number 155.

Dal', Vladimir. 1978. *Tolkovyi slovar' zhivago Velikoruskago yazyka*. [Practical Dictionary of the Great Russian Language]. Moscow: Russkii yazyk.

The Daughters of Hawaii. 1988. *Dining with the Daughters*. Honolulu, Hawaii: Daughters of Hawaii.

Dembinska, Maria, rev. and adapt. by William Woys Weaver, trans. Magdalena Thomas. 1999. *Food and Drink in Medieval Poland: Rediscovering a Cuisine of the Past*. Philadelphia: University of Pennsylvania Press.

Denisenko, L. ed. 1957. *Ukrainski stavi* [Ukrainian Dishes]. Kiev: Government Publisher of Technical Literature of URSR.

Dmitrovna, Elizavetta. 1946. *Samovar: A Russian Cookbook*. Richmond, Va: The Dietz Co.

Dmytryshyn, Basil. 1991. *Medieval Russia: A Source Book, 850-1700*. 3rd ed. New York: Harcourt Brace.

Evenshtein, Z.I. 1998. *Evreiskaya Kukhnya* [Jewish Cuisine]. Rostov-on-the-Don: Feniks.

Goldstein, Darra. 1999. *A Taste of Russia*. Rev. and updated. Montpelier, Vt: Russian Life Books.

Gluschenko, Irina. 2010. *Obschepit: Mikoyan i sovetskaya kukhnya* [Obschepit. Mikoyan and Soviet Cuisine]. Moscow: GU-VESh.

Gronow, Jukka and Sergey Zhuravlev. 2011. "The Book of Tasty and Healthy Food: the Establishment of Soviet Haute Cuisine " in *Educated Tastes: Food, Drink, and Connoisseur Culture*. Lincoln: University of Nebraska Press.

Grossinger, Jennie. 1977. *The Art of Jewish Cooking*. New York: Bantam.

Gurock, Jeffrey S. 1979. *When Harlem was Jewish, 1870-1930*. New York: Columbia University Press.

Hazen, Ruby, et. al. comp., 1988. *Recipes of San Francisco Russian Molokans*. 3rd edition. San Francisco, Ca.: Women's Circle First Russian Christian Molokan Church.

Henderson, Mary. 1980. *Paris Embassy Cookbook*. London: Weidenfeld and Nicolson.

Hutton, Marcelline J. 2001. *Russian and West European Women, 1860-1939: Dreams, Struggles, and Nightmares*. Lanham, Md.: Rowman & Littlefield Publishers.

Kaganova, A. ed. 1959. *Kulinariya* [Cookery]. 2nd ed., rev. Leningrad: Gostorgiszdat.

Katzen, Mollie. 2000. *The New Moosewood Cookbook*. Berkeley, Calif.:

Ten Speed Press.

Koehler, Margaret H. 1974. *Recipes from the Russians of San Francisco.* Riverside, Conn: The Chatham Press.

Kostomarov, I. I. 1860. *Ocherk domashnei zhizni i nravov velikorusskago naroda v XVI i XVII stoletiyakh* [Image of Domestic Life of the Great Russian Folk in the XVI and XVII centuries]. St. Petersburg: Karl Wolf.

Kovalev, V.M. and Mogilnyi, N.P. 1990. *Russkaya kuchnya: tradicii i obychai* [Russian Kitchen: Traditions and Customs]. Moscow: Sovetskaya Rossiya.

Kropotkin, Alexandra. 1993. *The Best of Russian Cooking*, exp. ed. New York: Hippocrene Books.

Leeds, Jeffrey C. 2001. *Simply Souper!* Troy, Mich.: Momentum Books Ltd.

Lutinova, I.S. 1997. *Slovo o pische russkoy* [The Word: About Russian Food]. St. Petersburg: St. Petersburg University.

Maddox, Gaynor and Ransom E. Noble, Jr., eds. 1943. *War-Time Edition Russian Cook Book for American Homes*. New York: Russian War Relief.

Margen, Sheldon, M.D. 1992. *The Wellness Encyclopedia of Food and Nutrition*. New York: Rebus.

Mikhalov, Vladimir S. 1996. *Orthodox Cuisine*. Moscow: KUbK-a.

Mindala, John and Kathy, eds. 1974. *Just a Pinch of Russian*. 3rd print. Cleveland, Ohio: The Cleveland R Club, Chapter 4/6 Federated Russian Orthodox Clubs.

Molokhovets, Elena and Joyce Toomre, trans. 1992. *Classic Russian Cooking, A Gift to Young Housewives*. Bloomington: Indiana University Press.

_____ . *Podarok molodym khozyaikam* [Gift to Young Housewives]. n.d. New York: N.N. Martianov.

Montagné, Prosper (Nina Froud, et al, trans.) 1961. *Larousse Gastronomique*. New York: Crown Publishers.

Nachiporovich, L.I. 1996. *Pravoslavnaya Kulinarya* [Orthodox Cookery] vols. 1 & 2. Minsk: Urodzhai.

Nicolaieff, Nina and Nancy Phelan. 1971. *Cooking with Nina A Book of*

Russian Food. London: Macmillan.
Norman, Barbara. 1970. *The Russian Cookbook*. New York: Bantam.
Papashvili, Helen and George. 1969. *Russian Cooking*. New York: Time-Life Books.
Petrovskaya, Kyra. 1992. *Russian Cookbook*. New York: Dover Publications.
Pininska, Mary. 1992. *A Little Polish Cookbook*. San Francisco: Chronicle Books.
Pokhlebkin, William V. 1988. *O kulinarii ot A do Ya: slovar spravochnik*. [About Cookery from A to Z: Dictionary and Reference] Minsk: Polymya.
_____. 1999. *Kulinarny slovar* [Dictionary of Cookery]. Moscow: Centograf.
_____. 2009. *Iz istorii russkoi kulinarnoy kultury* [From the History of the Russian Culinary Culture]. Moscow: Centograf.
_____. 2009. *Kukhni slavyanskikh narodov* [Cuisines of the Slavic Peoples]. Moscow: Centograf.
Pryakhin, G. ed. 1999. *Kulinaria: superkniga dlya gurmanov* [Gastromomy: Superbook for Gourmets], rev. with add. Moscow: Voskresenie.
Rombauer, Irma S. 1964. *Joy of Cooking*. New York: A Signet Special New American Library.
Shalimov, Sergey A., Elena A. Shadura. 1989. *Sovremennaya Ukrainskaya Kukhya* (Contemporary Ukrainian Cuisine). Kiev: Tekhnika.
Shuleman, Martha Rose. 1989. *Gourmet Vegetarian Feasts*. Rochester, Vt.: Healing Arts Press.
Sivolap, I. K. 1953. *Kniga o vkusnoy i zdorovoy pischeook* [Book of Tasty and Healthy Food]. Moscow: Pishepomizdat.
Smirnova, Marina, ed. 1994. *Retsepty pravoslavnoy kukhni vo dni posta*. [On the Days of Lent: Recipes from the Orthodox Kitchen.] Ivanovo: Sviato Vvedenskiy zhenskiiy monastyr.
Smith, Jeff. 1990. *The Frugal Gourmet on Our Immigrant Ancestors: Recipes You Should Have Gotten from Your Grandmother*. New York: William Morrow & Co.

Stoltz, Sidonie, ed. n.d. *Indy Cooks International.* Indianapolis: Nationalities Council of Indianapolis.

Suytkin, Olga and Pavel. 2011. *Nepredumannaya istoriya russkoy kukhni* [The Uninvented History of Russian Cuisine]. Moscow: Astrel.

The United Nations Nursery School. 1957. *Could I Have Your Recipe? A Cookbook of International Recipes*, 3rd Edition. Geneva, Switzerland: The United Nations Nursery School

Vasilieva, Larisa. 1992. *Kremlevskie zheny* [Kremlin Wives]. Moscow: Vagrius.

Vilenkin, B.V. and G.A. Levin. 1934. *Manual of Cookery.* Moscow: Soyuznarpit.

Visson, Lynn. 1982. *The Complete Russian Cookbook* Ann Arbor. Mich.: Ardis Press.

Volokh, Anne with Mavis Manus. 1989. *The Art of Russian Cuisine.* New York: MacMillan.

Voth, Norma Jost. 1990. *Mennonite Foods & Folkways from South Russia,* vols. 1 & 2. Intercourse, Penn.: Good Books.

Electronic

Alexandrova-Igatieva, Pelagia P. 1909. *Practical Foundations of the Art of Cooking.* 7th ed., St. Petersburg: M.M. Staulevich. Accessed 13 January 2013., http://rutracker.org/forum/viewtopic.php?t=3475397

Avdeeva, Ekaterina Pavlovna. 1848. *Ruchnaya kniga Russkoyi Opytnoyi Khozyaiki, sostavlennaya iz sorokoletnikh opytov dobpoyi khozyaiki russkoyi, K. Avdeevoyi* [Handbook of the Experienced Russian Mistress, Compiled from the Four Decade-long Experiences and Observations of the Good Russian Mistress K Avdeeva.] 6th ed., St. Petersburg. Accessed 2 January 2013.
http://www.xliby.ru/kulinarija/yetyudy_o_pitanii/p16.php

Burr, Hattie A. 1886. *The Woman Suffrage Cookbook: Containing Thoroughly Tested and Reliable Recipes for Cooking, Directions for the Care of the Sick, and Practical Suggestions.* Accessed 12 March 2013.

http://archive.lib.msu.edu/DMC/cookbooks/womansuffrage/wosu.xml

Contois, Emily. "The Woman Suffrage Cookbook of 1886: Culinary Evidence of Women Finding a New Voice in a Time of Great Transition." Accessed March 16, 2013., http://emilycontois.com/2012/07/13/the-woman-suffrage-cookbook-of-1886-culinary-evidence- of-women-finding-a-new-voice-in-a-time-of -great-transition/

Le Cordon Bleu. 1991. *Le Cordon Bleu at Home*. New York: William Morrow Cookbooks. http://food-reference.free-book.biz/Le-Cordon-Bleu-at-Home-ID361.pdf. Accessed 15 November 2012.

Dal, Vladimir I. 1869. Tolkovyi slovar' zhivogo velikorusskogo jazyka. [Practical Dictionary of the Living Great Russian Language]. St. Petersburg: Imperial Academy of Sciences. Accessed 5 January 2012. http://vidahl.agava.ru/W129.HTM

Demezer, A.A. and M.L. Dzjuba. 1957. *Domovodstvo* (Housekeeping). Moscow: Selkhoziz. Accessed 14 March, 2012.

Dvinina, Alyona. "Kulinarnaya kniga kak otrazhenie istorii," [Cookery Book as Reflection of History], *Proshloe –Nastoyaschee*. *Karelia*. No. 118. Accessed 21 Oct. 2004., http://www.gov.karelia.ru/Karelia/1249/14.html

Hartman, Ekbert and A.F. Smirnova, trans. "Elena Molokhovets," *Zvezda*, 2000, No. 3. Accessed 14 July 2011, http://magazines.russ ru/zvezda/2000/3/hartman.html

Klinovetska, Z. 1913. *Stravi i napitki na Ukraïni* [Dishes and Drinks in Ukraine]. Kiev and Lviv. Accessed 1 May 2013, http://narod.ru/disk/33111154001/Stravy.i.napitki.djvu.html.

Kovalev N. I. *Sovremennaya russkaya kulinariya* [Contemporary Russian Cuisine] Accessed 15 July 2013. http://www.litmir.net/br/?b=59485&p=1

Lebedev, Nikolai. "The Jewish Roots of Soviet Cuisine." Accessed 10 February 2012, *Jewish.ru*. http://www.jewish.ru/history/facts/2011/03/news994294917.php

Lippitt, Flora K. 1914. *The Neighborhood Cookbook*. 2nd ed., rev. and enl.

Portland, OR: Council of Jewish Women. Accessed 10 May, 2012., http://books.google.com/books?id=qNQsAQAAMAAJ&pg=PA5&lpg=PA5&dq=Lippitt,+Flora+K.&source=bl&ots=Jrnw8HoPPx&sig=zMyuTqKwXlBkNMLWeN18iF0XQy0&hl=en&sa=X&ei=8br6UbzqFYj84APznIDYAw&ved=0CEsQ6AEwBA#v=onepage&q=Lippitt%2C%20Flora%20K.&f=false

Meek, James. "The story of borshch," *The Guardian*. March 14, 2008. Accessed 2 March, 2013. http://www.theguardian.com/lifeandstyle/2008/mar/15/foodanddrink.travelfoodanddrink

Molokhovets, Elena Ivanovna. 1901. *Podarok molodym khozyikam, ili Sredstvo k umensheniyu raskhodov v domashnem kozaystve*. [Gift to Young Housewives or Means to Lowering Expenses in Housekeeping]. St. Petersburg: N.N. Klobukov. Accessed 16 February 2012, http://nuclphys.sinp.msu.ru/recipes/molohovec/

Petit, Alphonse. 1860. *La Gastonamie en Russie*. Paris: Émile Mellier. Accessed August 15, 2013, https://play.google.com/books/reader?id=5dQsAQAAMAAJ&printsec=frontcover&output=reader&authuser=0&hl=en&pg=GBS.PA3

Pokhlebkin, William V. 1997. *Povarnoye iskusstvo i povarskie prikladуное* [The Cook's Art and Applications]. Moscow: Tsentrpoligraf. Accessed 12 Jan 2013. http://depositfiles.com/files/dg7xd54gs

Radetsky N.M. comp. 1855. *Almanakh gastronomov* [Gastronomers' Almanac]. St. Petersburg, Vol. 3. Accessed. 22 Jan 2013. http://www.almanah-gastronomov.ru/

Sylvester, Archpriest. 1574. *Domostroy*. Accessed 13 Nov. 2012., http://www.bibliotekar.ru/index.files/2-3.htm

Zamyatina, Natalja. 2009. "My Friend Borschevik" (*Moy drug borschevik*) *Science and Life* (*Nauka I zhizn'*) No. 7. Accessed 5 Feb, 2012 http://www.nkj.ru/archive/articles/16099/

ABOUT THE AUTHOR

Nikolai Burlakoff is of Russian heritage. His long-standing interest in cultural studies and cooking finds expression in this work devoted to borsch, often associated with Russia. He has cooked since childhood when, at the tender age of three, he made cookies by mixing a carefully protected supply of post-war rationed sugar with sand. He survived this beginning to become an excellent cook.

His experience in institutional cooking encompasses cooking over an open fire at Russian Scouts camp in the Adirondacks, working the grill at Dunster House during his Harvard years, months as a cook's helper at Ft. Jackson, South Carolina, while awaiting the decision on conscientious objector status, and serving as the main cook on the replica ship *Halve Maen* whenever that vessel sailed.

To learn the technique of vegetable preparation for Chinese borsch (*luo song tang*) he volunteered at a Chinese monastery. Most recently he studied Living Food techniques with Hiawatha Cromer.

He contributed to the grassroots cookbook, *Indy Cooks International*, by the Nationalities Council of Indiana, and to *Foods of the Hudson: A Seasonal Sampling of the Region's Bounty*, by Peter G. Rose. His first book about borsch was the children's book, *How the Borsch Angel Got Its Name*, published by AElitaPress.org.

Currently he is working with an international team of poets, scholars, and translators preparing a book of poetry, ritual, history, recipes, and cooking techniques related to Kalmyk tea. The Kalmyks, a Mongolian people who have been living in Russia for over 400 years, brew a robust tea that is both a drink and a soup substitute adapted to the nomadic environment of traditional Kalmyk pastoral life. His books are available on Amazon.com and AElitaPress.org website: https://sites.google.com/site/aelitapressorg/Home